"Over the past few decades, Trinitarian theology has risen from the post-Enlightenment deluge in which it seemed to have sunk, and few have played as crucial a role in that development as the late Colin Gunton. Theologians and church leaders alike found in Gunton's work not only a rich theology of God but also the framework for a Trinitarian ontology, aesthetics, science, and cultural analysis—a Trinitarian theology useful in ways that Kant would never have dreamed. At the foundation of Gunton's work was the claim that Augustine early on steered Western theology into a reef, leaving contemporary theologians to gather the wreckage and rebuild. Through an appreciative yet critical examination of Gunton's project, and an equally cogent treatment of Augustine, Brad Green has gently corrected Gunton's reading of Augustine, showing that the Bishop of Hippo left Western theology far more seaworthy than Gunton believed. In the process, Green strengthens Gunton's case against modernity by providing some Augustinian equipment. This is theology of a high caliber—judicious, clear, convincing, and, above all, serviceable to the church as it navigates the roiling seas of modernity and postmodernity."

—Peter Leithart
New Saint Andrews College

"Brad Green set out to vindicate Colin Gunton's revolutionary critique of Augustine-namely, that he is a proto-Unitarian who imports the ancient Greek emphasis on the One into his own doctrine of the Trinity. Instead Green came to see, in ways that others have not, that Gunton is quite wrongheaded in tracing our modern and post-modern ills to an alleged monergism in Augustine. Far from failing to emphasize the communal character of the Trinity—allegedly denying the insights of the Cappadocians in this matter—Augustine has a robust doctrine of the three Persons as dwelling in utterly self-offering community. In his carefully argued and lucidly written dissertation, Green shows that Augustine's Trinitarian communalism—especially as it engaged ancient pagan culture—offers the real antidote to the perilous individualism that is the chief legacy of the Enlightenment."

—Ralph Wood
Baylor University

"Dr. Green is an accomplished scholar with a deep knowledge of Augustine and other church fathers. His proposed reply to the line recently taken by Colin Gunton and others is necessary and timely. Professor Gunton overplayed his hand and distorted Augustine's perspectives in various ways, which Dr. Green aims to elucidate. There is a growing body of secondary literature that takes Gunton at face value on this subject, and it is essential to refute it before it becomes a new orthodoxy. Dr. Green's proposal is therefore most welcome."

—Gerald Bray
Beeson Divinity School

Colin Gunton and the Failure of Augustine

Distinguished Dissertations in Christian Theology

Other titles in the series:

The Theology of the Cross in Historical Perspective
by Anna M. Madsen

REWIRED: Exploring Religious Conversion
by Paul N. Markham

Series Foreword

We are living in a vibrant season for academic Christian theology. After a hiatus of some decades, a real flowering of excellent systematic and moral theology has emerged. This situation calls for a series that showcases the contributions of newcomers to this ongoing and lively conversation. The journal *Word & World: Theology for Christian Ministry* and the academic society Christian Theological Research Fellowship (CTRF) are happy to cosponsor this series together with our publisher Pickwick Publications (an imprint of Wipf and Stock Publishers). Both the CTRF and *Word & World* are interested in excellence in academics but also in scholarship oriented toward Christ and the Church. The volumes in this series are distinguished for their combination of academic excellence with sensitivity to the primary context of Christian learning. We are happy to present the work of these young scholars to the wider world and are grateful to Luther Seminary for the support that helped make it possible.

Alan G. Padgett
Professor of Systematic Theology
Luther Seminary

Beth Felker Jones
Assistant Professor of Theology
Wheaton College

www.ctrf.info
www.luthersem.edu/word&world

Colin Gunton and the Failure of Augustine

The Theology of Colin Gunton in Light of Augustine

BRADLEY G. GREEN

Foreword by Lewis Ayres

☙PICKWICK *Publications* · Eugene, Oregon

COLIN GUNTON AND THE FAILURE OF AUGUSTINE
The Theology of Colin Gunton in Light of Augustine

Distinguished Dissertations in Christian Theology 4

Copyright © 2011 Bradley G. Green. All rights reserved. Except for brief quotations in critical publications or reviews, no part of this book may be reproduced in any manner without prior written permission from the publisher. Write: Permissions, Wipf & Stock, 199 W. 8th Ave., Suite 3, Eugene, OR 97401.

Pickwick Publications
An Imprint of Wipf and Stock Publishers
199 W. 8th Ave., Suite 3
Eugene, OR 97401

www.wipfandstock.com

ISBN 13: 978-1- 60899-268-3

Cataloging-in-Publication data:

Green, Bradley G.

    Colin Gunton and the failure of Augustine : the theology of Colin Gunton in light of Augustine / Bradley G. Green ; with a foreword by Lewis Ayres.

    xiv + 226 p. ; 23 cm. Includes bibliographical references and indexes.

    Distinguished Dissertations in Christian Theology 4

    ISBN 13: 978-1- 60899-268-3

    1. Gunton, Colin E. 2. Augustine, Saint, Bishop of Hippo. 3. Trinity. I. Ayres, Lewis. II. Title. III. Series.

BT10 .G80 2011

Manufactured in the U.S.A.

Contents

Foreword by Lewis Ayres • *ix*

Acknowledgments • *xiii*

1 Colin Gunton and the Failure of Augustine • 1

2 Creation and Redemption in the Theology of Colin Gunton • 30

3 Being and Ontology in the Theology of Colin Gunton • 67

4 Creation and Redemption in Augustine's *De Trinitate* • 88

5 Being and Ontology in Augustine's *De Trinitate* • 134

6 A Critique of Colin Gunton • 169

7 Conclusion • 202

Bibliography • 207

Index • 221

For Dianne,
my sine qua non

Foreword

ONE OF THE GREAT signs of hope in theological conversation across denominations is renewed interest in the fathers of the Church. Turning the life-giving earth of early Christian thought has been the preliminary to faithful reform in the Roman Catholic context for centuries. It is no accident that the meaning of the fathers was one of the fundamental subjects at issue in the reformations of the sixteenth century, and it is no accident that a renewed exploration of early Christian thought should now be the source of new and important conversation between Christian traditions, Catholic and reformed, Latin and Greek.

One of the most important areas of conversation in recent years has concerned the Trinity, the core mystery of Christian faith. For many decades, whether positively or negatively charged, the story of an essential separation between Eastern and Western Trinitarian theologies held sway. Against the background of such a narrative it became all too common for theologains to make an easy Eastward turn, rejecting the complex tradition of Latin discussion and argument, and yet never really engaging the complexities and differences within Eastern theology. The past two decades have seen an extensive reconsideration of the idea that an East/West division is fundamental in Trinitarian theology. The result has been the opening up of new scholarly conversations that mark new more complex divisions, new unities and which bring together figures one might previously have thought opposed. At the same time this new scholarship has begun to suggest the importance of new narratives by means of which we can think about the emergence of modern Western post-Hegelian, personalist and dramatic re-castings of the life of the Trinitarian God.

Brad Green's book takes its place within this new scholarship. He offers us an important examination of one of the central figures to hold out for what I have portrayed as the "old" narrative of division between

East and West, the late Colin Gunton. Gunton's large corpus of writing on the Trinity attempted to sustain the view of Augustine as the source of a distinctly Western and failed theology, one that tended toward monism, and one that had disastrous consequences for Western metaphysics and theology. Brad Green's treatment is always attentive, always respectful, even as it constitutes a significant critique of Gunton's work and suggests very different construals of Augustine's theology and significance. It is greatly to be hoped that the new trends in Trinitarian theology of which I have spoken develop in a variety of forms, that they not only converge on new unities but also open up new areas of discussion. Brad Green's book is thus to be greatly welcomed to the emerging body of new Trinitarian literature, taking on an important figure, and bringing from his critique perspectives and vistas that can help to revitalize our thinking. Through such acts of rethinking and recovery the Christian faith grows in intellectual power and force, it shows its vitality and witnesses to Logos through whom and in whom all exists.

Lewis Ayres
Bede Chair in Catholic Theology
in the Department of Theology and Religion
University of Durham

Acknowledgments

THE VOLUME YOU ARE holding in your hand was originally written as a dissertation for a PhD in Theological Studies at Baylor University. I am thankful to those who served on my committee: Bob Patterson (chair), A. J. "Chip" Conyers, Carl Vaught, and Ralph Wood. All helped me think through the issues and I am thankful to each of them. My employer, Union University, has encouraged my scholarship, and I am thankful to the administration and Board of Trustees at Union, and to my colleagues—both inside and outside of the School of Theology and Missions, where I teach. I am particularly grateful for Ray Van Neste and Hal Poe, who have always spurred me on in my scholarship. I am thankful to the late Colin E. Gunton, with whom I visited (both through correspondence and in person) about the trajectory of my thinking. I began the work on this project quite smitten with Gunton's understanding of the theological roots of modernity. While I remain very grateful to Professor Gunton and his excellent theological mind, I came to see things a bit differently—which is evident in this book. Nonetheless, I suspect I have been forever shaped by Gunton, and I will always be in debt to him. I appreciate the folks at Wipf & Stock, and am glad this monograph is being published with Wipf & Stock. It has been a joy to work with them. Several persons were willing to read the manuscript, and to offer recommendations for publication, as well as endorsements: Gerald Bray, Stephen Holmes, Peter Leithart, and Ralph Wood. Lewis Ayres also supported the publication of this work, and I appreciate his willingness to write the Foreword. I am appreciative of my children. Caleb, Daniel, and Victoria have all been patient while Daddy has done the work to prepare this volume for publication. Thank you children. Dianne, my wife, has been especially patient, as she has now supported this project twice. Thank you Dianne. This book is dedicated to you.

CHAPTER 1

Colin Gunton and the Failure of Augustine

Does Augustine lie at the heart of certain problems in contemporary theology? Does Augustine, the fount of much of Western theology, bequeath to the West a theological tradition destined for failure? While this may at first sound improbable or overstated, Colin E. Gunton of King's College (University of London) argues persuasively that key weaknesses in contemporary Western thought—modernism in particular—are the result of old issues, *very* old issues. Gunton is surely accurate in affirming the magnitude and significance of Augustine's place in the history of Western thought. Hans von Campenhausen assesses Augustine as follows:

> Augustine is the only church father who even today remains an intellectual power. Irrespective of school and denomination he attracts pagans and Christians, philosophers and theologians alike by his writings and makes them come to terms with his intentions and his person. He also has an abiding indirect influence, more or less modified and broken, as a conscious or unconscious tradition in Western churches, and through them in the general heritage of culture.[1]

Stanislaus J. Grabowski offers no small praise: "The name of St. Augustine is undoubtedly the most outstanding in the annals of the patristic age. He towers above all the Fathers who have preceded him, and casts a shadow

---

1. Campenhausen, *Fathers of the Church*, 183.

upon all who have come after."[2] If such praise be true, can Augustine also be the font of some of the key errors in Western thought? Is Augustine a major source of our contemporary malaise?

The doctrines of the Trinity and creation are central to Gunton's concerns, and Gunton is not alone in affirming the centrality of such doctrines. David S. Cunningham has recently written, "Many of the difficulties that Christian theologians have faced, as they have attempted to shore up various structures of the faith over the past several centuries, can be traced in part to the faulty construction (or in some cases, the complete absence) of this all-important keystone [i.e., the doctrine of the Trinity]."[3] Thomas Torrance similarly argues that the Trinity is not a peripheral doctrine of the Christian tradition to be included at the end of one's theological studies. Rather, the Trinity is at the very heart of the Christian gospel: "the very essence of the Gospel and the whole of the Christian Faith depend on the centrality and primacy of the relation in being and agency between Jesus Christ and God the Father."[4]

For Gunton, at the heart of contemporary problems is a truncated or confused gospel, which errs in its understanding and articulation of the Trinity and creation. Indeed, Gunton affirms William Morris' notion that "Modernism began and continues wherever civilisation began and continues to *deny* Christ."[5] As one works through Gunton's writings, this same theme continues to appear. Gunton's *The One, the Three and the Many: God, Creation and the Culture of Modernity*, given as the 1992 Bampton Lectures, is the best work for understanding Gunton's thesis regarding the far-reaching effects of confusion relating to the doctrine of God. In this volume the problem of the One and the Many provides the schematic background upon which Gunton works. The One and the Many is a recurring problem in the history of philosophy. Is reality primarily One (e.g., Parmenides), or is reality primarily Many (e.g., Heraclitus)? There is little agreement or consensus regarding a settlement to this perennial issue.[6] For Gunton, the issue of the One and the Many provides *the* con-

---

2. Grabowski, *All-Present God*, vii.
3. Cunningham, *These Three are One*, 6–7.
4. T. Torrance, *Trinitarian Faith*, 3.
5. Cited by Gunton, *One, the Three and the Many*, 1. Cf. Fuller, *Theoria*, 139.
6. Rousas J. Rushdoony suggests, in his summary of Cornelius Van Til's position on the One and the Many, that the secular philosophical community has exhausted its resources in attempting to wrestle with this issue. For Rushdoony, secular philosophy has

ceptual backdrop upon which to understand the development of Western thought. In one sense, Western thought *is* the question of the One and the Many. How does this relate to our thesis in this work? In short, Gunton's position is that in the West the One has prevailed over the Many. The "victory" of the One is not just an accidental or peripheral issue, and its cause is not foreign to Christian thought. Indeed, at the heart of the One's victory in the West is one of the key figures in Western thought—St. Augustine. Indeed, Gunton traces the primacy of the One to St. Augustine. Hence our title, the *failure* of Augustine. While Augustine serves as a hero for many Christians, Gunton laments the legacy of Augustine, and this antipathy toward Augustine shows up in the vast majority of Gunton's writings. Augustine errs in positing an "unknown substance *supporting* the three persons."[7] The One is so emphasized that the Many are virtually made superfluous. Thus Gunton can write that with Augustine's construal of the Trinity, we are led to "an essentially singular deity for whom community is epiphenomenal or secondary."[8] With Augustine we are left with "some unknown and unknowable substance underlying the economy."[9] Augustine simply lacks the "conceptual equipment" to avoid such heresies as Arianism and modalism, and therefore the Western tradition has struggled with such heresies (particularly the latter).[10] We have erred in our understanding of God, and according to Gunton we strayed from the best paths largely due to the thought and impact of Augustine. We are now reaping the consequences in realms as diverse as the theological, ecclesiastical, cultural and political spheres.[11] That is, central to contem-

---

exhausted itself because it simply does not *have* the resources with which to come to terms with the problem of the One and the Many. The only solution to the One and Many question is to be found in the reality of the Triune God, a conclusion with which, on the whole, Gunton would agree. See Rushdoony, "Van Til and the One and the Many." Vernon Bourke does not do a lot with it, but he briefly suggests that Augustine was able to bring together both Parmenides and Heraclitus in his own thought. He writes, "One might say that he has made room in his thinking for the permanent being of Parmenides and for the flux of Heraclitus." See Bourke, *Augustine's View of Reality*, 5.

7. Gunton, *Promise of Trinitarian Theology*, 43.

8. Ibid., 53.

9. Ibid., 54.

10. Ibid., 55.

11. These four specific areas are dealt with in Gunton, "Trinity in Modern Theology," 937–57. Although other works by Gunton are more well-known and thorough, if someone was completely new to Gunton's writings, and wanted a brief introduction to his thought, particularly as it relates to the Trinity and the weaknesses in Augustine, this article would be an excellent place to start.

porary difficulties, theological or otherwise, is a confused understanding of God. We might say that for Gunton confusion in modern life is in direct proportion to confusion in our understanding of God. Let us try to make Gunton's point perfectly clear. Gunton offers two main complaints against Augustine which succinctly summarize Gunton's position.

First, Gunton contends that Augustine's attempt to fuse neoplatonic and Christian categories resulted in a dualism between the sensible and the intelligible, and between the material and the ideal, and in effect "neutralized" the concept of "relational being" which Gunton holds was "made possible by the *homoousion*." That is, Nicaea's *homoousion* had opened up a new way of conceiving of "being," and Augustine's dualism in effect had no room for such a concept. Augustine's failure to appropriate the Nicene conceptual advance led to three key developments: (1) the concept of person was undermined. Thus, the primary emphasis is on *essence* or *being* rather than person. (2) The unity of God was stressed at the expanse of plurality. Or, we might say, the One was gaining its victory over the Many. This was in effect a trend toward modalism, for the "real" God is One, where "the real being of God underlies rather than consists in the three Persons."[12] (3) Consistent with Augustine's Platonism, the material world was disparaged. Hence, the doctrine of creation was marginalized, and the Incarnation was "reduced to a timeless point, so that the importance of the human and historical Jesus was minimized."[13]

Second, Augustine squandered the Cappadocian ontology, which affirmed that God is "a sort of continuous and indivisible community."[14] Augustine sought trinitarian analogies in the human mind, pushing social, ecclesiastical and practical considerations to the periphery. Also, by seeing trinitarian analogies in the mind, Augustine failed to draw (or at least emphasize) the conceptual connections between the "internal," "transcendent," or "immanent" Trinity and God's work in creation and redemption. Thus, in the Western tradition, "God" could be dealt with in theological treatises, say with treatments of omniscience, omnipotence, timelessness, etc., with little necessary reference to the work of Son and Spirit in creation and redemption—again, this is due to a tendency to emphasize the oneness of God at the expense of the threeness of God. Or

---

12. Ibid., 940. This claim is crucial to Gunton's scheme, and we will see this charge again.

13. Ibid.

14. Ibid., 941.

better put, Augustine, and the West in his train, failed to grasp the important insight that it is impossible even to *conceive* of God without speaking of Father, Son and Spirit. There *is* no "oneness" before "threeness." Gunton contends that this signal failure in the development of Christian thought has had serious repercussions in the areas of theology, ecclesiology, culture and politics. We briefly note these repercussions here, and they will be treated in more detail later in the monograph.

First, theologically the Trinity has, over time, simply seemed irrelevant. If what is *really* important is the *One* God, why worry about a logical conundrum like the Trinity? Related to this, there appears to be little organic connection between *who* God is (the being of God) and what he does in history (e.g., creation and redemption). For again, if the timeless, simple, immutable God is the object of our attention, the crucial connection between who God is and what He does is diminished.[15]

Second, in the ecclesial realm the failure to appropriate the riches of trinitarian theology has resulted in the concomitant failure to see the Church as a "communion in the image of the Trinity."[16] Other images and paradigms have rushed to fill this gap, such as political and military models. Sectarian and millenarian groups, bristling at the authoritarian tendencies which often attach themselves to such images and models, have split from the larger Church, and the result has been a fragmented and broken Church.

Third, in terms of culture, the overemphasis on the One found in Augustine and his Western heirs has ultimately led to Modernity—the rejection of the One in favor of the Many. Likewise, we have seen the emergence of contemporary atheism—a rejection of God conceived of as an authoritarian One.[17]

Fourth, politically the emphasis on the oneness of God led to associating Christianity with repression. That is, a radical monotheism, instead of trinitarianism, often was seen as a type of repressive monism, and Christianity was often associated with repressive political systems.[18]

As we work through Gunton's writings we will see this same constellation of concerns and themes. Gunton contends that antiquity over-

15. Ibid.
16. Ibid., 942.
17. Ibid.
18. Ibid.

emphasized the One over the Many, and modernity, seeing this as ultimately authoritarian and oppressive to individuality, rebelled, and in turn overemphasized the Many (with modernity's radical emphasis on individuality). God was displaced "from the transcendent to the immanent sphere," in that whereas once there was considered to be a God "out there," moderns have essentially become their own God.[19] This displacement of God has led to the fragmenting of culture, including the spheres of truth, goodness, and beauty.[20] While moderns "displaced" God in the name of freedom and individuality, the result has been a true *lack* of freedom and individuality—what Gunton calls the "homogenization" of culture.[21] In rejecting the authoritarian One, man has displaced God and man has become "disengaged," in that man does not have proper relations to others or to the non-personal world.[22] That is, there is no God "out there" to provide coordinates for man's existence. In sum, "What makes modernity distinctive is its displacement of God. Modernity as an ideology arises not only out of antiquity, but also by means of an attempt in various ways to displace God as the transcendent focus of life in the world, that is, as the one who provides our being with its coordinates."[23]

For Gunton, Plato's emphasis on the One can be seen in the "Platonizing minds" of both Origen and Augustine (particularly his doctrines of creation and Trinity).[24] In this "monist" view of God, Western theology has had difficulty affirming the value of the particular. Indeed, (1) creation is severed from (2) redemption, since redemption requires the continued activity of God with particulars, and particulars appear to be problematic for much of Western theology.[25] Gunton writes, "*The root of modern disarray is accordingly to be located in the divorce of the willing of creation from the historical economy of salvation.*"[26]

So here is the problem as Gunton sees it. The inability to deal adequately with the problem of the One and the Many has caused a fun-

---

19. Gunton, *One, the Three and the Many*, 6.
20. Ibid.
21. Ibid., 33–34.
22. Ibid., 13–16.
23. Ibid., 101.
24. Ibid., 2. Cf. "The History: Augustine, the Trinity, and the Theological Crisis of the West," in his *Promise of Trinitarian Theology*, 31–57.
25. Gunton, *One, the Three and the Many*, 2.
26. Ibid., 55. Italics his.

damental deficiency in our understanding of God. The privileging of the One over the Many has led to an impasse in much of Western theology. First, Gunton clams that *creation* has been severed from *redemption*. This may seem like a sweeping claim, considering the fact that Augustine wrote extensively on both creation *and* redemption. Nonetheless, Gunton contends that in Augustine's thought creation is not *inherently* connected to redemption, but rather creation is an arbitrary act of the will. Also, redemption is a problematic issue for Augustine, for redemption requires a "high view" of the particular, and the particular—or the material—plays a small role in Western thought. That is, because the West has privileged the One, it has been difficult for the West to affirm the essential importance of the Many (i.e., particulars), and hence the importance of the continuing life and redemption of the created order.

Second, this deficient view of the One and the Many, and hence a deficient view of God, where the relationality of God as seen in the Trinity was diminished, led the West to fail to develop a fully Trinitarian ontology. This has led to the *disengagement* of Man from the world, and the *displacement* of God from his rightful transcendent place to the immanent sphere of man's mind. Because of this displacement, God no longer is "there" to provide coordinates for our being.

Gunton's favored solution to the problems spawned by this error in Western theology is the trinitarian theology of the Cappadocian Fathers and Irenaeus. Gunton's goal, in forging a solution, is "a renewed theological vision of truth that does justice to the concerns of modernity and offers a way forward that is free of some of the weaknesses of the Western tradition."[27] Gunton proposes that a trinitarian theology of creation is the best "antidote" to the problem of the One and the Many—and Gunton seeks to offer a theologically-informed way or responding to two trends that can be traced to Augustine: (1) the severing of creation and redemption, and (2) the failure to develop a thoroughly relational and trinitarian ontology.

First, in trying to respond to the supposed severing of creation and redemption, Gunton turns to Irenaeus, with his idea of the "two hands of God" (the Son the Spirit). Gunton sees in Irenaeus a theological model affirming the goodness of creation and an affirmation of God's continued relationship to, and working with, his creation in the working out of

---

27. Ibid., 130.

redemption.[28] Redemption is not a "rescue" of persons from createdness (an error Gunton associates with much of Western theology—especially Augustine), but is rather the bringing of creation to its appointed end (an emphasis Gunton also sees in Basil the Great).

Second, in response to the allegedly inadequate ontology that developed in the West, Gunton looks to the Cappadocian Fathers (particularly Basil), who offer a view of the Trinity, and hence of "being," which does not subsume the Many under the One. The Cappadocians forged a "new" Christian ontology which gives proper place to the concrete personhood of the three members of the Trinity and to their relationships as constitutive of "being," but these insights were ultimately squandered by Augustine.

The purpose of this monograph is to offer an analysis of key components of Gunton's thought in light of the trinitarian theology of Augustine as seen in his *De Trinitate*. To that end, the monograph seeks to come to grips with the trinitarian theology of Augustine, and to ask if Gunton's largely negative assessment of Augustine can stand up to scrutiny. This topic is worthy of study for several reasons: (1) Gunton's construal of Augustine is in many ways representative of a general trend in contemporary theology, and is therefore worthy of attention; (2) in contemporary theology (both academic and popular) there is a fascination with the Eastern Orthodox tradition (and it is largely to this tradition which Gunton looks for theological resources which can be used as a corrective to Augustine); (3) there is a resurgent interest in trinitarian theology, and many of those who write in this area—Thomas Torrance,[29] James Torrance,[30] Alan Torrance,[31] Robert Jenson,[32] John Zizioulas,[33] and Colin Gunton, among others, often have a general sympathy for the East—particularly the Cappadocians—as well as varying measures of antipathy toward Augustine. While Gunton's work can be viewed as part of

---

28. Throughout Gunton's corpus he holds up Irenaeus as the exemplar of systematic theology at its best. For example, at one place Gunton writes, "It is my view that Irenaeus is a model for all systematic theologians." See his "Historical and Systematic Theology," 15.

29. T. Torrance, *Trinitarian Faith*.

30. J. Torrance, *Worship, Community and the Triune God of Grace*.

31. A. Torrance, *Persons in Communion*.

32. Jenson, *Triune Identity*.

33. Zizioulas, *Being as Communion*.

this larger trinitarian theological resurgence, a resurgence which would be worthy of a broader analysis, this study will limit itself largely to a theological analysis of key themes in Augustine's *De Trinitate*, via the contemporary work of Colin Gunton.[34] The monograph will proceed along the following general format.

Following this introductory chapter, the second and third chapters, by an exposition of Gunton's writings, will show how Gunton's largely negative critique of Augustine runs virtually through all of Gunton's writings and is by no means an isolated or peripheral subject in Gunton's theological corpus. Rather, Gunton's thesis that much blame should be laid at the feet of Augustine is a consistent theme in Gunton's theological writings. Chapter Two will look at the theme of creation and redemption in Gunton's writings, summarizing Gunton's position, and summarizing Gunton's perspective on how Augustine erred in those areas.

The third chapter will continue to exposit Gunton's writings, and here we will analyze key issues of ontology: nature, persons and relations. We will summarize Gunton's own position, a position which is sympathetic to, and draws heavily from the Cappadocians. We will also summarize Gunton's critique of Augustine on these issues, for Gunton argues that Augustine simply squandered the ontology forged by the Cappadocians, and that in squandering this inheritance Augustine left a disastrous legacy for the history of Western thought.

The fourth chapter will turn to Augustine's *De Trinitate*. In particular, we will look at the themes of creation and redemption in *De Trinitate*. Attention will be given to the place of the created order in *De Trinitate* as well as how the work of Christ relates to Augustine's efforts in *De Trinitate*. These themes in Augustine will be expounded in light of Gunton's critique, and we will save a full critique of Gunton for later.

The fifth chapter will be devoted to the issue of ontology in *De Trinitate*: nature, persons and relations. What is Augustine's position on these key themes? We will exposit Augustine's writing on these themes, with an eye toward Gunton's criticisms of Augustine.

The sixth chapter will engage in a critique of Gunton in light of our analysis of key themes in *De Trinitate* and other writings of Augustine. We will argue that Gunton's writings are thoroughly helpful and constructive

---

34. Hence, this work is not a manual, or step-by-step, verse-by-verse exposition and critique of *either* Gunton *or* Augustine's *De Trinitate*. Rather, we go to Augustine with Gunton's thesis in mind, and offer a critique of Gunton in light of Augustine.

in a number of areas. Gunton points us in the right direction by looking at the theological roots of contemporary problems (theological or otherwise). Additionally, he helps Western theologians to look at the potential weaknesses of their own tradition, and what might be done to correct the tradition. Specifically, Gunton encourages Western theologians to look to the East (particularly the Cappadocians) and to Irenaeus in order to find theological and conceptual resources and tools which may help theologians to more faithfully communicate and articulate the essentials of the Christian faith. However, we will also point to certain weaknesses in Gunton's writings, particularly to his writings on Augustine, and how Augustine figures in Gunton's theological picture.

Finally, it is important to reiterate what we are *not* arguing. (1) We are not trying to block or defeat Gunton's argument, presented most thoroughly in *The One, the Three and the Many*, that the weaknesses in Augustine's thought will ultimately lead to modernism and postmodernism. The path from Augustine to contemporary problems and issues ultimately is not our concern here. We are asking more fundamental questions about Augustine and Gunton's understanding of him. (2) Related to what has just been mentioned, while we will argue that there are theological and conceptual strengths in Augustine to which Gunton should pay more attention, and that Augustine does a better job of construing persons, nature and relationships in the Trinity than Gunton allows, we will not here deny that there are *tendencies* which may exist in Augustine's thought, which, over time, may be exaggerated by later theologians.

Developments and Critiques of Augustinian Trinitarianism from Anselm to Zizioulas

Before engaging in an exposition of Gunton's work it might be helpful briefly to outline the main contours of how Augustine's construal of the Trinity has been received from Anselm to the present. This will help us to see where Gunton's position falls within the Christian tradition. Is he plowing new ground? Or is he articulating a position which is well-attested in the Christian tradition? Augustine is claimed as a hero by both Protestants and Roman Catholics, and he has had both numerous apologists and antagonists. Where does Gunton fit (if he even does) in the historical lineup of Augustine's friends and foes?

When one looks at the broad picture of trinitarian reflection in the West, and sees the influence which Augustine has had, it is truly impressive. Bracketing for the moment Augustine's obvious use of Scripture in his own construal of the Trinity, and whether Augustine's themes are simply the themes of Scripture, a number of themes in Western trinitarian thought can be traced straight to Augustine: the Holy Spirit as the link between the Father and the Son, the unity of the work of the Trinity, etc. Even when writers differ from Augustine they are almost always *aware* that they are differing, and they take this fact seriously.

Anselm, Richard of St. Victor, and Aquinas

Anselm is best seen as maintaining, on the whole, his Augustinian inheritance. In the Prologue to his *Monologion* Anselm is explicit regarding his appreciation of, and debt to Augustine. He writes, "In the course of frequent readings of this treatise I have been unable to find anything which is inconsistent with the writings of the Catholic Fathers, and in particular with those of the blessed Augustine." He continues, speaking to those who might criticize his work as too "modern" or otherwise in error: "I ask that they first make a careful and thorough reading of the books *On the Trinity* of aforementioned learned Augustine and then judge my little treatise on the basis of them."[35] Anselm followed Augustine closely, but also followed Boethius closely, and did not simply reproduce Augustine's position.[36] Additionally, Anselm was more concerned to defend the *Filioque* clause. His defense of this doctrine in *On the Incarnation of the Word*, *On the Procession of the Holy Spirit*, and briefly in *Monologion* are well-crafted and determined, trying to claim as much common ground with the East as possible, but nonetheless affirming the importance of the *Filioque*.[37] Like Augustine, he did not offer a very satisfactory explanation of the distinction between "generation" and "procession." In fact, it appears that the generation of the Son was virtually subsumed under the procession of the Spirit.[38]

---

35. Anselm, Prologue to *Monologion*, 6.

36. Evans, *Anselm*, 56.

37. See Anselm's essays, *On the Incarnation of the Word* and *On the Procession of the Holy Spirit*. Cf. *Monologion*, 55.

38. Bray, *Doctrine of God*, 181–82.

As a key theologian in medieval scholasticism, Anselm's writings on the Trinity differ markedly from Augustine's in style. Whereas to read Augustine's *De Trinitate* is to embark with Augustine on a dense and technical quest to understand and see the Triune God, to read Anselm is to work through a dense and technical defense of trinitarian dogma as forged in the Western tradition.

Richard of St. Victor (d. 1173) worked with Augustinian themes, expanding or developing Augustine's psychological motif. Like Anselm, Richard worked with the presupposition that God is "perfect existence."[39] Like Augustine, Richard held that love was central to the Divine Being. However, while Augustine did give attention to the Holy Spirit as the love between the Father and Son, Richard was more explicit on the *necessity* of the existence of three persons in order for love to be truly and fully shared. That is, "a Trinity of divine persons *must* exist."[40] But why? One person needs a second person if the first person is going to be able to express love. But a third person is needed as well, because love is not ultimately complete unless a third person also is loved with the same love with which one is loved. Thus, while the Son receives love from the Father, both the Father and Son love the Spirit.

However, the key difference between Richard of St. Victor and Augustine is their respective emphases on nature and persons. Without denying a divine nature, Richard's attention is more centered on the role of the *persons*, and on the three persons as agents of divine love. While the centrality of love is an Augustinian theme, the centrality of persons in Richard's thought is an emphasis worth noting.[41]

Most agree that Aquinas is largely following Augustine on the doctrine of the Trinity.[42] Like Augustine, Aquinas affirms the *received* doctrine of the Trinity as reflected in Scripture, the creeds, and Christian tradition

---

39. Clark, "Trinity in Latin Christianity," 286.

40. Richard of St. Victor, *De Trinitate*, 149.4–150.35 (emphasis mine).

41. Cf. Fortman, *Triune God*, 194.

42. Cf. Davies, *Thought of Thomas Aquinas*, 187. Davies quotes a succinct summary of trinitarian doctrine from Augustine's' *De Trinitate* I.7, where Augustine summarizes the trinitarian dogma he accepts on faith, and then Davies notes that "Aquinas is of the same mind." Davies later notes, Aquinas' "procedure, we might say, is more or less the same as that of St Augustine, whose fifth-century treatise *De Trinitate* was the first really major, systematic, and powerfully influential theological statement of how we think of God as three in one" (192).

in general.[43] Starting with an affirmation of the doctrine itself, Aquinas then explores—like Augustine—certain analogies of the Trinity, and how the general coherence of the doctrine might be articulated and defended. The analogies are worth exploring, but they are truly limited in describing who God is.[44] But for our purposes, what is more revealing is the ways in which Aquinas deviates from, or develops the trinitarian thought of Augustine, and why.

We note here simply a key point at which Aquinas differed from Augustine. As we will see below, throughout Augustine's *De Trinitate* the distinction between procession and generation (or, why the Holy Spirit is said to "proceed" and not said to be "begotten") is broached. By the end of the volume Augustine has not truly answered the question as to why the Holy Spirit is said to proceed, and is not said to be begotten.[45] Aquinas, on the other hand, offers a way of distinguishing between begetting and proceeding. The "coming forth" of the Son (being begotten) is associated with the *intellect*, and the "coming forth" of the Spirit (procession) is associated with the *will* (or *love*). Aquinas writes, "Mind and will are identical in God, but their difference in notion requires a relatedness between an issuing of a word and an issuing of love; for will loves only what mind conceives."[46]

Aquinas' picture of God is also more "tidy" than Augustine's.[47] Again, while Augustine's *De Trinitate* reads like a quest, Thomas' construal of the

---

43. *Summa Theologiae*, I.32.1. Aquinas writes: "Natural reason cannot discover the Trinity of persons in God; it learns about God from his causing of creatures, and knows only what characterizes him as the source of everything that exists." That is, natural reason can discern that there is a cause or source behind things, but natural reason cannot discern that this cause or source is a triune being.

44. *Summa Theologiae*, I.27.1.

45. Towards the very end (Book XV.48—and the last section is 51) Augustine notes, "It still remains of course extremely difficult to distinguish generation from procession in that co-eternal and equal and incorporeal and inexpressibly unchangeable trinity." Instead of actually answering the question, Augustine proceeds to quote a long passage from a sermon on the gospel of John (*Homilies on the Gospel of John* 99, 8–9). The closest he comes to answering the question is as follows: the question still persists as to "why the Holy Spirit is not said to be born but rather to proceed. For if he were called Son he would be called the Son of them both, which is the height of absurdity" (433). In short, to say the Holy Spirit is *begotten* is to say that the Holy Spirit is the Son of both the Father and the Son, which is absurd.

46. *Summa Theologiae*, II.27.3.

47. The following summary of Aquinas is an attempt to make sense of some fairly dense concepts, found in *Summa Theologiae*, 1a, 28. The following sources have been

Triune God is an orderly and impressive summary and defense of the Trinity. Specifically, Thomas contends that there are four *real* relations in God: Paternity, Filiation, Spiration and Procession. These four real relations correspond to the two processions mentioned above: (1) the procession of the Word, which is called *generation* or *begetting* (an act of the Intellect), and (2) the procession of Love, which is called *procession* (an act of the Will). The procession of the Word concerns the relationship of Father and Son to one another: *Paternity* (i.e., the relationship of the Father to the Son, founded on the act of begetting) and *Filiation* (i.e., the relationship of the Son to the Father, founded on the act of being begotten). The procession of Love concerns the relationship of the Holy Spirit to the Father and Son: *Spiration* (i.e., the relationship of Father and Son to Holy Spirit, founded on the act—common to Father of Son—of "spiration," or breathing-out the Holy Spirit) and *Procession* (i.e., the relationship of Holy Spirit to Father and Son, founded on the act of proceeding from Father and Son).

If there are *four* real relations, and if the relations are basically equated with the persons of the Trinity, why is there not *four* members of the Trinity? In short, and this issue is worthy of longer treatment, Aquinas differentiates between *real* relations and *subsistent* relations. While a *real* relation, when speaking of God, is one which is grounded in an act of God, a *subsistent* relation is one which is self-grounded, and is opposite to other relations. In our case, a *subsistent* relation in the Trinity must be truly distinguished from, and opposite to, other relations in the Trinity. David Cunningham's definition is helpful here: "in God, a subsistent relation is only subsistent if it is distinct from the other relations; and this distinction requires a relative contrast."[48] Of the four real relations (Paternity, Filiation, Spiration, Procession), all are also *subsistent* except Spiration. Why? Spiration is *common* to both Father and Son as well as not truly opposition or distinct from Procession. Therefore, Spiration is not a subsistent relation.

Aquinas' reasoning is dense and technical. Working within an Augustinian framework, he has systematized and organized the basic scheme of Augustine. Without being slavishly committed to repristinat-

---

helpful: Cunningham, *These Three Are One*, 59–71; Fortman, *Triune God*, 204–10; perhaps the most concise and helpful treatment is to be found in Hill, *Mystery*, 97–98.

48. Cunningham, *These Three Are One*, 62.

ing the tradition of Augustine, he has nonetheless ushered the Western-Augustinian trinitarian construal to its climax.

John Calvin

There is no question that Calvin was indebted to Augustine, and besides Scripture, Calvin quoted Augustine more than any one other source. However, to simply pass by Calvin with the quick summary that he was in essence "Augustinian" would miss the point. For with Calvin the key issue is not that he was influenced by Augustine, but how Calvin learned from Augustine without leaving Augustine the way he found him.[49]

Of particular interest to our concerns is possible continuities between Calvin and the Cappadocian Fathers, whom Gunton holds up as exemplars. Thomas F. Torrance has written, "Gregory the Theologian [i.e., Gregory Nazianzen] and Calvin the Theologian together build a firm bridge in Christian doctrine between East and West."[50] While Calvin is indebted to Augustine's construal of the Trinity, he is an independent thinker who also develops certain Cappadocian themes.[51]

---

49. Bray, *Doctrine of God*, 197–224, has argued that Calvin's construal of the Trinity is cognizant of both the Cappadocians and Augustine, retaining the strengths of both while ultimately offering his own doctrine, which surpasses them both. Bray contends that after Chalcedon, in which the concept of *person* was so crucial, it was easier for theologians to emphasize primacy of the *person* (rather than *nature*). Bray writes, "It therefore comes as something of a surprise to discover that the Protestant Reformers, in spite of their links with the Augustinian tradition, and not withstanding Karl Barth's claim that he was walking in their footsteps, had a vision of God which was fundamentally different from anything which had gone before, or which has appeared since" (197).

50. T. Torrance, "Doctrine of the Holy Trinity," 21. It is certainly true that Calvin made explicit use of the Cappadocians in his own doctrine of the Trinity. Indeed, in speaking of the threeness of God Calvin turns to Gregory Nazianzen to help explicate his theme, and says, "that passage in Gregory of Nazianzus vastly delights me." (*Institutes*, I.XIII.17; he is quoting Gregory Nazianzen, *On Holy Baptism*, oration xl). It is worth raising a question at this point. If Calvin is Augustinian, yet makes great use of Cappadocian themes, and if Calvin is largely responsible for mediating Augustine to those who followed in the West, could it be that Augustine's impact on the West has thus been, in a sense, "easternized" via Calvin? And hence, what kind of impact would this have on Gunton's thesis that in modernity and postmodernity the West is rebelling against its Augustinian heritage (the overemphasis on the One)?

51. Bray, *Doctrine of God*, 197–98, contends that most of the great Reformation themes flow out of certain trinitarian convictions which are a distinct advance on previous construals of the Trinity: "The great issues of Reformation theology—justification by faith, election, assurance of salvation—can be properly understood only against the background of a trinitarian theology."

Perhaps most significantly, Calvin transcended—to some degree—both the East and the West in emphasizing the thoroughgoing manner in which Father, Son, and Holy Spirit are each *autotheos*—God in himself.[52] Whereas both Augustine and (especially) the Cappadocians emphasized the monarchy of the Father, Calvin was more concerned to emphasize that each person is *autotheos*—God in himself. Thus, Calvin can write, "For in each hypostasis the whole divine nature is understood, with this qualification—that to each belongs his own peculiar quality."[53] Calvin has just mentioned the *differences* between Father, Son and Holy Spirit, and appears to want to stress that such differences (e.g., the Father is the fountain/wellspring, the Son is the wisdom/counsel/ordered disposition of all things, while the Holy Spirit is "assigned the power and efficacy of that activity") by no means mitigate the divine nature of each person. Thomas F. Torrance makes the same basic point this way:

> While Calvin regarded the Father as the focus of divine unity, he did not think of the *Person* of the Father in the same unifying way as Basil of Caesarea or his brother Gregory Nyssen, both because he did not operate with their generic notion of being in the Godhead, and because, like Athanasius and Gregory Nazianzen, he would have nothing to do with "degrees of deity," for there is no greater or less in respect of the Being of consubstantial Persons.[54]

What is significant in this quote for our purposes is not the last remark about the consubstantiality of the three persons, for this was clearly affirmed by Augustine as well. What is significant is Torrance's remark about Calvin's understanding (or rather de-emphasis on) the "unifying" role of the Father. While Calvin, with both Augustine and the Cappadocians, affirms that the Father is the "source" or "fount" of wisdom, Calvin appears anxious *also* to stress that each of the three persons are still *autotheos*—God in himself. As Torrance proceeds to note, "the fullness of the one Godhead applies to each of the three divine Persons as well as to all of them together."[55] In Calvin's words, each of the three persons are God *in solidum* (which translates something like, "in entirety"). Calvin

---

52. Ibid., 201ff. Cf. Warfield, "Calvin's Doctrine of the Trinity."
53. *Institutes*, I.13.19.
54. T. Torrance, "Calvin's Doctrine of the Trinity," 72.
55. Ibid., 73.

writes, "each person *in solidum* is God."⁵⁶ Calvin also wishes to distance himself from the notion that the Son has been given his essence from the Father, a principle held by both Augustine and the Cappadocians. For Calvin, for the Son to receive his essence from the Father tends to undermine the deity of the Son. Calvin writes, "For whoever says that the Son has been given his essence from the Father denies that he has being from himself."⁵⁷ Thus, while Calvin looks to both Augustine and the Cappadocians, he offers a significant shift, in that the emphasis is now on the primacy of persons, and the Son (and the Spirit), along with the Father, are each explicitly considered to be *autotheos*—God in himself, or God *in solidum*—in entirety.

Friedrich Schleiermacher

Schleiermacher is included here, not because of his particular critique of Augustine, but rather because of his role as a transitional figure between the Reformation and modern theology. Karl Barth called Schleiermacher the "Church Father of the 19th century," and most students are introduced to him as the father of liberal theology.⁵⁸ For Schleiermacher the key to religion is "feeling" or the "feeling of absolute dependence," and this feeling is the key motif in understanding his theology.⁵⁹ Christian doctrines ultimately "are accounts of the Christian religious affections set forth in speech."⁶⁰ Christian doctrine—in the best sense of the word—must be "the direct description of the religious affections themselves,"⁶¹ and attention must first be given to those doctrines "which come nearest to the direct exposition of the religious affections."⁶² In light of Schleiermacher's theological method, it comes as little surprise that the doctrine of the Trinity is treated as a conclusion at the very end of *The Christian Faith*. When the center of theology (indeed of Christianity in general) is the "feeling

---

56. *Institutes*, I.13.2. The Latin text of the *Institutes* (I.13.2) reads: *quorum quisque in solidum sit Deus*, which is translated: "of which each person in entirety is God." I.13.23 reads *restat ut tota et in solidum patris et filii sit communis*, which is translated: "It remains that [the essence] is wholly and in entirety common to Father and Son."

57. *Institutes*, I.13.23.

58. Barth, *Protestant Thought*, 306.

59. Schleiermacher, *Christian Faith*, 3–93.

60. Ibid., 76.

61. Ibid., 127.

62. Ibid., 128.

of absolute dependence," and when doctrines are ultimately "expositions" of religious affections, and when only those doctrines which somehow directly flow out of, or concerns one's "feeling of absolute dependence" (or "Christian self-consciousness") are considered worthy of full consideration, it is easy to see how a doctrine like the Trinity might be treated only at the very end of a theological summary.

It is worth noting also that the feeling of absolute dependence, as construed by Schleiermacher, tends towards an emphasis on the unity of God rather than the triunity of God. As Schleiermacher writes, "The feeling of absolute dependence, accordingly, is not to be explained as an awareness of the world's existence, but only as an awareness of the existence of God, as the *absolute undivided unity.*"[63]

Schleiermacher's discussion of the Trinity follows the second of two main sections of the Christian Faith, and this section has been concerned with man, sin, the person and work of Christ, the Christian life and the Church. Thus, Schleiermacher begins his discussion of the Trinity as follows, "An essential element of our exposition in this Part has been the doctrine of the union of the Divine Essence with human nature, both in the personality of Christ and in the common Spirit of the Church."[64] Thus, like the best of the Christian tradition, Schleiermacher couches his discussion of the Trinity in the context of salvation. But, while the doctrine of the Trinity might be true, for Schleiermacher it is nigh impossible to move from the Christian self-consciousness to the doctrine of the Trinity. For, while Christ is the Divine Essence which was united to human nature, and the Holy Spirit is the Divine Essence which pervades the Church, this distinction in the Divine Essence is "not an utterance concerning the religious consciousness, for there it could never emerge."[65] Indeed, Schleiermacher is emphatic that he is *not* saying that "the orthodox doctrine of the Trinity is to be regarded as an immediate or even a necessary combination of utterances concerning the Christian self-consciousness."[66] That is, while Schleiermacher affirms the reality of Christ and the Holy Spirit (however those might be conceived), a distinction in God is *not* something which flows directly out of the Christian

---

63. Ibid., 132; italicizing mine.
64. Ibid., 738.
65. Ibid., 739.
66. Ibid., 740.

self-consciousness or the feeling of absolute dependence, and therefore this distinction in the Godhead (and thus ultimately the Trinity) is not considered essential. As Schleiermacher writes, the key doctrines of the incarnation and the presence of the Holy Spirit in the Church "are independent of the doctrine of the Trinity."[67]

Schleiermacher also contends that the historical affirmation of the Trinity involves one in an impossibility. As Schleiermacher writes, "The ecclesiastical doctrine of the Trinity demands that we think of the three Persons as equal to the Divine Essence, and *vice versa*, and each of the three Persons as equal to the others." Here Schleiermacher has nicely summarized the general historical affirmation of the Trinity. But he continues, "Yet we cannot do either the one or the other, but can only represent the Persons in a gradation, and thus either represent the unity of the Essence as less real than the three Persons, or *vice versa*."[68]

Ultimately, Schleiermacher contends that no one has been able adequately to construe the unity of the Divine Essence and the equality of the three Persons without subordinating one to the other. He even suggests that the New Testament texts which have been the seedbed of trinitarian reflection might be handled and interpreted within a Sabellian paradigm— and to the extent that Schleiermacher believes the Sabellian alternative is a good or adequate way to deal with those texts Schleiermacher would here be guilty of the latent modalism which Gunton sees in the West, and traces to Augustine.[69] Additionally, Schleiermacher concludes that the historical construals of the Trinity have been unable to avoid subsuming the three Persons under the Divine Essence—a point with which Gunton would heartily agree.[70]

Karl Barth

Barth both borrowed from and challenged Augustine in key areas, including the doctrine of the Trinity. For example, like Augustine Barth pictures evil in fully negative terms. In fact, Augustine could call evil the *privatio boni* (privation of the good), and both Augustine and Barth could speak of

---

67. Ibid., 741.
68. Ibid., 742.
69. Ibid., 750.
70. Ibid., 751.

evil as "nothingness."[71] In his work, *The Holy Spirit and the Christian Life* Barth argues fervently that while Augustine is remembered as the great "doctor of grace" who passionately fought Pelagius, Augustine nonetheless erred by seeing too much good in the created order. Indeed, Barth argues that Augustine actually paved the way for those various movements which would emphasize man's work to the diminishing of God's grace.[72]

The concerns which Barth raise in *The Holy Spirit and the Christian Life* are also seen in Barth's reticence and ultimate rejection of the tradition of finding "vestiges" of the Trinity in the created order. Barth held that the idea that one can find traces of the Trinity in the created order opened up the dangerous Pandora's box of natural theology, and its concomitant dangers: the elevation of reason and turning theology into anthropology.[73] However, as we will argue later, Augustine's use of vestiges is *also* very nuanced and reticent. Augustine is quite clear that one *begins* with the theological commitment to the truth of the doctrine of the Trinity. Indeed, the starting point of the theological endeavor is faith. Indeed, Augustine affirms at the beginning of *De Trinitate* that he already believes in the doctrine of the Trinity on the basis of authority (primarily Scripture and Church teaching), and that the quest in *De Trinitate* to understand this Trinity is undertaken with a precommitment to the truth of the doctrine of the Trinity. Indeed, the very first line of *De Trinitate* (besides the prefatory letter to his bishop) reads: "The reader of these reflections of mine on the Trinity should bear in mind that my pen is on the watch against the sophistries of those who scorn the starting-point of faith, and allow themselves to be deceived through an unseasonable and misguided love of reason."[74]

---

71. Barth, *Church Dogmatics*, II/2, 170; III/1, 108; III/3, 352ff. Cf. Thielicke, *Modern Faith and Thought*, 404–5.

72. Barth, *Holy Spirit and the Christian Life*, esp. chapter 1 (pp. 3–11).

73. Cf. Cunningham, *These Three are One*, 94.

74. *De Trinitate* I.1 (p. 65). We note that Thomas Aquinas says virtually the same thing. Aquinas, and here he is very similar to Augustine, says that when we see causation we don't see evidence of a Trinity, but only of a cause (Augustine will argue that we see evidence of the one divine *substance*, but of nothing *trinitarian*; cf. *De Trinitate*, XV, 6–7 [399–400]). On the centrality of faith, Aquinas contends that "though natural reason can learn things about God's nature and unity it knows nothing about the distinction of God's persons." Indeed, "Trying to prove the Trinity by reason would injure the faith by denying the surpassing dignity of its subject-matter, and making it a laughing-stock to unbelievers, who would think our belief relied on such unconvincing arguments." Cf. *Summa Theologiae* I.32.1. Following this, Aquinas virtually echoes Augustine: "An anal-

The first thing Augustine must do is "establish by the authority of the holy scriptures whether the faith is in fact like that."[75] Thus, the quest for the (trinitarian) image of God in man in the latter half of *De Trinitate* must be seen against the backdrop of Augustine's acceptance of the Trinity on the basis of authority, which as the first chapters of *De Trinitate* show, is ultimately Scripture. Initially Barth seems quite friendly to Augustine's effort to find vestiges of the Trinity in creation, as long as one's knowledge of the Trinity is first founded on revelation. This nuance—that we must always begin with God and his revelation—is repeatedly affirmed by Augustine and those who follow him. David Cunningham is correct when he writes that Barth "cites a number of Christian theologians who have described various *vestigia*; [but] he also admits that they seem to have gladly accepted the caveat that one must always move from God to the *vestigia*, not the reverse."[76] Thus, Barth at one point can write that it is legitimate to try to see traces or vestiges of the Trinity in the created order, "because those who knew God's revelation in Scripture thought they might be given the power to say what in and of themselves they naturally do not say and cannot say."[77] This is quite friendly to Augustine's own position, but eventually Barth will contend that the path which is open to the vestiges is a dangerous path indeed. Any theology which seeks to give significant place to the effort of finding vestiges of the Trinity in creation has opened up the door to the loss of revelation and the loss—in the ultimate sense—of *theo*logy.

Karl Rahner

Karl Rahner lamented that in the West theological manuals from the work of Thomas Aquinas forward almost universally treat *De Deo Uno* first, followed by *De Deo Trino*.[78] Rahner writes, "St. Thomas does not begin with God the Father as the unengendered origin in the Godhead, the origin of all reality in the world, but with the nature common to all three

---

ogy from our minds cannot conclusively prove anything about God, since mind does not mean exactly the same thing in God and in us." (I.32.1).

75. *De Trinitate* I.4.
76. Cunningham, *These Three are One*, 98.
77. *Church Dogmatics*, I/1, 340.
78. See Rahner, *The Trinity*, 17. Also see Rahner, "Remarks on the Dogmatic Treatise 'De Trinitate,'" 77–102.

persons. And the procedure became well-nigh universal." Thus, because of this tendency to separate the "One God" and the "Triune God," the Trinity has come "into still greater danger than that of being found without interest for religious existence: *it looks as though everything important about God which touches ourselves has already been said in the treatise* De Deo Uno."[79] Gunton latches on to this phrase, and this criticism from Rahner plays heavily in Gunton's own writings.[80] Ultimately, Rahner concedes, the *order* of the treatises is not as important as the *content* of the treatises. Nonetheless, "in the present division and order of the treatises," their unity and interconnexion is not well enough worked out."[81] Rahner proceeds to suggest that this tendency to emphasize the "one single nature" is possibly to be traced back to Augustine. Rahner suggests that Augustine's desire to start with this "one single nature" risks positing a *fourth* "element" which is prior to the three persons (clearly echoes of Gunton here). Rahner prefers the Eastern way of starting with "the one absolutely unoriginated God, who is still the Father."[82] This discussion leads eventually to Rahner's well-known contention that ultimately, "The Trinity of the economy of salvation *is* the immanent Trinity and vice versa," or as is sometimes abbreviated, "the economic Trinity *is* the immanent Trinity."[83] And for Rahner, keeping the economy at the forefront of the explication of the doctrine of the Trinity is the best way to keep from "losing" the three persons: "Starting from the presence of God the Father himself, communicated in the *economy of salvation* through the Word in the Spirit, one could show that the differentiation in the 'God for us' is also that of the 'God in himself,' and go on simply to explain that this three-fold quality of God in himself may be called triune 'personality.'"[84]

Jürgen Moltmann

Jürgen Moltmann explicitly favors a "social" Trinity over those construals which begin with the One God and then move to the three. Moltmann notes, "My own teachers, Karl Barth and Karl Rahner, decided the ques-

---

79. Rahner, "Remarks," 84–85; emphasis mine.
80. *Promise of Trinitarian Theology*, 32–33.
81. Rahner, "Remarks," 86.
82. Ibid., 84.
83. Ibid., 87.
84. Ibid., 102; emphasis mine.

tion in favour of the sovereignty of the One God and were then able to talk about the Trinity only as the 'three modes of being' or the 'three modes of subsistence of that one God." Moltmann chooses another option: "I myself have proposed instead that the question be decided in favour of the Trinity, and here I have developed a *social doctrine of the Trinity*, according to which God is a community of Father, Son and Spirit, whose unity is constituted by mutual indwelling and reciprocal interpenetration."[85] At least one factor driving Moltmann at this point is that the "social" doctrine of the Trinity allows one to find God's unity not in his sovereignty, but in is "unitedness or at-oneness." With the social Trinity Moltmann is enabled to avoid the language of domination, social systems favoring the "autocracy of a single ruler," the "lordship of the man over the woman," and "ecclesiastical hierarchy," and therefore to affirm "the democratic community of free people," the "equal mutuality" of men and women, and "fellowship church."[86]

In comparing Augustine and Eastern traditions of the Trinity, Moltmann clearly favors the East. He writes, "The first [i.e., Augustine and the West] shows a tendency towards monotheism in the concept of God, and a trend towards individualism in anthropology; whereas the second finds in the triune God the archetype of true human community."[87] The social doctrine of the Trinity found in the East is "a way of overcoming the one-sidedness of Western anthropology."[88] Moltmann contends that Augustine's construal of the Trinity dangerously overemphasizes the One, and has ultimately led to the denigration of the body (by centering the image in the mind), and to the oppression of woman (by seeing man as the primary bearer of the image).[89] The weakness in the Western tradition (typified here in Augustine and Aquinas) is that they "proceeded from the unity of the Trinity in the divine being, and from the divine sovereignty 'outwards.'" Their error?: "In this way they raised to divine dignity the human subject of reason, will and domination."[90] The better option is the East, which "started from the essential fellowship of the Trinity

---

85. Moltmann, *Trinity and the Kingdom*, viii.
86. Ibid., viii–ix.
87. Moltmann, *God in Creation*, 234.
88. Ibid., 234–35.
89. Ibid., 239.
90. Ibid., 242.

(*perichoresis*) and found the *imago Dei* in the primal human community."[91] Finally, contra Augustine, Moltmann wishes to argue that it is the image of *Christ* which is crucial to human existence: "contrary to Augustine's view, human beings are in fact fashioned according to a single Person of the Trinity: the person of the Son."[92] Moltmann could easily be misinterpreted here. He appears to say that we are *created* in the image of God, but the means by which we are "gathered into the open Trinity" [or, one might say, partake or share in the life of the Triune God], is by being conformed to the image of the Son: "As God's image, human beings are the image of the whole Trinity in that they are 'conformed' to the image of the Son: the Father creates, redeems and perfects human beings through the Spirit in the image of the Son."[93]

Moltmann clearly wishes to distance himself from Augustine and is attracted to Eastern construals and conceptions. Gunton and Moltmann have some similar interests. Gunton contends that Augustine's legacy is theological confusion, modernity and postmodernity, and the loss of the particular, relatedness, meaning and truth in contemporary culture. Moltmann emphasizes that Augustine's legacy is the domination and oppression seen in much of Western society. Gunton is cognizant of this, but interestingly does not necessarily embrace Moltmann as a complete kindred spirit. In fact, Gunton claims that for all of Moltmann's strengths—and not withstanding Moltmann's stated preference for Eastern construals of the Trinity—even Moltmann has failed truly to appropriate the ontological and conceptual advance and resources of the Cappadocians.[94] It is the Cappadocian ontology—a truly *Christian* ontology—which must be recovered. Indeed, "Underlying the concerns [of Moltmann] . . . is the matter of ontology, without which none of the questions will receive satisfactory treatment."[95] Nonetheless, Moltmann represents a contemporary trend which is on the same general trajectory which Gunton is attempting to propagate.[96]

91. Ibid.
92. Ibid.
93. Ibid., 243.
94. We will detail these details in a later chapter.
95. *Promise of Trinitarian Theology*, 23.
96. A. J. Conyers argues that in order for Moltmann's theology to work or succeed, Moltmann actually *needs* the hierarchy that he so passionately rejects. Cf. Conyers, *God, Hope, and History*. For an analysis of Moltmann and Pannenberg, see Olson, "Trinity and Eschatology," 213–27.

Wolfhart Pannenberg

Pannenberg offers a slightly more appreciative interpretation of Augustine. Pannenberg correctly points to the limited nature of Augustine's analogies, and that Augustine did *not* try to derive threeness from the one essence. As Pannenberg notes, "Augustine's psychological analogies should not be used to derive the trinity from the unity but simply to illustrate the Trinity in whom one already believes."[97] Indeed, "The psychological analogies that [Augustine] suggested and developed in his work on the Trinity were simply meant to offer a very general way of linking the unity and trinity and thus creating some plausibility for trinitarian statements." The "picture of God in the human soul" ultimately "falls far short of the original," and Augustine ultimately emphasized the inadequacy and limited nature of the psychological analogies.[98]

Like Gunton, Pannenberg worries about an emphasis on the oneness of God that diminishes the importance of the three. Indeed, "The moment it appears that the one God can be better understood without rather than with the doctrine of the Trinity, the latter seems to be a superfluous addition to the concept of the one God even though it is reverently treated as a mystery of revelation." This surely resonates with Gunton's own concerns. This tendency to deemphasize or neglect the Trinity is pinpointed by Pannenberg, and is to be traced, in large part to the failure in the seventeenth and eighteenth centuries to affirm "an inner systematic connection between the trinitarian statements and the divine unity."[99] When this lack of an "inner systematic connection" is combined with certain strands of biblical interpretation and historical criticism, the groundwork is laid for the loss of the doctrine of the Trinity.[100] For our purposes we simply note that for Pannenberg, the plight of the Trinity (at least until Barth) in modern times is not traced primarily to Augustine, as in Gunton. Rather, Pannenberg's historical reconstruction centers on the conceptual failure to maintain a unity between the oneness and threeness of God, and it was into this stage that certain movements in biblical studies began to question finding the Trinity in the biblical documents.

---

97. Pannenberg, *Systematic Theology*, 287.
98. Ibid., 284–85.
99. Ibid., 291.
100. Ibid., 291–92.

However, we should not drive a wedge between Pannenberg and Gunton, either. For while Pannenberg does not trace the difficulties mainly to Augustine, Pannenberg still finds weaknesses in Augustine's construal of the Trinity, and Pannenberg's constructive proposals mirror Gunton's at points.

First, like Gunton, Pannenberg wishes to emphasize particularity—in Pannenberg's case the particularity of Jesus Christ. Thus, in formulating one's conception of the Trinity, the starting point is "the revelation of God in Jesus Christ."[101] Likewise Pannenberg notes, "the concrete relation of Jesus to the Father, not the thought of the self-communication of God by the Son and Spirit, must be the starting point for trinitarian reflection."[102] Whether one can fully move from Jesus of Nazareth to a full-orbed affirmation of the Trinity is a question we will leave for later.[103]

Second, Pannenberg somewhat criticizes Augustine's notion that the Spirit is the love between the Father and Son. That is, Pannenberg affirms that the Spirit is the "bond of union between the Father and the Son." However, Pannenberg rejects the double procession of the Spirit.[104] Nonetheless, the notion that the Spirit is the love that unites Father and Son does diminish the distinct personhood of the Spirit.[105] Pannenberg also criticizes Augustine for his tendency to gloss over or ignore those biblical texts which speak of Jesus *receiving* the Spirit, for in doing so, Augustine gives inadequate attention to the relationship between Son and Spirit.[106] Where Augustine (and the West in his trail) *and* Eastern theologians have gone astray has been in interpreting fellowship vocabulary in terms of a relation of origin, for in so doing Augustine *and* Eastern theologians "cannot do justice to the reciprocity in the relations."[107]

---

101. Ibid., 301.

102. Ibid., 307.

103. Henri Blocher is rather skeptical: Pannenberg "cannot solve the contradiction between his sound concern to maintain the ontological Trinity ("concrete monotheism"), and the construction of *his* Trinity from the man Jesus." See his "Immanence and Transcendence in Trinitarian Theology," 119.

104. Ibid., 316–17. Of course, the double-procession of the Spirit is not unique to Augustine, and its rejection is not unique to Pannenberg.

105. Ibid., 316.

106. Ibid., 316 n. 179.

107. Ibid., 318–19.

Third, and following from the second point, Pannenberg laments the tendency in the West to reduce the three persons to individual relations, a tendency which Pannenberg associates with Augustine.[108] Pannenberg wishes to say that the trinitarian relations *constitute* the "different distinctions of the persons," yet the persons cannot simply be *reduced* to relations, largely because the nexus of relations is more complex and multi-faceted than perhaps was once thought.

Fourth, contra Augustine and the Cappadocian Fathers, Pannenberg argues against the notion that the Son and Spirit "derive" their deity from the Father. This notion is found in both Augustine and the Cappadocians, and Pannenberg wishes to retrieve the work of Athanasius, among others, in order to affirm that even the deity of the Father is in a real sense dependent on the Son.[109]

Fifth, Pannenberg, like Gunton, wishes to emphasize the economy of salvation as central to one's construal of the Trinity.[110] This is of course concomitant to Pannenberg's emphasis on the "revelation of God in Jesus Christ as the starting point" of one's doctrine of the Trinity.[111] Pannenberg generally affirms Rahner's dictum that "the immanent trinity is the economic trinity," as long as the immanent trinity is not ultimately absorbed into the economic trinity.[112]

Finally, we note that as much similarity there is between Pannenberg and Gunton, Pannenberg closes his chapter on the Trinity by refuting an option which, as we shall see, Gunton shall defend. Pannenberg calls for a "new way" of expressing the "unity of the three persons in the one God," but offers little concrete direction. Whereas Gunton will argue that the communion of the three persons of the Trinity *is* the being of God, Pannenberg appears to explicitly reject this option. Pannenberg writes, "the unity of the persons in mutual perichoresis" does not give us "the thought of the unity of the persons," for perichoresis "presupposes another basis of the unity of the three persons." Indeed, the "inward and outward working together of the three persons cannot be the basis of the premise

---

108. Ibid., 320.
109. Ibid., 322.
110. Ibid., 327ff.
111. Ibid., 300ff.
112. Ibid., 327–28.

of their unity, though their essential unity, which has its basis elsewhere, can find expression in it."[113]

John D. Zizioulas

Perhaps the most significant Eastern influence on Colin Gunton is John D. Zizioulas.[114] Zizioulas is one of the chief contemporary trinitarian theologians working within the Eastern Orthodox tradition. To a large degree, Gunton's indebtedness to the Cappadocian Fathers can be traced to the influence of Zizioulas.[115] Zizioulas' work is most accessible to the English reader in his *Being as Communion: Studies in Personhood and the Church*.[116] Gunton follows Zizioulas in affirming that the Patristic Fathers, particularly the Cappadocians, forged a new ontology which was able to move beyond the monistic ontology of the ancient Greeks. Zizioulas contends that the "creation of this ontology was perhaps the greatest philosophical achievement of patristic thought."[117] This "new" ontology is captured in the title of his book, "being as communion." That is, being *is* communion. Thanks to such theologians as Athanasius and especially the Cappadocian Fathers, "the ancient world heard for the first time that it is communion which makes beings 'be': nothing exists without it, not even God."[118] Patristic thought is led to two theses regarding ontology: (1) "There is no true being without communion," thus "Communion is an ontological category"; and (2) communion must originate in a hypostasis, a "concrete and free person."[119] Thus, communion is not something a preexisting Church "does"; rather, communion *constitutes* the Church as the Church. As Zizioulas writes: "Thus the eucharist was not the act of a preexisting Church; it was an event *constitutive* of the being of the Church, enabling the Church to *be*. The eucharist *constituted* the Church's being."[120]

---

113. Ibid., 334. For further analysis of Pannenberg see Roger Olson, "Wolfhart Pannenberg's Doctrine of the Trinity," 175–206. Cf. Olson, "Trinity and Eschatology."

114. This summary of Zizioulas is by necessity brief. We will be treating these themes in more detail below. For a recent exposition of the trinitarian thought of Zizioulas and Joseph Cardinal Ratzinger, see Volf, *After Our Likeness*.

115. Personal conversation with Colin Gunton, Regent College, June 1998.

116. Zizioulas, *Being as Communion*.

117. Ibid., 16.

118. Ibid., 17.

119. Ibid., 18.

120. Ibid., 21.

As we will discuss later, Gunton clearly leans upon Zizioulas. However, Gunton's position is less concerned with "communion" *per se*, and more with relationship. Thus, Gunton essentially modifies Zizioulas' "being as communion" to the effect of, "being in relationship." That is, for Gunton the being of God *is* the three persons in relationship.

Conclusion

Having briefly summarized some of the main contours of historical responses to Augustine, we note that Gunton is by no means alone in criticizing Augustine, nor in looking to the East for direction. Thus, Gunton is clearly not writing in a theological or historical "vacuum." There are "fellow travellers" who share many of the same convictions and concerns. However, to grasp the force of Gunton's thought, and perhaps its uniqueness, and to understand the continuities and discontinuities between Gunton and others, we must engage in a more thorough exposition and analysis of his work. To such exposition and analysis we now turn.

CHAPTER 2

Creation and Redemption in the Theology of Colin Gunton

WHAT EXACTLY ARE GUNTON's objections to the theology of Augustine? Gunton's criticisms of Augustine show up in practically all of his works, whether on Christology,[1] creation,[2] the atonement,[3] and the Church,[4] and one of the clearest expositions of Gunton's position on Augustine is found in Gunton's *The Promise of Trinitarian Theology*. For example, in the opening pages Gunton writes: "One of the theses to be argued in this set of essays is that there is much to be said for the claim that the way in which Augustine formulated the doctrine of the Trinity did bequeath problems to the West, and that in solving them some help is to be sought from the Cappadocian Fathers."[5] It is fair to say that this remark summarizes the thought of much of Gunton's theological writing: Augustine has led us astray, and the way back is to be found (in part) through the Cappadocians (as well as Irenaeus). Gunton notes, "the shape of the Western tradition has not always enabled believers to rejoice in the triune being of God. The Trinity has more often been presented as a dogma to be believed than as the living focus of life and thought.... [Thus] if the real God is known as one, the tacking on of his threeness

1. *Christ and Creation*.
2. In addition to *Christ and Creation*, see especially *The One, the Three and the Many*.
3. *Actuality of the Atonement*.
4. "Church on Earth," 48–80.
5. *Promise*, 1–2.

simply appears as an unnecessary complicating of the simple belief in God." Gunton continues: "Hence there developed the apparent mathematical dimensions: the hopeless quest for analogies that will somehow make sense of the otherwise illogical."[6] And Gunton concludes: "As we shall see, this has much to do with Augustine's famous quest in the latter part of his *De Trinitate* for threefold patterns in experience, and particularly mental experience, which might be seen in some way to mirror the being of God as three."[7]

In our exposition of Gunton's thought, particularly as it reflects on the trinitarian theology of Augustine, we survey Gunton's thought with an eye to the problem of the One and the Many. This is a key theme for Gunton, and it generally pervades most of his writing in one way or another. But two other key themes are the categories of (1) Creation and Redemption, and (2) Ontology (particularly nature, persons, and relations). But undergirding the entire discussion will be the over-arching matrix of the One and the Many, which is *the* conceptual backdrop for Gunton's understanding of the history of Western thought. At the heart of Gunton's critique is Gunton's claim that Augustine *begins* with the oneness of God and that Augustine also *overemphasizes* the One at the expense of the Three. As Gunton reads Augustine, this orientation was key to Augustine's own theology and had a thoroughgoing (and ultimately disastrous) influence on the history of Western thought. While this preeminence of the One in Augustine's theology serves as a summary of Gunton's general critique of Augustine, this "problem" flows quickly into, or is intricately related to, other difficulties that Gunton sees with Augustine and his legacy, problems we will treat in turn.

In *The One, the Three and the Many*, the ancient philosophical problem of the One and the Many serves as *the* conceptual backdrop for Gunton's analysis of modernity and how we got there. While Parmenides emphasized the One (i.e., reality is totally unchanging), and Heraclitus the Many (i.e., reality is flux and change), Western thought has struggled with how to hold the One and the Many together.[8] The question of the

6. Ibid., 3.
7. Ibid.
8. Gunton, *One, the Three and the Many*, 18, posits that "the dialectic of the one and the many has provided the framework for most subsequent thinking about many of the basic topics of thought."

One and the Many is crucial, and one's position on the nature of reality (i.e., the One and the Many) is constitutive of one's view of the world and life in general. When considered theologically, we could say that one's view of God shapes one's view of everything else. As Gunton writes: "from the beginning of Western thought the concept of God, or its equivalent, has served to provide a focus for the unity of the world."[9] Thus, the chief error of Augustine is that Augustine, like Parmenides and Plato, overemphasizes the One at the expense of the Many. This is the heart of Gunton's quarrel with Augustine. Augustine, with his "monist" God has bequeathed to the West a plethora of problems, which has now manifested itself in modernity and even post-modernity (which in Gunton's view is best seen as a type of "late modernity"). Specifically, Augustine's emphasis on the One led to modernity because modernity is ultimately the rejection of the authoritarian One which has pervaded so much of Western thought. As Gunton writes: "The Western theological tradition . . . was strongly Parmenidean in much of its thrust, so that modernity has rebelled against God, the one, in the name of the many."[10] Indeed the modern (including the postmodern) penchant for unrelated particulars (or, one might say, radical "diversity") is in part an understandable reaction to the oppressive One: "The unity of God has been stressed at the expense of his triunity, and to that extent the modern critique must be understood as a recalling of theology to its own trinitarian roots."[11] In short, modernity is finally the ultimate rejection of the One in favor of the Many, and the blame for this tendency to emphasize the one is to be laid at the feet of Augustine.

In this chapter we will engage in a close reading of Gunton's writings with attention to the theme of creation and redemption. This rubric of "creation and redemption" will serve as the backdrop for our discussion of Gunton's position on the classical doctrines of the Christian faith. The use

---

9. Ibid., 22. We will treat the whole issue of whether or not the Trinity is a "model" (e.g., for the Church or for the world) in more detail later. Gunton believes the Trinity serves as an example for both the Church and the world. Miroslav Volf also wishes to see the Trinity as a model for the Church in his *After Our Likeness*. Adam, "The Trinity and Human Community," 63, offers a more cautious note when he states that while "the Trinity may be a model for the church and for the world, it is worth remembering that these are minor themes in the Bible." He concludes, "The focus of the Bible is not on the model of the Trinity but on the message of the Trinity: and that message is the gospel of Jesus Christ."

10. *One, the Three and the Many*, 41.

11. Ibid., 39.

of this rubric should both help us to see the coherency of Gunton's theological writings, and see how Gunton's negative portrayal of Augustine is a generally pervasive theme in Gunton's writings. We now turn to Gunton's writings and will examine them under the heading of creation and redemption.

Creation and the Created Order

At the heart of Gunton's theology is a strong doctrine of creation. In the sense that creation is perhaps *the* central doctrine in Gunton's thought, he echoes H. H. Schmid's assertion that "all theology is creation theology, even when it does not speak expressly of creation but speaks of faith, justification, the reign of God, or whatever, if it does so in relation to the world."[12] One could say that this doctrine is a cornerstone to the rest of Gunton's thought. We will see in Gunton's writing on creation his recurring themes: the centrality of the Trinity to a full and complete understanding of creation, and key weaknesses in Western construals of creation—largely traceable to Augustine. Gunton notes three key features of a Christian understanding of creation, and seven key doctrinal features that flow from these three key features.[13] The three key features of a Christian understanding of creation are: (1) "creation as an article of the creed"; (2) "creation out of nothing"; (3) "creation as a work of the whole Trinity."

Seven doctrinal themes flow out of these three key Christian contributions to the doctrine of creation.[14] First, in creating out of nothing God did not use anything external to himself. God did not need anything outside himself in order to create. Additionally, the created order had a definite beginning in space and time.

Second, *creatio ex nihilo* does *not* imply that creation was an arbitrary act of the will on God's part. Rather creation is purposive in that (1) it flows from the love of God, and (2) creation exists for a reason—creation

---

12. Schmid, "Creation, Righteousness, and Salvation, 115.

13. A succinct and helpful summary of Gunton's doctrine of creation, and his perspective on how this doctrine has fared in the history of Christian thought can be found in Gunton, "Doctrine of Creation," 141–57. For a longer treatment see Gunton's *Triune Creator*. For a more detailed treatment of the christological nature of creation see his *Christ and Creation*.

14. Unless otherwise noted, these seven themes are explicated in Gunton, "Doctrine of Creation," 141–44.

has a *telos*; it is "going somewhere." Thus, creation is not somehow "necessary," as if God was "compelled" to create. Rather, God chose to freely create as an act of love. *But*, since God was already a loving community of three persons, the act of creation was not a necessary one that was needed in order for God to express love.

Third, a Christian doctrine of creation affirms that creation is in a sense both dependent and independent, and is moving toward a *telos*. That is, the world is indeed not God, and is indeed a separate entity, but that God—through the Son and Spirit (the "two hands" of Irenaeus)—is continually relating to the world, allowing and moving the world toward its appointed end.

Fourth, closely related to the third feature above, a proper understanding of how God is related to the created order helps us to understand such themes as conservation, preservation, providence and redemption. All of these works of God are carried out through the Son and Spirit, with particular emphasis to the incarnation. Conservation and preservation refer to God's continued maintenance and upholding of the created order, while providence and redemption look more forward to God's work, through the Son and Spirit, of moving the world to its appropriate *telos*.

Fifth, a Christian doctrine of creation has a certain perspective on the perennial problem of evil. Christianity does not have the option of tracing evil to matter, since creation is ultimately "good." Rather, evil should be seen as somehow parasitic upon, and a perversion of, the good. Evil is "that which corrupts the good creation and so thwarts God's purpose for it."[15] Due to the reality of evil and sin, the created order must be redirected to its proper end, indeed redeemed, and this work of God again must be conceived of in trinitarian—christological and pneumatological—terms.

Sixth, for historic Christianity, creation includes a preeminent place for man, who is made in God's image. Rather than locating the image in some human endowment, like reason, it is better to see the image in terms of "a conception of the whole of human being as existing in relation to God, other human beings and the rest of the created order." And this image must be understood christologically. We truly image God more and

---

15. Gunton, and indeed the Christian tradition as a whole, is clearly indebted to Augustine at this point. Cf. *Triune Creator*, 203, where Gunton writes that evil "is not intrinsic to the creation, but some corruption of, or invasion into, that which is essentially good."

more as we are being conformed to the image of Christ, and we shall fulfill our "dominion" role properly only as we are being conformed to Christ.

Seventh, the doctrine of creation implies a certain ethical standard and mission. Since God has created the world, and since redemption entails the perfecting of the world, a bringing of the world to its appointed end, Christians are called to live their lives ethically, in response to God.

We might summarize Gunton's analysis with the following three propositions. The first main theme in Gunton's doctrine of creation is the goodness and limited independence of creation.[16] The material world is good, and there is no matter/spirit dualism. Additionally, creation has a limited independence. That is God created the world, and the world has a purpose which must be fulfilled.

The second main theme in Gunton's doctrine of creation is the concern to affirm the continuity between creation and redemption. Redemption is not simply a "rescue operation" out the world. Rather, redemption is to be seen as bringing or moving creation to its true end, of perfecting creation.

Third, Christ is central to creation. Christ is both the mediator of creation, and Christ is the mediator of redemption. Any doctrine of creation which does not keep Christ at the center really does not deserve the name "Christian."

Having summarized Gunton, how does Augustine fit into Gunton's construal? Gunton summarizes the history of the doctrine of creation by pointing to several key figures who offered positive construals and are exemplars of helpful developments of the doctrine. Justin Martyr helped differentiate Christianity from Platonism, and by differentiating man from God opened up the possibility of his contention that knowledge of God is possible only through the work of the Holy Spirit.[17] Irenaeus affirmed *creatio ex nihilo*, the goodness of the created order, the eschatological, or redemptive *telos* at the heart of the created order, a redemption which is brought about by the "two hands" of God, the Son and Spirit.[18] Basil the Great argued, against Aristotle, that all things are created, and that matter is not eternal, while John Philoponos (sixth century) also argued against the eternality of the universe.

---

16. *Christ and Creation*, 91.
17. "Doctrine of Creation," 148.
18. Ibid.

But not all the developments in Christian thought were helpful or faithful to the tradition which preceded them, and particular blame is to be directed against platonizing tendencies found in thinkers like Origen and Augustine. Origen errs in his two-fold doctrine of creation, which affirms a matter/spirit dualism, in which spirit is superior to matter, and Origen failed to fully appreciate the goodness of the created order, which is seen largely as simply a means toward redemption.[19]

But it is Augustine who comes under particular fire. The interconnectedness of creation and redemption is a key theme in Gunton's analysis, and he sees serious deficiencies in Augustine's thought on this score. Indeed, Augustine's failure to affirm the interconnectedness or continuity between creation and redemption is simply an outgrowth of his insufficient construal of the Trinity—i.e., his failure to properly construe the One and the Many. Thus, as Gunton sees it, this problem of the One and Many flows quickly into other problems. In Gunton's view, Augustine's trinitarian construal diminishes the link between creation and redemption. This is tragic, because as Gunton sees it there is an intricate relation between creation and redemption. He writes: "Creation was not simply the making of the world out of nothing, not even that world continually upheld by the providence of God, but the making of a world destined for perfection, completedness."[20] Both creation and redemption are ultimately trinitarian acts, and Gunton (looking to Basil), sees the Holy Spirit as the "perfecting cause of creation." Indeed, for Gunton, the Holy Spirit is the agent through whom God perfects *this* creation into a perfect order, rather than *simply* the "replacing" this order with another.[21] Gunton follows Karl Rahner in criticizing Augustine, for following Augustine theological writers generally write separate treatises, *On the One God* and *On the Triune God* (and Gunton and Rahner lament both the fact that they are separate treatises, and that *On the One God* precedes *On the Triune God*). On Gunton's view, such separate treatments, and the fact that the *oneness* of God is primary results in severing creation from redemption. Indeed, the result of Augustine's trinitarian doctrine is "that salvation history comes to appear irrelevant to the doctrine of God."[22] But how exactly

---

19. Ibid., 149.
20. *Christ and Creation*, 45.
21. Ibid., 46.
22. *Promise of Trinitarian Theology*, 33.

is this so? How is it that Augustine's (alleged) over emphasis on the one results in a diminishing of the link between creation and redemption?

Ultimately, creation is severed from redemption, since redemption requires the continued activity of God with particulars, and particulars appear to be problematic for Augustine.[23] That is, Augustine so emphasizes the one essence that he finds it difficult to make sense of the three (i.e., the particulars), and hence it is also difficult to conceive of God as *redemptively* related to particulars. Gunton contends that for Augustine, the "true ontological foundations of the doctrine of the Trinity ... are to be found in the conception of a threefold mind and not in the economy of salvation."[24] That is, Augustine looks to the human mind rather than the redemptive work of God in the world for analogies of the Trinity. Therefore, Augustine's attempt to articulate psychological analogies for the Trinity tends to divide creation from redemption and reveals Augustine's antipathy for the material world: "*The crucial analogy for Augustine is between the inner structure of the human mind and the inner being of God, because it is in the former* [the human mind] *than the latter* [the inner being of God] *is made known, this side of eternity at any rate, more really than in the 'outer' economy of grace.*"[25] Indeed, as Gunton writes: "*The root of modern disarray is accordingly to be located in the divorce of the willing of creation from the historical economy of salvation.*"[26]

For Gunton, Augustine's neoplatonism taints his doctrine of creation, as seen in the fact that Augustine—even after his Christian conversion—maintains something of an antipathy for the created order.[27] Gunton contends that for Augustine, "Because God is timelessly eternal, nothing that he does can be understood to take time."[28] Thus, for Augustine creation *had* to be instantaneous, since creation certainly could not have taken *time*. But this type of doctrine of creation, according to Gunton, is in error, and ultimately leads to Deism. How? Ultimately, Augustine's emphasis on the timelessness of God "means that his theology is in the outcome far more 'other-worldly' than Irenaeus', and less able to be affirmative of the

---

23. *One, the Three and the Many*, 2.
24. *Promise of Trinitarian Theology*, 42–43.
25. Ibid., 45.
26. Ibid., 55; italics his.
27. *Triune Creator*, 73ff.
28. Ibid., 77.

world of time and space."²⁹ Thus, since Augustine finds it difficult to articulate the relation of God and the world, his God ends up being the god of deism, exiled outside of time, with no meaningful relationship with *this world*.³⁰

Related to the above, Gunton contends that Augustine's inadequate doctrine of creation helped keep Augustine from properly construing the relation of this world to the reality of redemption. That is, Augustine's doctrine of creation kept him from being able to affirm the continuity between creation and redemption. As Gunton writes, it is with Augustine "that there comes into theology the notion of creation as the product of a kind of abstract omnipotence, inadequately related to the economy of salvation."³¹ That is, it is "sheer will" which drives Augustine's God to create.³²

In Gunton's view, Augustine's two-stage creation echoes Philo. God first creates "a kind of intellectual creature," and only secondly creates an inferior material world.³³ Thus, we see again a matter/spirit type of dualism. Whereas Irenaeus had, in combating the Gnostics, argued that there were ultimately only two orders of being—God and the world, Augustine has forfeited this truth by positing a dualism within the world. Instead of two ontological categories of God and creation, we have with Augustine an ontological dualism *within* creation between matter and spirit, or between the material and non-material world. Gunton is generally not positive about Augustine, so we must mention a certain place at which Gunton is generally favorable to Augustine, at least at first. Gunton affirms Augustine's contention that time is created *with* the world. That is, creation took place *with* time, but not *in* time, such that we must say that time only came into being with the creation of all things.³⁴ However, the problems begin when one tries to conceive of the relation of a timeless God to the world. That is, it is one thing to say that time was only created when the rest of creation came into being. It is another thing to *continue* to conceive of God as timeless while trying to construe this God

---

29. Ibid., 83.

30. Gunton is also wary of a tendency he sees in Augustine of equating (1) being in time/being created with (2) fallenness. See ibid., 83.

31. Ibid., 16.

32. Ibid., 76.

33. Ibid., 78. Gunton is quoting Augustine's *Confessiones* 12.9.

34. *Triune Creator*, 83.

Creation and Redemption in the Theology of Colin Gunton 39

as actively relating to his creation. And it is Augustine's effort to *continue* to picture God as timeless that is problematic for Gunton. As Gunton writes, "Augustine tends to conclude that because creation is the act of the timeless God, then all God's acts must be conceived to be timeless."[35] The problem, as Gunton contends, is that since "for Augustine God is by definition timeless, it becomes difficult to conceive of any involvement of God in time."[36] Thus, *time* itself is problematic for Augustine.[37] Indeed, since for Augustine the fact that events in time actually *take* time is a sign of fallenness, it becomes virtually impossible to conceive of God's continued relations with the created order. Thus, we are back to Gunton's repeated theme of the cleavage between creation and redemption, a problem found particularly in Augustine, and mediated to much of Western theology through him. Since time, by its very nature is concomitant with fallenness, and since this world exists in time, it is difficult for Augustine to hold creation and redemption together, since redemption requires an intimate relation to *this* world.

Another key component of Gunton's criticisms of Augustine is the charge that whereas Basil affirmed an ontological homogeneity of the created order, where all of creation was on the same plane ontologically, Augustine affirmed a hierarchy of being, where the highest strata had divine-like qualities, and the lower strata—matter—was "close to being nothing."[38] Gunton also quotes Augustine in the *City of God*, where Augustine can write that God "created man's nature as a kind of mean

---

35. Ibid.

36. Ibid.

37. Gunton's conclusion is interesting. We should conceive of God neither in terms of timelessness nor temporality. Rather, we should simply be apophatic. We simply should remain silent on the issue of God and time. We know that the "work of Christ and the Spirit indeed indicate God's positive relation with time, demonstrating both his freedom and sovereignty over it and the fact that it is not entirely foreign to his being." But we should stop there, for "anything beyond that is necessarily mere speculation. See *Triune Creator*, 92.

38. See *Triune Creator*, 78; 92ff. Gunton is quoting Augustine, *Confessiones* 12.7. However, we should note in the context Augustine is arguing from Wisdom 11:18 that in the first stage of creation God created a type of formless matter. In 12.8 he writes, "But at that first stage the whole was almost nothing because it was still totally formless. However, it was already capable of receiving form. For you, Lord, 'made the world of formless matter' (Wisd. 11:18)." Then Augustine writes, that out of this formless matter God makes the rest of the universe: "You made this next-to-nothing out of nothing, and from it you made great things at which the sons of men wonder."

between angels and beasts."[39] In such tendencies, Augustine is squandering the Cappadocian inheritance (here particularly Basil), which affirmed that all of creation is ontologically equal

Man, the Imago Dei, and Sin

While discussing Gunton's doctrine of creation it is appropriate to speak a word about man and sin in Gunton's writings. Gunton has written full volumes on neither man nor sin. However, we can see the outlines of his perspective by looking at his work as a whole. Gunton is eager to affirm the goodness of the created order, including man. Rejecting any matter/spirit dualism, Gunton affirms the goodness of the created order, and as we have seen, he is eager to see redemption as bringing about the true end of the created order. That is, redemption is not "rescuing" persons out of the world. Rather, creation has always had a certain *telos*, and redemption is God's work of bringing about that proper end. Within the created order, man does have a place of preeminence. Man is the image-bearer, and has been given dominion over the created order.[40] Gunton, against many current trends, affirms the centrality and supremacy of man in creation. Nonetheless, while man is at the apex of creation, and is at the center of redemption, the whole created order is included in God's redemptive work.[41]

As image-bearers the doctrine of man must be understood in a christological sense, in that we only truly fulfill our role as image-bearers by being in, and relating to Christ. As Gunton contends, "Just as, therefore, we cannot understand the creation apart from Christ, so we fail even more completely to understand human being apart from Christ, and particularly apart from Christ crucified."[42] Gunton here understands the *imago dei* less in terms of "reason" or some other human endowment, and more in terms of "the whole of human being as existing in relation to God, other human beings and the rest of the created order."[43] That is,

---

39. *De civitate Dei* 12.21. It should be noted here that the context for Augustine's discussion is the responsibility man had to obey the commands of God given him in the garden, and the dominion role man is to exercise over the rest of the created order below him.

40. Ibid., 143–44.

41. *Christ and Creation*, 33.

42. *Triune Creator*, 196.

43. "Doctrine of Creation," 144.

"To be in the image of God is not, therefore, to have some timeless quality like reason, or anything else, but to exist in a directedness, between our coming from nothing and our being brought through Christ before the throne of the Father."[44]

This last point deserves elaboration. At the heart of Gunton's attempt to appropriate the riches of trinitarian theology is the centrality of *relationship* as constituting the being of God. That is, the three persons in relationship *is* the being of God. In relationship to anthropology, Gunton wishes to extrapolate and say that we, like God, are duly constituted as relational beings. That is, being in relationship is what it *means* to be a human person. We are constituted by both "horizontal" and "vertical" relationships, "horizontal" in that we relate to the rest of the created order, and "vertical" in that we relate to God.[45] Gunton writes, "In sum, then, we know ourselves, we come to learn about the kind of beings that we are, as we live in terms of three different kinds of relations: as we live in the created world, with each other and before God our creator and redeemer." Indeed, "To ignore any of the three is to fail to know who and what we are."[46] While the most full way to relate to God is as a believer in the Triune God, and as one who confesses the lordship of Christ, God nonetheless is preserving the whole of the created order. Gunton contends that we image God in a trinitarian fashion. Our imaging of God is somehow modeled on how God images himself. So Gunton: "Imaging is therefore a triune act: the Son images the Father as through the Spirit he realises a particular pattern of life on earth." Hence, "The representative bearer of the image becomes, as the channel of the Spirit the vehicle of the renewal of the image in those who enter into relation with him." Thus, for those who are in Christ, there "is a 'change into his likeness' (2 Cor. 3:18), a being renewed in knowledge after the image of the creator' (Col. 3:10)."[47] What Gunton appears to be saying here is that as we are in Christ, Christ renews the image of God in us. As Gunton writes, "Jesus is the true image of God and means of the restoration of its true form in others—those who are 'conformed' to his image (Romans 8:29)."[48]

---

44. *Christ and Creation*, 102.
45. Ibid., 36f.
46. Ibid., 74.
47. Ibid., 101.
48. *Triune Creator*, 198.

Gunton summarizes two dimensions as to what it means for us to image God. First, the fact that man is made male and female is "a finite echo of the relatedness of Father, Son and Holy Spirit."[49] In other words, God is ultimately a community of persons, and man as both male and female, echoes or models this on a finite level. Second, as image-bearers we have dominion over the rest of the created order. But Gunton's understanding of this is a bit different than might be expected. "Dominion" for Gunton means that our human calling is "to enable the creation to praise its maker."[50] Gunton concludes, "*To be in the image of God is therefore to be called to represent God to the creation and creation to God*, so enabling it to reach its perfection."[51] Elsewhere, Gunton states, "the doctrine of the image of God represents a relation, primarily to God and secondarily to the other creatures, animate and inanimate alike."[52]

Relation is for Gunton an *ontological* category. I shall treat ontology separately in the next chapter, but it should be noted briefly here. Concerning what it means to be human, it is the failure to see the centrality of relationship which has caused confusion over the *imago Dei*. As Gunton notes, "relation constitutes who and what we are. Many of the difficulties facing the image doctrine derive from a failure to see this, and to construe the image as something characterizing us as individuals, rather than as persons in relation."[53] Ultimately, the image of God must be seen in trinitarian and relational terms—and for Gunton these terms are virtually coextensive. That is, we image God in that we as human persons somehow reflect the three persons in relationship who constitute the Triune God. As Gunton writes, " Just as Father, Son and Holy Spirit constitute the being of God, so created persons are those who, insofar as they are authentically personal . . . are characterized by subsisting in mutually constitutive relations with one another."[54] Thus, "To be in the image of God is therefore to be in necessary relation to others so made."[55] It is just at this point that Augustine is in err, for

---

49. *Christ and Creation*, 101.
50. Ibid., 102.
51. Ibid., 102–3.
52. *Triune Creator*, 198.
53. Ibid., 206.
54. Ibid., 208.
55. Ibid.

Gunton contends that this relational emphasis is missing in Augustine's thought. Augustine erred in affirming that man by himself is the image of God, rather than seeing that the *imago Dei* is actually constituted by man's relationships with God and others.[56] Our dominion over the rest of the created order should also be seen as a relationship with the created order, and this dominion is at least a necessary outgrowth of the *imago Dei*, if not actually constituting that image.[57]

This relational emphasis regarding the *imago Dei* is seen by Gunton as giving man a certain "status," a status which entails a certain mode of being, or ontology.[58] But this new status is one which must be perfected eschatologically. Hence, we again see the recurring theme of continuity between creation and redemption in Gunton's thought. That is, the *imago Dei* is real—and is to be seen primarily in man's relationships—but it is a real status that must be perfected. Thus, in relation to redemption, the *imago Dei* is something *given* in the creation of each person, but it must be *perfected* or *completed* in that redemption that is only complete in the eschatological future. And again, this redemption is in continuity, not discontinuity with God's act of creation. So Gunton can write that "redemption is not a creation out of nothing but a perfecting of that which has been made."[59] This perfecting of the image is indeed part and parcel with the perfecting of creation as a whole. This redemption is centered in Christ, and is mediated to the world through the Church.[60] But for the image to be in need of redemption raises the question of sin, to which we now turn. Although Gunton has not written a treatise on "sin," several key themes appear to run through Gunton's writings related to this topic. The key themes are: (1) sin as idolatry; (2) the impact of sin on relationships—both towards God and towards the rest of the created order; (3) sin as pollution.[61] Other themes such as guilt, transgression, etc., are rather sparse in Gunton's writings.[62] Indeed, the first theme, idolatry, leads directly to

---

56. Ibid. Gunton quotes Augustine from *De Trinitate* 12.7.10: "man by himself alone is the image of God, just as fully as when he and the woman are joined together in one."

57. Ibid. 209.

58. We will treat the whole issue of ontology in more depth next chapter.

59. *Triune Creator*, 204.

60. We treat the doctrine of the Church more fully later in this chapter, as well as in the following chapter.

61. *Christ and Creation*, 103ff. Cf. *Atonement*, 150–52; 185–87.

62. One occasionally sees reference to such themes as guilt and transgression, but not often. However see *Triune Creator*, 203, where Gunton speaks of man: "In the case of

the second theme, disordered relationships, for in idolatry we give too much reverence to the creature over the creator—hence the distorted relationships. Indeed, as Gunton writes, "sin and fallenness derive from that distortion of relatedness to God that takes shape in idolatry."[63] The third theme—sin as pollution—is seen in Gunton's repeated use of this theme. He writes of "human fallenness and its tendency to pollute whatever it touches."[64]

In short, the divide between creation and redemption is ultimately to be laid at the feet of Augustine's emphasis on the One over the Many, an emphasis which in effect jettisons God's involvement with particulars and materiality (i.e., the created order), or one could say, jettisons God's redemptive involvement with his creation.

Revelation

Gunton's concerns relating to creation and redemption can be seen in his doctrine of revelation. In his work *A Brief Theology of Revelation*, Gunton expounds a doctrine of revelation which flows out of his larger trinitarian theology. At the heart of Gunton's doctrine of revelation is the issue of mediation. Gunton stresses that revelation is always mediated, and the key agent of mediation is the Holy Spirit.[65] He argues (referring to Michael Polanyi) that revelation is always mediated. That is, revelation is not simply mind-to-mind or soul-to-soul knowledge, that is, some sort of "inner entirely unmediated and private experience."[66] He notes two reasons why this is so: (1) "knowledge of other persons is not simply knowledge of minds and souls, but of persons, that is to say, beings whose embodiment is essential to their being"; (2) "self-knowledge also has to be mediated, because here too we are beings only in relation, and cannot know our-

---

the human creature, we have the case of one not only capable, but also guilty, of offences against others made in the image of God which too often confound the imagination."

63. *Christ and Creation*, 106.

64. Ibid., 105.

65. Interestingly, one would expect Gunton—who wishes to follow Irenaeus' "two hands" as a model for so much of his theology—would equally emphasize the Son here. But Gunton appears to want to emphasize the Spirit as the agent of mediation, perhaps out of a concern to correct the de-emphasis on the Spirit in so much of Western theology.

66. *Brief Theology of Revelation*, 24.

selves without the mediation of others."[67] Without embracing either (1) "anti-foundationalism" nor (2) the radical emphasis on "community" and "interpretive communities," Gunton does emphasize the importance of the other, stressing that our own life as a knowing being is a life which takes place in the context of relationships to others.[68]

Revelation and creation, are intricately related, and revelation takes place in the world, our *created* world. God reveals Himself in *this* good world. He notes, "A belief that truth about the world, ourselves and each other is attainable by the human mind cannot be held apart from other deep-seated convictions about the nature of reality" (i.e., the created order).[69] That is, we see here that *creation* itself is a good part of the way God reveals Himself to his creatures. As Gunton notes, "a doctrine of divine revelation—of revelation of and by God—is supported by a doctrine of creation that holds that the created world is the kind of world within whose structures there can be revelation."[70] We see here Gunton's concern to avoid any sort of matter/spirit dualism (the type of dualism he sees in Augustine), and also to avoid driving a wedge between creation and redemption.

While revelation takes place within the created order, it requires both a doctrine of man and a doctrine of the Holy Spirit. Concerning man, Gunton argues that we are both limited, but that as limited, created beings we can "transcend" ourselves and understand and know things above and outside of ourselves. That is, we are a part of nature, but we can also "transcend" nature, and "understand that of which we are a part." In short, "We understand the world through and in our being part of it."[71] Throughout his writings Gunton appears to wish to "rescue" the Holy Spirit from the fringes. We see this in his doctrine of revelation, for it is the Holy Spirit who enables revelation to take place. The "creator Spirit brings it about

---

67. Ibid. Note the term "being in relation." This recurs repeatedly in Gunton's writings and reflects his understanding of "being," or ontology, as well as his debt to the Cappadocians and John Zizioulas. "Being" is not a static principle or thing. Rather, "being" cannot be spoken of without speaking of "being in relation." Indeed, at the very heart of what it means to be is the reality of relating. There is not a "thing" that *then* relates. Rather, to *be* simply *is* to relate.

68. Ibid.

69. Ibid., 33.

70. Ibid.

71. Ibid., 34.

that human rationality is able, within the limits set to it, to encompass the truth of the creation."[72] Indeed, for Gunton *all* knowledge is only possible because of revelation, because it is the Spirit who brings it about that this world is a world which can be known and understood.[73]

According to Gunton, many articulations of a doctrine of revelation fall short because they simply lack an adequate pneumatology and epistemology. That is, there is a failure to grasp that it is the Holy Spirit who mediates *all* revelation.[74] The context of Gunton's discussion here is Hans Frei,[75] Rudolf Bultmann, Karl Barth, and authoritative church bodies. He contends that in the work of these figures/institutions, one of several things happens. The Spirit's work: (1) is replaced by the activity of the human intellect (with those whom Frei is criticizing); or (2) becomes centered in the "subjective human response" (with Bultmann or Barth); or (3) becomes virtually equated with an institutional authority—a church body.[76]

As Gunton proceeds, it becomes clear that the real problems of a contemporary doctrine of revelation are quite old. Indeed, as in so many areas, the problem is to be laid at the feet of Augustine and his kindred spirits. Indeed, Augustine and his Platonic heritage had an (almost) deadly effect on the development of a Christian doctrine of revelation, and we are still seeing the repercussions of Augustine's influence today. Gunton contends that Philonic and Augustinian philosophy essentially crowded out a trinitarian god and *almost* replaced it with the eternal Platonic forms: "The Philonic and Augustinian development brought it about that the co-eternal and personal mediator of God's creating work was effectively replaced by the *almost* eternal Platonic forms."[77] Put another way, "the *Logos* was crowded out by the *logoi*" (i.e., the platonic forms). These *logoi*,

---

72. Ibid., 35–36.

73. Ibid., 38.

74. Ibid., 68. Gunton is here dealing with Hans Frei, Rudolf Bultmann, and—to a lesser extent—Karl Barth.

75. Gunton summarizes the two views which Frei himself sees as inadequate as follows. Emphasis is either put on: (1) "facts ascertained by historical enquiry of the same kind as that sought by secular methods of historiography"; or (2) "timeless didactic ideas indicated by the narratives."

76. *Revelation*, 68.

77. Ibid., 42–43.

Creation and Redemption in the Theology of Colin Gunton 47

in much of (particularly Augustinian) Western thought, became the effective mediators of creation." In short, "Christ is displaced by the forms."[78]

Gunton contends that Augustine's effective displacement of Christ in fact results in a "twofold contamination of the doctrine of creation": (1) ontological and (2) rational and epistemological. In terms of (1) ontology, Gunton concludes that Christ was effectively displaced by the eternal forms or *rationes*, and the Christian doctrine of revelation was contaminated by "pagan hierarchies of being."[79] In terms of (2) rationality and epistemology, Gunton concludes that the human mind was seen to have virtually an unmediated relation to the divine mind, which in effect made revelation unnecessary or superfluous.[80] Gunton also notes that "The exclusion of christological mediation is definitive for the thought this era takes, because the structuring of the created order comes to be provided not by the one who became incarnate, *Christus creator*, but by *intellectual forms of patterns*."[81]

Gunton contends that whereas in Irenaeus creation is both explicitly christological and pneumatological, and creation is continuous with redemption, for Augustine ultimately creation is "the outcome of arbitrary will."[82] This deficiency in Augustine is due to the fact that whereas in Irenaeus the "two hands" (the Son and the Spirit) are the means by which God continues to relate to and sustain the created order, for Augustine, the Platonic universals or ideas replace Christ. After reading and re-reading Gunton, I am still puzzled by Gunton at this point. Gunton explicates his position as follows, in the midst of discussion of William of Ockham. The will of God in Augustine becomes severed from christology and pneumatology. Hence, "If there are no universals, then only the will of God is able [to] hold things together. But it is a divine will of a very distinctive kind. The link between the particulars of our experience is made by a God essentially conceived after the image of the individual rational will so prominent in theological anthropology after Augustine. It is so applied

---

78. Ibid.
79. Ibid., 44–45.
80. Ibid., 45.
81. *Triune Creator*, 98.
82. Cf. the section titled "The West's Double Mind," in *One, the Three and the Many*, 51–61 (here, 54).

to God that it makes the world appear to be simply the arbitrary product of the divine will, abstractly conceived and essentially unknown."[83]

Gunton, leaning on the work of Michael Buckley, contends that this non-christological and non-pneumatological way of construing God's relation to the world will eventually pave the way for atheism: "According to Michael Buckley, the development of a non-christological and non-pneumatological account of the relation of God and the world was crucial in the development of modern atheism, and indeed provides a recurring refrain in his account."[84] It is within this context that Gunton can make the point, "*The root of the modern disarray is accordingly to be located in the divorce of the willing of creation from the historical economy of salvation.*" That is, the link between creation and redemption is severed in Augustine's thought, due largely to the fact that he construes his doctrines of creation and of God's continued relation to creation in non-christological and non-pneumatological terms (*and* since Christ is replaced by the Platonic universals/ideas).

Another issue which we will treat in detail is whether Gunton has truly understood Augustine correctly on the issue of the knowledge of God. Indeed, perhaps *the* key biblical text which serves as a type of backdrop to Augustine's search for God in *De Trinitate* is 1 Cor 13:12: "For now we see in a mirror dimly, but then face to face. Now I know in part; then I shall understand fully, even as I have been fully understood." Part of the angst or tension that seems to run through *De Trinitate* is due to the fact that Augustine recognizes the radical limitations on our knowledge of God while in this world. Additionally, the critic of Augustine must deal seriously with the role of *Christ himself* in the knowing process. In Augustine's *De Magistro* (*The Teacher*), the key conclusion as to how we can know that a certain word refers to a certain thing is because Christ is the teacher who shows us or teaches us. Indeed, one might make the case that *all* knowledge for Augustine is ultimately knowledge that is brought about, mediated or taught us by Christ.

For Gunton, revelation and creation must be seen in explicitly trinitarian terms. We might summarize his position as follows. The doctrine of creation is essentially not simply a *product* of revelation, but rather the doctrine of creation is a *function* of revelation. Creation itself is revela-

---

83. Ibid., 58.
84. Buckley, *At the Origins of Modern Atheism*, 55.

tory, mainly in three ways. First, creation is in itself worthwhile. The affirmation by a culture of the rationality of the world has only developed in cultures that are steeped in the Bible. That is, even the view that the world is rational is something that has been revealed.[85] Second, the world reveals who God is simply by the fact that the created world is a framework for culture.[86] Third, creation is revelatory in that creation reflects something of the trinitarian being of God. Gunton writes: creation "suggests that not the patterns of Platonic formality or of Aristotelian causality but trinitarian relationality offer possibilities for drawing analogies between the being of God and that of the world." That is, God's created world gives evidence of unity and diversity, relationality and particularity, which are analogous to unity and diversity found in the triune God.[87] This unity and diversity, as well as relationality and particularity, are most truly seen in the Trinity, and is reflected in the world.

Rationality is also related to the Trinity. Rationality is established "on . . . the free personal relation of God to the world through his Son and Spirit." That is, "It is the trinitarian formulation of a doctrine of creation which allows God to be God, the world to be the world, distinct beings and yet personally related by the personal mediation as creator and creation."[88] Only when the Trinity is viewed correctly—i.e., where both unity and diversity, relationality and particularity are viewed correctly—can one understand the legitimate basis of rationality.

Gunton contends that the doctrine of revelation is a function of the doctrine of salvation, or of the "divine saving economy."[89] This whole emphasis is important in understanding Gunton, for here Gunton wishes to bring together (1) his emphasis on the continuity between creation and redemption with (2) his doctrine of revelation. Indeed, Gunton wishes to center his doctrine of revelation "on the saving action of God in Christ [redemption is emphasized] who is the mediator also of creation [creation is emphasized]."[90] Here Gunton is indebted to Irenaeus, for redemption is seen not as simply an intervention into a world gone wrong, but as the continuation and fulfillment of God's plan for his creation.

85. *Revelation*, 61–62.
86. Ibid., 62.
87. Ibid.
88. Ibid., 63.
89. Ibid., 111ff.
90. Ibid.

Gunton expounds the connection between (1) revelation and (2) creation and redemption by a brief look at the Gospels, particularly the Gospel of John. Gunton reveals his thesis towards the end of the book: "The Spirit is revealed, that is to say, as the mediator of relation to God through Christ and *consequently* as the mediator of revelation." Indeed, "That is the heart of the theology of mediation that is being outlined in these lectures."[91] Ultimately, revelation is trinitarian, because, "Wherever there is revelation of any kind, there is the work of the creator and redeemer Spirit."[92] One final word from Gunton should help tie together Christ and Spirit, creation and redemption, as they relate to revelation: "If Christ is the mediator of creation, then he is the basis of created rationality and therefore of human knowledge, wherever and whatever; we might say, of all human culture."[93] But even this christocentric rationality must keep in mind the Spirit: "all rationality, truth and beauty are seen to be realised through the perfecting agency of God the Spirit, who enables things to be known by human minds and made by human hands."[94]

Christ

Throughout Gunton's writings he gives evidence of a desire to appropriate the strengths of the theological past without simply engaging in a work of repristination. However, while Gunton is not engaged in *simply* repristination, he does see his own theology of the incarnation as in fundamental continuity with the early Church fathers. This is particularly clear in his treatment of Christology.[95] Gunton, against much of modern theology

---

91. Ibid., 121.

92. Ibid.

93. Again, we note that Augustine's epistemology is radically christocentric. As noted above, in *De Magistro* (The Teacher) the only way someone knows that *this* word refers to *that* thing is because *Christ* is the "teacher" who instructs us that this word refers to that thing.

94. *Revelation*, 125.

95. Much of the following comes from Gunton's work, *Yesterday and Today*. Many of the themes found in this earlier work have been reworked in various ways in later volumes, but there are insights and positions found here which demand treatment. We should also note that this volumes differs from his later work in its emphases. Although *Yesterday and Today*, when it deals with Augustine, generally does so in a negative sense (cf. 108–11), it does not spend a lot of time with either the Cappadocians nor Irenaeus. The only exception here is a treatment of Gregory of Nazianzus's notion that, "that which is not assumed he has not healed" (173–76).

wishes to affirm that ontology is simply inescapable. This is true in theology in general, and in Christology in particular. Ontological terms or categories are not to be jettisoned in favor of moral, ethical, or other categories. Thus, Gunton can write that "the unity of God and man in Jesus can be expressed in ontological terms."[96]

Rather than simply arguing that the contemporary skepticism regarding incarnational Christology and "two natures" language is rooted *simply* in certain modern or Enlightenment sympathies, Gunton contends that moderns struggle with traditional christological affirmations are actually due to modern *continuities* with ancient problems. For example, Gunton can argue that Kant was skeptical about the possibility of knowledge of the transcendent or supernatural world because Kant was struggling with an ancient problem. Both Kant and Plato believed that this temporal world could not yield knowledge of the transcendent or supernatural world. Whereas Plato thus posited, or affirmed the world of eternal forms (which *were* stable and knowable), Kant posited that the mind imposes order on the world. Although Plato and Kant reach different conclusions, they were both working from common presuppositions: skepticism of any true, knowable order which is a constituent part of this temporal world.[97]

Whereas the era of the Church fathers more easily dealt with the eternal, our age is more comfortable (fixated?) with the temporal. Thus, past ages were quite comfortable with a Christology "from above," while ours has seen an emphasis on a Christology "from below." Gunton's own position appears to be that we ultimately need to reach the same *conclusion* as the Church fathers, even if our *starting point* is a bit different. Thus, he can write, "because we are in Christology above all concerned with *God's* love, we cannot avoid working through to the same kind of conclusions to which the Father's came."[98] Indeed, "If we begin with the preoccupations of our times, we cannot remain there any more than they did." If the early Church fathers "began" with a Christ from above, but eventually had to conclude that Jesus of Nazareth was "the place where the eternal was temporally and spatially located," then our age may begin with the earthly Jesus but we "may come to see that in this temporal and

---

96. Ibid., 170.
97. Ibid., 105–8.
98. Ibid., 135.

spatial reality not only immanent phenomena but also the eternal God are to be found."[99]

On one level, Gunton's writings on Christology allows him to work on a common theme in his work, that theme being that modernity in many ways is *not* new, but is the working out, and coming-to-fruition of certain ideas and tendencies which are themselves quite old. That is, it is *not* the case that modernity need set the stage—and define the rules—for the practice of theology by contemporary Christians. Modernity was not simply an "advance" in all areas of human endeavor. Modernity, like most eras, has a mixed record when its attempts at wrestling with classical problems are measured. Gunton can therefore write that one of the main theses in his *Yesterday and Today* is that older christological formulations can be still (on the whole) retrieved by contemporary Christians: "it is not impossible for the modern Christian to affirm, albeit critically, a large part of both the form and the content of Christian orthodoxy."[100] Stated a bit differently, it is simply not the case that "Christology since the Enlightenment had become an entirely different enterprise."[101]

As in so many areas, the key to a true and genuine Christology is relationship. Gunton argues for a theory of language in which language does not simply "mirror" reality. This idea that language mirrors reality in a sense sets itself up for failure, for no language fully or truly mirrors reality. Thus, language is too easily said to have failed when it mirrors imperfectly. Gunton argues that proper language emerges as people relate in worship to Christ. That is, the proper language is in a sense generated out of a life of worshipping Christ. Gunton writes: "The personal relation of worship gives rise to doxological language; and as this language is, in its turn, indwelt, a more systematic account becomes possible of the one through whom indwelling becomes actual."[102] Thus, Gunton continues, "the God whom we worship through Jesus Christ comes to appropriate linguistic expression, as the personal relationship gives rise to a considered rational and indirect expression."[103] In a refreshing way which runs counter to much contemporary thinking about language, Gunton really

99. Ibid.,. 135.
100. Ibid., 146.
101. Ibid., 165.
102. Ibid., 148.
103. Ibid.

believes in the meaningfulness of language, because language ultimately has an organic connection with that to which it refers. As Gunton writes, "If we are to find an authentically modern christological language it must be that which reality gives us as we orient ourselves *to* it *through* the language of worship."[104] Indeed, "Words for the present do not come out of the blue, but emerge only as the present converses with the past in the light of the faith they both share."[105]

There is one particular aspect of Gunton's christology which should be briefly noted. Gunton appears to affirm Edward Irving's contention that in the incarnation the Son took on not a sinless humanity or flesh, but took on truly sinful and fallen humanity, or flesh. To deny this would be a denial of a thoroughgoing incarnation.[106] Gunton contends that Irving was not denying the Christian tradition in such an affirmation, but rather that "Irving's argument is a version of the classic patristic teaching that what Christ does not assume, he does not heal."[107] The notion that Christ took on fallen human flesh leads to a common theme in Gunton's work: it is the Holy Spirit who sustains and perseveres the incarnate Christ, so that one can say *both* (1) Christ took on fallen human flesh *and* (2) Christ was not actually sinful.[108]

In the end, Gunton wishes to affirm a generally traditional Christology. In describing the incarnation, Gunton writes, "What happened, at a particular time, was that the eternal Word became flesh."[109] The "hypostatic union" "is a model which provides a conceptual link between historical event and eternal reality."[110] Indeed, "When the eternal love of God takes to itself this human reality, there is a created being at once divine and human, the person Jesus Christ."[111] While the older theological terms cannot simply be repeated, they nonetheless helpfully pointed to aspects of the life, teachings and work of Christ, aspects which Christians today also want to truthfully speak. Words like *hypostasis* and *ousia* were used to try to articulate fundamental concepts. The use of such words and concepts

---

104. Ibid., 149.
105. Ibid.
106. Gunton, "Christology: Two Dogmas Revisited—Edward Irving's Christology."
107. Ibid., 159.
108. Ibid., 161–64.
109. *Yesterday and Today*, 158.
110. Ibid.
111. Ibid.

are "an attempt *to map the implications for ontology of the life in which the divine love took human form.*"[112] Such words as *homoousios* do not simply deal with other words, but are concerned with ontology, "with what is really there."[113] We have no need to jettison the classical Christological confessions and creeds (e.g., Chalcedon) due to some "hellenizing" influence exercised upon them. Gunton can say plainly: "contemporary theology should be able gladly to affirm the relative validity of the great christological creeds of the first few centuries."[114] Although human claims are not absolute (thus the reference to "relative" validity), they can still be true. Gunton does want to affirm the uniqueness of Jesus, as he write: "What is being claimed in continuity with the New Testament and the mainstream Christian tradition is that we are here [i.e., in Jesus] presented with the reality of God in a manner that is unique."[115] Although Gunton does not want to opt for a "functional" rather than an "ontological" Christology (indeed, throughout his works Gunton rigorously defends the necessity of ontology), he does want to argue that the ultimate reason why Christians claim a uniqueness for Jesus is soteriology: "Jesus is unique because he is the way by which God restores his human creation—and, along with it, his whole creation—to a wholeness of relationship with him."[116] For Gunton there really are ontological and soteriological realities which stand "behind" and inform our attempts to speak truthfully about God. In the end, Gunton argues, "Christological statements obtain their claim to truth and rationality from the prior ontological and soteriological claim that Jesus of Nazareth is the logic of the holy love of God."[117]

Holy Spirit

Gunton's doctrine of the Holy Spirit is worked out in close to relation to other central concerns such as christology and creation. At the heart of Gunton's christological concerns is the relationship between Christ and creation, and between creation and redemption. In short, Christ is the

---

112. Ibid., 159.
113. Ibid.
114. Ibid., 160.
115. Ibid., 163.
116. Ibid., 164.
117. Ibid., 165.

Creator *and* Redeemer: the same Lord who created the world is redeeming the world. What must be avoided is "the tearing apart of creation and redemption, so that redemption comes to appear to consist in salvation out of and apart from the rest of the world."[118] Indeed, as Gunton notes, "Creation was not simply the making of the world out of nothing, not even that world continually upheld by the providence of God, but the making of a world destined for perfection, completedness."[119] We see here the organic connection between creation, redemption, Christology, *and* eschatology.[120] Thus, it is clear for Gunton that the continuity between creation and redemption is *christological* continuity.

According to Gunton there has been a failure in the West fully to affirm the humanity of Christ, a failure related to a deficient doctrine of the Holy Spirit. As Gunton notes, "Many of the features of the mainstream Western theology of the Spirit . . . can be seen to derive at least in part from Augustine's influence, or, if it thought dangerous to draw direct lines of historical causality, to echo the kind of things that he says."[121] Gunton's criticisms of Augustine's view of the Holy Spirit are particularly harsh. Gunton writes that Augustine "is notoriously weak on the Spirit, subordinating the eschatological freedom of a person to a timeless function in a Platonic triad."[122] According to Gunton there are two chief weaknesses in Augustine's construal of the Holy Spirit.

First, Augustine's conception of the Spirit as the "link" between Father and Son is flawed. As Gunton sees it, Augustine's view of the Holy Spirit as link is a means to "close" (or we might say "complete") an inward circle. That is, the Holy Spirit is construed in such a way as to demarcate the "immanent" Trinity from the work of the economy: contra Rahner, the immanent Trinity is *not* the economic Trinity. As Gunton concludes, "This breach between economy and theology is of a piece with, and a

---

118. *Christ and Creation*, 32.

119. Ibid., 45.

120. Another issue that we broach, but cannot be treated in detail, is the whole constellation of issues that flow from a "tight" connection between creation and redemption. That is, since Gunton wants to see redemption as the perfecting of creation (indeed, "built into" creation is the *telos* of redemption), Gunton would presumably favor a generally Reformed theological outlook.

121. Gunton, "God the Holy Spirit," 111.

122. "Christology," 167.

partial consequence of, the failure of Augustine to give the Spirit adequate weight economically."[123]

Second, and this is also related to Augustine's supposed preference for a "Platonic" (or "immanent") Trinity over an economy Trinity, Gunton laments Augustine's tendency towards intellectualism. That is, by emphasizing the immanent Trinity Augustine effectively shifted attention away from God's work in history towards the epistemological quest. Here, at least in part is a root cause of the West's myopic concern for epistemology.[124]

Gunton summarizes these two main weaknesses by contending that in Augustine there is simply a failure to come to terms with the eschatological role of the Spirit.[125] This eschatological emphasis has been restricted in Augustine's thought due to his emphasis on the psychological analogies, which has tended "close-off" the Trinity from relations in and to the world. What is needed, says Gunton, is not a wholesale rejection of Augustine's conception of the Spirit as "love," but rather a better understanding of *how* the Spirit might be construed as love. Thus, instead of the Spirit as "love" simply between the Father and Son, a construal which seems to demarcate the Trinity from external relations, we need a construal of the Trinity which is constituted by two key features. First, the Spirit *is* the dynamic of divine love, but one which is other-oriented in that the Spirit "seeks to involve the other in the movement of giving and receiving that is the Trinity." Here the Spirit's role is "*to perfect the love of Father and Son by moving it beyond itself.*" And this leads to the second key feature of a better understanding of the Spirit. Second, the Triune God does not simply love Himself, but is moved by love outwards to the created order, and the role of the Spirit is that of "perfecting" the created order, or, we might say, redemption. Are we forced to say that God *must* create, since creation (and redemption) are overflows of His love? No. Creation and redemption are not "necessary" or "required," but are free

---

123. Ibid., 124.

124. A key aspect of any analysis of Gunton's quarrel with Augustine is whether Augustine can be acquitted of the charge of deemphasizing the Spirit's role in the economy by pointing to Augustine's contention that the missions in *time* reveal the processions in *eternity*. Or said otherwise, what God does in time (send the Son and Spirit for our salvation) reveals who God is in eternity (the Son and the Spirit eternally proceeding from the Father). That is, if the sending of the Spirit in time for our redemption reflects who God is in eternity, then there *does* seem to be an organic connection between the economy and the being of God in the thought of Augustine.

125. Ibid., 126.

acts of God, nonetheless rooted in the love of God. Thus, Gunton tries to affirm Augustine's concept of the Spirit as love, but wants to go further, emphasizing the eschatological role of the Spirit. That is, God is not simply a being who is focused on Himself, but who, by means of the Spirit, reaches out to the world in creation and redemption.[126]

The Holy Spirit and the Church are closely linked in much of Gunton's writings. This close link is demonstrated in his essay, "The Church: John Owen and John Zizioulas on the Church."[127] Two themes which Gunton wishes to hold together are," the freedom, transcendence and particularity of the Holy Spirit; and the nature of the Church as community." It is in the Church "that we must seek an identification of the Spirit's particular work."[128] That is, it is in the Church that believers benefit from the work of the Holy Spirit. Specifically, in the life of the Church freedom and community must be understood in terms of the Holy Spirit. Thus, on Gunton's view, "unless, . . . our concept of churchly freedom is the freedom given by the Spirit who creates community, we shall be in danger of collapse into the kind of individualistic autonomy that encourages us to think that we do it all by ourselves, and which, as I have already suggested, sometimes marks later times."[129] The Holy Spirit's actual eschatological role is to constitute the Church. As Gunton writes, "The Spirit lifts the community to the Father through the Son: and therefore we must say that the Church is constituted as the Spirit, through the word of the gospel—the risen Christ becoming concrete in the present—calls the community into being."[130]

The role of the Holy Spirit is to perfect the humanity of Christ. It is the Holy Spirit who allows Jesus to resist temptation "by virtue of his

---

126. Gunton seems to waffle on whether this "outward" move towards the world in creation and redemption is somehow necessary or required. The thrust of Gunton's logic is that at the heart of what it means for the Spirit to be the Spirit is the whole realm of the Spirit's eschatological activities, but there *are* no eschatological activities apart from creation and redemption. And, Gunton dismisses rather quickly the notion that God is "satisfied" in and by Himself: "if God's love is essentially self-satisfied rather than self-sufficient, an inward-turning circle, there is to be found within it no reason at all for God's creating but arbitrary will." (Ibid., 127–28). I am unclear how to square Gunton's apparent denial of God's "self-satisfaction" with Gunton's affirmation that God need not create.

127. This essay is found in Gunton, *Theology through the Theologians*, 187–204.

128. Ibid., 190.

129. Ibid., 194.

130. Ibid., 202.

obedience to the guidance of the Spirit."[131] Indeed, it is through the empowering power of the Spirit that Jesus can be the ultimate priest,[132] and it is through the Spirit that Jesus on the cross "perfected the obedience that he had learned through his temptation and ministry,"[133] and it is the Spirit who is the agent of Christ's resurrection.[134]

Gunton provides a helpful summary of his thought in regard to Christ, Spirit, creation and redemption in his discussion of the *imago Dei*: "That the image of God is centered on Christ means therefore not only that he is the pattern for our approach to the world, but that the creation can be truly itself only by being conformed to him through the Spirit."[135] Thus, Christ in an ultimate sense images God, and through Christ, creation (including both human and non-human creation) is redeemed (i.e., allowed to "be truly itself"), and all this takes place through the Spirit.

Redemption

We need to ask exactly how the work of Christ relates to the rest of Gunton's theology. We note that for Gunton it is in the Church that the reality of the person and work of Jesus Christ is mediated or, or furthered in, the world. That is, in the Church the Spirit makes particular the work of Christ.[136] But how more specifically does the work of Christ—in particular the cross—fit into Gunton's scheme?[137] In working with a number of metaphors, Gunton posits that as *victory* the work of Christ ultimately

---

131. *Christ and Creation*, 54.
132. Ibid., 56.
133. Ibid., 59.
134. Ibid., 63.
135. Ibid., 107.

136. Ibid., 110. For Gunton, redemption is seen also as a restoring of two sets of relationships: (1) with others and (2) with the rest of the created order. The Holy Spirit and the Church are both necessary for this reordering: "the church is the place where we must locate our first account of the re-forming of the image of God. The image is re-formed and so realised in the process of human conformation to Christ by the action of the eschatological Spirit" (ibid., 115–16).

137. Interestingly, Gunton's main work devoted to the atonement, *Actuality of the Atonement*, concerns itself little with Augustine. Indeed, Augustine is largely absent from the work. It should be noted that the strengths of this volume are many, and is a particularly insightful critique (although often subtle) of the more destructive strands of postmodernism.

provides a new vision of our world.[138] The emphasis on the metaphor of the *justice* of God, which Gunton associates with Anselm, is also legitimate. But Gunton claims that even though Anselm *begins* with the legal metaphor, Anselm has a broader theological understanding of the nature of the atonement which cannot be *simply* or *solely* summarized as a "legal" view. While Gunton affirms the legitimacy of seeing the cross in terms of a legal metaphor, Gunton wishes to affirm a broader conception of what happens on the cross: "if sin is cosmic disorder, then salvation is the action of God [here portrayed in terms of the cross] as he takes responsibility for the whole context of our lives, setting us free to live in the universe he does not allow to go to ruin."[139] In short, Gunton affirms the cross in legal/justice terms, but he wants a broader articulation of this theme. He concludes:

> The heart of the matter is the use of the metaphor: that a concept whose apparently primary meaning is to be found in matters of legality is now used chiefly to explicate relationships between persons, and in particular the all determining relationship between the creator and his erring but never abandoned children.[140]

The metaphor of *sacrifice* is the key metaphor in helping to understanding the meaning of the atonement.[141] The metaphor of sacrifice helps us to understand that human life has been "soiled," and has lost its direction due to sin and the consequences of sin. The metaphor of sacrifice teaches us that "the giving of life, the greatest gift of the creator, demolishes the barrier that uncleanness erects, and so restores relationship."[142]

The most important way in which Gunton's view of the atonement relates to his larger thesis which we are trying to expound here, is that the atonement is not an "intervention" into the world, and neither is the atonement somehow radically distinct from what God has done in the past. In short, with the atonement (God's redemptive work on the cross)

---

138. *Atonement*, 80. And the Spirit is never very far away: "Metaphor [and here *victory* is in view], then,—when it, too, is filled with meaning by the gift of that same Spirit—expresses the truth of this matter, which is God present savingly to the world, but in ways appropriate to the nature of the world in its createdness and fallenness; that is, in the victory that is the life of Jesus Christ."

139. Ibid., 96.

140. Ibid., 113.

141. Personal conversation with Colin Gunton, August 6, 1999, Brentwood, England.

142. *Atonement*, 138.

there is no wedge between creation and redemption. As Gunton notes, the "'intervention of God for his world is not isolated from the rest of his action, because it is the mediator of creation who comes to ensure that the original purposes of God do not founder in futility.'"[143] Indeed, "the redemptive action of God in Jesus" should be seen as "of a piece with his just and sacrificial ordering of all things,"[144] and redemption should be seen as the completing of what God began with creation.[145] Ultimately, the atonement should be viewed "in terms of the perfection of creation, in the Son's bringing to the Father a renewed and completed world."[146]

Church

The work of Christ on the cross is ultimately made real in the world by means of the Church. That is, Gunton wishes "to show how the reconciliation between God and the world achieved on the cross may take shape in a God-given community [i.e., the Church] ordered to that purpose."[147] The cross of Christ ultimately "wins" a "victory," allowing persons a space to live and be in *this* creation.[148] Indeed, at the heart of the Church is the atonement, for the life of the Church is rooted in the atonement.[149]

The Church is not "only" rooted in that atonement, but is also seen to be the temporal embodiment of the life of the Trinity. That is, the Church is "the community that is created and called to be the finite embodiment of the eternal communion of Father, Son and Spirit."[150] Gunton contends, "The church is called to be the echo of the very being of God, and is enabled to be so as it is taken up in worship into the life of the Trinity." The Church is the *locus* where persons come to know and experience and learn how to follow Christ: "The Church is the concrete place where certain human beings accept a call to associate themselves with the reality of him who is the logic of divine love."[151] Ultimately *all* of the created order

---

143. Ibid., 146.
144. Ibid., 150.
145. Ibid., 153.
146. Ibid., 154.
147. Ibid., 177.
148. Ibid., 182.
149. Ibid., 194.
150. Ibid., 199.
151. *Yesterday and Today*, 176.

(i.e., not simply the human created order) is called to share in the praise of God, and the Church is responsible for all creation, calling all creation "in its own way" to be reconciled to Christ.[152]

Gunton is quite clear that Augustine is a chief culprit in formulating an inferior understanding of the Church. One of the chief weaknesses in Augustine's doctrine of the Church is ultimately a pneumatological weakness, indeed a trinitarian error. Gunton's concern is that in Augustine's doctrine of the Spirit there is no notion of how the Spirit realizes "future" blessings now through the creation of community (i.e., the Church). Indeed, "In Augustine we are near the beginning of the era in which the church is conceived essentially as an institution mediating grace to the individual rather than of the community formed on the analogy of the Trinity's *interpersonal* relationships."[153]

In sum, Augustine has erred in his understanding of Christ, Spirit, and Church. These errors have manifested themselves in a number of different ways in the history of Christian thought. The way forward is a fuller and better understanding of (1) the centrality of Christ in both creation and redemption, (2) the centrality of the Spirit in the life of Christ and the redemption of the world and (3) the centrality of the Church as the locus of the work of the Spirit. We will see how these and other issues come together in eschatology, to which we now turn.

Eschatology

Appropriately, we save eschatology for last, but in reality it has been present all along. Since Gunton wishes to see redemption as creation fulfilling its true purpose, it is natural that eschatology would be central to Gunton's theology. Ultimately, for Gunton, there is an eschatological component to all of Christian doctrine, since "the end" (i.e., redemption in the fullest sense) is always that to which the created order is pointed. One can say that in eschatology all of the "pieces" of Gunton's theology come together. Whereas in Gunton's view the Western tradition (following Augustine) has severed creation and redemption, and has failed to give attention to the organic connection between creation and redemption, another strain in the theological tradition (seen above all others, in Irenaeus) has managed to more properly see this connection between creation and redemp-

152. *Atonement*, 200.
153. *Promise*, 50–51.

tion. This organic relationship between creation and redemption should be seen in one's eschatology. Eschatology should be the fulfillment of all that God has intended for creation. Eschatology is not simply the final "stage" of God's rescue effort. Rather, eschatology witnesses the fulfillment of God's redemptive purposes, which are in turn in radical continuity with, and the purposeful fulfillment of God's work of creation.

To be truly a creature is to be oriented toward a *telos*. This *telos* is not "foreign" to the creature, nor is it something "added" along the way. Rather, the *telos* is integral to what it means to be a creature. As Gunton writes, "Creation was not simply the making of the world out of nothing, not even that world continually upheld by the providence of God, but the making of a world destined for perfection, completedness."[154] Indeed, as Gunton contends, "To *be* a creature *means* to be a being called and directed to a future perfection."[155] And again, Gunton sees the Western tradition in general as seriously deficient, and he sees in Irenaeus a better construal. Whereas the West generally moves from paradise to fall to restoration, in Irenaeus the picture is more of God completing what was begun in creation.[156]

Eschatology for Gunton is thoroughly trinitarian, as both Christ and Spirit are active and present. Gunton, following Basil, sees the Holy Spirit as the "perfecting cause of creation." That is, Gunton wishes to see more continuity between this age and the next, or between creation, and the final, completed perfected order.[157] While Basil is held up as an exemplar, Augustine is again held up as a liability. While "the eschatological dimension to the work of the Spirit . . . is so prominent in the New Testament," its "virtual absence from Augustine must be said to have been one of his worst legacies to the Western tradition."[158] Indeed, what is missing from Augustine is "a conception of the Spirit as realising the conditions of the age to come particularly through the creation of community."[159] Augustine's deficient view of the Spirit is tied closely to his deficient view of the Church. Rather than seeing the Church as a community which

---

154. *Christ and Creation*, 45.
155. Ibid., 46 (emphasis mine).
156. *Atonement*, 153.
157. *Christ and Creation*, 46.
158. *Promise*, 50.
159. Ibid., 50–51

is analogically modeled after the relations of the Trinity (Gunton's preferred construal), Augustine erred in seeing the Church as essentially an institution which mediates grace.[160] The emphasis on the Church as an "institution," which Gunton sees as more of a Western emphasis, led many "heretical" movements in Europe to bristle at the authoritarian nature of the Church, and the *chief* motive for their discomfort with the Church was that these movements saw "the institution as *claiming* too much of a realisation of eschatology, while *expecting* too little of the community as a whole."[161]

In *Christ and Creation* Gunton emphasizes the christological and pneumatological nature of eschatology. In particular he treats the christological nature of both creation, redemption and consummation. He asks, "Who then is the Christ of the Bible, and what is his relation to creation?" Christ is both the agent of creation, but as the incarnate Lord, he is *part of* creation, and how this incarnate Lord is the focus of redemptive (and hence teleological, or eschatological) work of God is central to Gunton's theology. Indeed, Christ is both the "one through whom all was created," as well as "the means of the re-establishment of the image in humanity."[162] Christ is thus central to creation, redemption and eschatology as a whole.

Gunton treats five "episodes" in the life of Jesus Christ: (1) its beginning, (2) the baptism and temptation, (3) death, (4) resurrection, and (5) ascension. While all five episodes *ultimately* have an eschatological thrust, Gunton spends more time explicating the eschatological importance of death, resurrection and ascension. Christ's death points forward eschatologically in that his work on the cross Christ achieves a sacrifice

---

160. Ibid. Although Gunton's writings seem to affirm the idea that the Trinity is appropriately a "model" for anthropology, as well as the Church, in personal conversation Gunton has said that he shies away from the idea of the Trinity as "model." However, on the notion of the Trinity as "model" see the appropriate sections in Chapter Three below. Miroslav Volf also wants to see the Church as "modeled" after the Trinity, or in Volf's words, the "image" of the Trinity. See his *After Our Likeness*. Peter Adam is much more cautious about seeing the Trinity (particularly the interpersonal relations of the Trinity). as a model for Christians. See his "Trinity and Human Community," 52–65. For one, in the Bible we have little *detailed* knowledge about the inner life or workings of the Trinity. Ultimately, the Trinity may provide some general help as to how human community, and in particular the Church should model its life, but more central is the fact that in the gospel of the Trinity we have the message of "salvation through Jesus Christ" (64).

161. *Promise*, 65.

162. *Christ and Creation*, 119.

which can be offered to the Father, a sacrifice which is "a renewed and cleansed sample of the life in the flesh in which human being consists."[163] This "sample" points forward in that it stands for the created order, which "in due time" will "be taken up into the recapitulation there accomplished" [i.e., on the cross].[164] It is important to note again, that Jesus accomplishes his work on the cross "through the Spirit," for on the cross he "perfected the obedience that he had learned through his temptation and ministry" [and he had been taught by the Spirit].[165]

The resurrection of Jesus is accomplished by the Spirit, who in this act is doing the work of the Father. The resurrection is an eschatological act "taking place in the midst of time."[166] The resurrection is chiefly concerned with Jesus' "horizontal" relations (i.e., with the rest of the created order), while the ascension is chiefly concerned with his "vertical" relations (i.e., with the non-created order, God).[167] Gunton wishes to contend that there is a "universalizing" element to the resurrection, in that the resurrection brings it about that Christ's "eschatological rule is universal."[168] The destiny of the world is tied up with the resurrection, in that since Jesus Christ now participates in "the conditions of the age to come," then "the perfection promised for the creation and realised through the work of the Spirit is centered here" [i.e., in the resurrected Jesus Christ].[169] Jesus, in light of the resurrection, is indeed the "first fruits of the transformation of the whole creation," the "down payment" (2 Cor 1:22), of what is to come.[170] The resurrected Jesus Christ, as the first-fruits, is our representative (a representation *itself* established by the resurrection), and is "the means whereby, through the Spirit, other created reality becomes perfected."[171] In short, "The resurrection is thus the anticipatory realisation of the eschatological destiny of the whole creation."[172]

163. Ibid., 58–59.
164. Ibid. 59.
165. Ibid.
166. *Christ and Creation*, 63.
167. Ibid., 60. Gunton notes that ultimately the nature of resurrection and ascension tends to relativize the distinction between "horizontal" and "vertical."
168. Ibid., 61.
169. Ibid.
170. Ibid., 63.
171. Ibid., 64.
172. *Triune Creator*, 224.

The ascension is also eschatological in that "it clearly involves ... the taking up of [Christ's] humanity into God," and thus provides a "bridge" between earth and heaven.[173] The ascension truly "brings about a new state of affairs," and "is concerned to bring out the character of the mediation that he represents and is."[174] The ascension points forward eschatologically in that "it is the ascension that establishes Jesus as the eternal mediator between heaven and earth, by virtue of that which he did and suffered as a man."[175]

At the heart of Gunton's eschatology is a recurring theme: the unity between creation and redemption. Gunton's goal is "to develop an eschatology which is concerned with the completing of that which was once established in the beginning."[176] And while the desire to reaffirm the unity between creation and redemption is so important to Gunton, it is Augustine, as Gunton sees it, who so drove a wedge between creation and redemption, and who mediated to the Western theological tradition a tendency for others to do the same. Again, the better theological model is to be found in Irenaeus, for in summarizing Irenaeus Gunton notes, "It is thus that there is a continuity of creation and redemption, according to which the latter can be understood as a new act of creation—perhaps better, recreation—on the basis of the old, which is thus renewed and redirected to its true end."[177]

Ultimately, Gunton wishes to find the end in the beginning, and the beginning completed in the end. Eschatology sees God's purposes for *creation* come to fruition in *redemption*. Whether this conception is missing in, or foreign to Augustine is an issue we will investigate in a later chapter.

Conclusion

We have seen that the theme of creation and redemption is central to Gunton's thinking. Gunton's concern to vindicate the continuity between creation and redemption runs through virtually all of his writings. Gunton contends that Irenaeus is the earliest and most significant proponent of

173. *Christ and Creation*, 65.
174. Ibid., 66.
175. Ibid., 67.
176. *Triune Creator*, 222.
177. Ibid., 223.

this insight, and that this insight has in many ways been lost, particularly in Western theology. At the heart of the West's failure to appropriate this insight is Augustine, who, by a poor construal of the doctrine of God diminished the role of the particular, and effectively severed creation from redemption. This trend in Western thought has eventually led to modernity, for in the modern age we have seen a true rebellion against the overpowering One in favor of the diffused Many.

Gunton has constructed a type of architectonic sweep of the history of thought, and the blame which he has laid at Augustine's feet is significant. In order to offer a critique of Gunton, we must look at Augustine in some detail, and ask if Gunton has offered a construal of the history of Western thought which is fair to Augustine. But before we look at Augustine we must look at another key theme in the writing of Gunton, the question of ontology. To that we now turn.

CHAPTER 3

Being and Ontology in the Theology of Colin Gunton

IN ATTEMPTING TO EXPOSIT the thought of Gunton, our first theme was that of creation and redemption. The theme of creation and redemption, and how Augustine failed in numerous areas that relate to that theme provided the focus of chapter two. In this chapter, we will focus on a different key theme in Gunton's writings: the issue of being and ontology. We kept bumping against this topic in the last chapter, but postponed a fuller treatment until now. Again, Gunton's view of Augustine is largely negative, and we wish to explicate exactly what is the thrust of Gunton's critique. This issue flows naturally from the rest of Gunton's critique and can be summarized as follows: Augustine so emphasizes the One that there is little room left for particulars—especially persons. And again, this weakness is ultimately a trinitarian error. Whereas Augustine is so concerned to guard the oneness of God, it is hard for him to truly affirm the real personhood of each of the three members of the Trinity. As Gunton writes, "since Augustine theology has always tended in a modalistic direction, conceiving the real God as the pure being underlying the distinctions of the persons who, when examined critically, behave like the Cheshire cat."[1] Gunton looks to the Cappadocian Fathers, who offer a better construal of the three persons of the Trinity that does not subsume the three persons under the oneness of God—the Many are not subsumed under the One. It is common to summarize the difference between the Eastern and Western conception of the Trinity by saying that the Cappadocians

1. Gunton, "Christology," 166.

begin with the three and then move to the one.² While Gunton affirms that Augustine indeed does begin with the One, and *then* tries to make sense of the three, it is inaccurate to summarize the Cappadocians by saying they do the reverse—begin with the three and move to the one. Not at all says Gunton. Rather, the Cappadocians simply never were trying to solve a mathematical conundrum, whether it involves beginning with the one or with the three.³ Rather, the Cappadocians emphasized the persons of the Trinity, but not in a way that they could be said to have "begun" with the "three." According to Gunton, it is best simply to understand the Cappadocians as emphasizing the persons.

Gunton contends that by construing the Trinity in a way which sees the three person as *really* persons, and not simply as mathematical difficulties which must be somehow squared with the oneness of God, the Cappadocians offer a vision of the Trinity which is not only true, but if recovered, could offer a paradigm for healing the ravages of modernity. At the heart of Gunton's position is ontology. Ontology is not optional, for there will always be a certain ontology at the heart of our endeavors, theological or otherwise. Thus, the only real task is that of coming to terms with what is a true ontology. Gunton's position is most clearly explicated in *The Promise of Trinitarian Theology*, but we will see these same

---

2. This is a common way of construing the differences between Greek and Latin approaches to the Trinity. For example T. R. Martland writes: "Augustine's doctrine of the Trinity contributed to a fuller understanding of what the Christian means when he asserts that God is one, but the cost of this contribution was a failure to take seriously the Christian assertion that God of his nature is multiple." See his article, "A Study of Cappadocian and Augustinian Trinitarian Methodology," 252–63 (here, 252). Edmund J. Fortman writes, "One way, that of the Greek Fathers and of the Latin Fathers before Augustine, starts from the plurality of Persons and proceeds to the assertion that the three really distinct Persons subsist in a nature that is numerically one." On the other hand, Augustine's way "starts out from the unity of nature and moves to the trinity of Persons." See Fortman, *Triune God*, 140. Many similar quotes could be offered. Others are more skeptical of such approach. Michel René Barnes argues that most modern writing on the Trinity buys into a false "Greek/Latin" antithesis (i.e., the Greeks begin with the three and the Latins begin with the one) which can be traced to the work of Theodore de Régnon last century: *Études de théologie positive sur la Sainte Trinité*. Barnes can argue that a "belief in the existence of this Greek/Latin paradigm is a unique property of modern trinitarian theology," such that "only theologians of the last one hundred years have ever thought that it was true." (238). See Barnes' article, "Augustine in Contemporary Trinitarian Theology," 237–50. Cf. Wesche, "Triadological Shaping of Latin and Greek Christianity. Part 1," 63–75; idem, "Triadological Shaping of Latin and Greek Christianity. Part 2, 84–105.

3. Personal conversation with Colin Gunton, August 6, 1999, Brentwood, England.

themes elsewhere in Gunton's work.[4] First, we should note that central to Gunton's efforts is a desire to recover and advance an ontology which can be traced to the Cappadocians but was largely lost and abandoned by Augustine and his successors. We will explicate this as we proceed, but in short, Gunton wishes to argue that for the Cappadocians, *relationality*, or *communion* constitutes "being," and supposedly this is an achievement ignored or not understood by Augustine.[5] The issue of ontology is crucial for Gunton, because as he sees it the option is either a Christian ontology or an ontology which is foreign to Christianity: "Where there is not explicitly Christian theological ontology, an implicit and foreign one will fill and has filled the vacuum."[6]

Additionally, we should say that although we are treating the whole issue of "nature, persons, and relation" in a different chapter from "creation and redemption," these two groups of issues are not isolated, and there are many areas of convergence and overlap. The theme of the One and the Many is our overarching paradigm for trying to exposit and critique Gunton, but there are not hard and fast lines between issues related to "being and relationship" and issues related to "creation and redemption." As we shall see, Augustine's supposed failure to construe an appropriate ontology is a key factor which dovetails with his supposed weaknesses in holding together creation and redemption.

In the "Preface" to *Promise*, Gunton speaks of "a quest for ontology."[7] He also notes that one of the concerns motivating the volume is "to hold

---

4. In *Promise of Trinitarian Theology*, see chapter 3, "The History. Augustine, the Trinity and the Theological Crisis of the West" (31–57), and chapter 5, "The Concept of the Person. The One, the Three and the Many" (86–103).

5. Gunton is self-consciously dependent on John Zizioulas, particularly Zizioulas' work, *Being as Communion*, as we shall see.

6. *Promise*, 71. Gunton also laments that an ontology derived from, or rooted in the Trinity was not "extended into ecclesiology." As a result of this failure to apply a trinitarian ontology to the doctrine of the Church, a vacuum was created, and this "vacuum was readily filled by rival ontologies" (62). While Gunton will argue that Christian theology took a wrong turn (especially with Augustine), and Christian theology generally failed to appropriate the riches of a trinitarian ontology, he does not want to say with Harnack that "the whole apparatus of early dogmatic theology was the imposition of a false metaphysic upon the gospel" (61; Gunton's summary of Harnack). Rather, Gunton writes, "I would hold rather, with John Zizioulas, that the development of the doctrine of the Trinity was the creation, true to the gospel, of a distinctively Christian ontology; but would add that its insights were for the most part not extended into ecclesiology" (61–62).

7. Unless otherwise noted, the references and quotations in this paragraph are found in *Promise*, ix–xii.

creation and redemption together." Thus, while we are treating "creation and redemption" and "ontology" in separate chapters, we should not drive a wedge between them. The key for Gunton is clearly found in the doctrine of the Trinity: "And the doctrine of the Trinity *is* crucial to ontology—to any ontology that would hold together creation and redemption—although its implication in this field are rarely explored." Even in the first page of the "Preface" the reader gets a hint that Augustine stands ominously in the background of Gunton's study: "the reasons for the modern belief in the irrelevance of trinitarian theology lie in large part in the shape the Western tradition took after Augustine, so that in many respects the Enlightenment can be seen as less as a rejection of traditional Western thought than as the reinforcement and radicalization of some of its leading features." The Cappadocians are also nearby, and will be featured in this volume as largely the best way ahead. While Gunton does not want to "romanticize" the contributions of the Cappadocians, due in part to "a history of abstraction" in the Eastern tradition, nonetheless, "to the Cappadocians are owed crucial steps in a process of conceptual development which, despite some parallels in the West, has for the most part been neglected." Indeed, "Many of the papers in this volume are intended to carry forward a programme of ontological exploration in the light of concepts which owe much of their shape to the Cappadocians." Gunton even notes that at one time *The Promise of Trinitarian Theology* was tentatively titled *Homage to Cappadocia*.[8]

Ontology and Relationship

Gunton contends that the Cappadocians, in their trinitarian work, ultimately forged a new ontology. But before looking at the Cappadocians themselves, it is worth pointing again to the work of John Zizioulas, and its impact on Gunton's thought. When Gunton approaches the issue of ontology, Zizioulas is almost always in the background. Zizioulas' *Being in Communion* looms large on the pages of Gunton's writings. Indeed, it would not be unfair to say that the Cappadocians have been mediated to Gunton through the work of Zizioulas. Zizioulas' emphasis on "being as communion" is appropriated by Gunton in Gunton's "being in relationship," the idea that the "being" of God *is* simply the three Persons—Father, Son and Spirit—in relationship.

---

8. *Promise*, 174.

To understand Gunton's perspective on the Cappadocians and Augustine's alleged misunderstanding of them, we must back up and trace out Gunton's historical reconstruction of the development of ontology, particularly as it relates to Christian thought. For Gunton, the relationship between ontology and cosmology is a close one, for in much of the development of Christian thought, ontology was being hammered out against the backdrop of Christian efforts to understand and articulate a Christian understanding of the world, and God's relationship to it. Thus, our discussion of ontology at first follows Gunton's discussion of the historical development of cosmology in Christian thought, before getting into a detailed discussion of the Cappadocian construal of ontology, and Augustine's subsequent misunderstanding of the Cappadocian tradition.

Whereas the Greeks in general affirmed a type of pantheistic ontology, the Bible affirms creation by a personal agent. Gunton suggests that these are ultimately the only two ontologies: (1) pantheism and (2) creation by a personal agent. As Gunton notes, "The choice is inescapable: either God or the world itself provides the reason why things are as they are."[9] Justin Martyr (died c. 165 AD) makes some headway towards a Christian ontology, although only in an incipient manner. In Justin's thought "the leaven of biblical teaching is beginning to permeate," in that he makes a significant break from his platonist past and affirms the importance of the doctrine of creation, and also affirms a true discontinuity between the human mind and God, hence requiring the concomitant affirmation that our mind must be taught by the Holy Spirit if we are to know the things of God.[10]

A more significant breakthrough comes with Irenaeus, who Gunton considers to be one of the Christian Church's finest theologians.[11] Irenaeus held that God created by His two hands, the Son and the Spirit, and that God is free in relation to the created universe. What this leads to is what Gunton calls "the classic Christian ontology," which is "that there are no degrees of being but two realities, God and everything else that he has made, the created order."[12] By both (1) construing creation through a trinitarian matrix—God creates by his two hands, Son and Spirit—and

---

9. *Triune Creator*, 39.

10. Ibid., 51.

11. Gunton, in "Historical and Systematic Theology," 15, comments, "It is my view that Irenaeus is a model for all systematic theologians."

12. *Triune Creator*, 54.

(2) drawing a clear distinction between Creator and created, a position which Justin approached, but did not completely embrace, Irenaeus more clearly affirmed a more Christian ontology, which consists of two realities: God and the created order. Particularly important for Gunton is that within the created order there is not an ontological dualism of spirit/matter, where the material world is somehow "lower" on the chain of being than the spiritual or non-material realm.[13]

While admitting there are different ways to read Origen of Alexandria, Gunton contends that Origen failed to appropriate the strengths of Irenaeus' doctrine of creation, and erred in falling back into Greek/Platonist tendencies, particularly the tendency to posit a dualism between spirit and matter.[14] Additionally, Origen, with his two-stage doctrine of creation, in a sense "reverts" to the weaknesses of Philo's similar construal, and fails to appreciate the conceptual advance seen in Irenaeus.[15] Rather than a truly Christian ontology which posits two ontological realities (i.e., God and creation) Origen, by his suspicion of the material world ends up positing a middle realm—in general, the platonic realm of ideals—between God and creation. In short, Origen posits *another* realm of being.[16]

Athanasius (c. 275–373 AD) fares better than Origen in Gunton's view, but does not climb to the heights of Irenaeus. Athanasius properly argued for the eternality and divinity of the Son, and affirmed the "absolute ontological distinction" between God and creation.[17] However, in his concern to stress the deity of the Son, Athanasius did not articulate as well as Irenaeus the Son's full "human and so material involvement with the world."[18] In short, by stressing that the Son was *homoousion* with the Father, the full humanity of the incarnate Son may have been subtly neglected.

Although Gunton is extremely favorable to Irenaeus, he spends more time expounding the conceptual advances found in the ontology forged by the Cappadocian Fathers. It is with the Cappadocians that a new ontology is more fully worked-out. Additionally, Gunton contends that it is

---

13. Ibid.
14. Ibid., 57–61.
15. Ibid., 57.
16. Ibid., 60.
17. Ibid., 66–67.
18. Ibid., 67.

the work of the Cappadocians which Augustine failed to understand, and hence failed to appropriate. It is to the Cappadocians that we now turn.

According to Gunton, the Cappadocian Fathers, in reflecting on, and articulating and defending the doctrine God, forged a new ontology. Basil's key ontological contribution is seen in his work on creation, found primarily in his *Hexaemeron*, his discourse on creation. According to Gunton, Basil's key contribution was what Gunton calls "the ontological homogeneity of creation."[19] That is, there are not degrees of being: "everything created has the same ontological status."[20] This affirmation that all creation is on the same ontological plane is the same positive contribution Gunton saw in Irenaeus.[21]

While Gunton is partial to Irenaeus, Athanasius, and Basil, and more is critical of Origen and the platonizing tradition in general, his harshest criticisms are directed against Augustine. Augustine never shook his platonic background, and these platonic tendencies subvert his doctrine of creation, and reintroduce a non-biblical ontology. Whereas Irenaeus and Basil had appropriately affirmed that the only two ontological categories are God and creation, Augustine reverted to a misguided material/non-material dualism, in which there is a hierarchy of being within the created order. The material world is seen as inferior, and redemption is seen as an escape *from* the material world, rather than including the transformation *of* the material world.[22] We have outlined Gunton's view of Augustine on creation in the previous chapter, and we will expound his misunderstanding of the Cappadocians below.

Gunton contends that the Cappadocians forged a new ontology, indeed a truly Christian ontology, and that this ontology was effectively lost in the West (due largely to Augustine). Gunton wishes to reclaim such an ontology:

> a more satisfactory ontological basis will be found if we pay attention to the doctrine of the Trinity, which was, when first formulated [again, the Cappadocians appear to be largely in view here], the means to an ontology alternative to those of the intellectual worlds in which Christianity once took shape, and must now re-

---

19. Ibid., 71.
20. Ibid.
21. Ibid., 52–56.
22. Ibid., 73–79.

shape its form of life if it is to be adequate to the challenge of the modern conditions.[23]

The Cappadocians, Gunton contends, affirm that there really are three *persons*, "beings whose reality can only be understood in terms of their relations to each other, relations by virtue of which they together constitute the being (*ousia*) of the one God."[24] This construal achieves two main things. First, the Cappadocians are able to distinguish between the oneness and threeness of God: "concepts are developed, that is to say, by means of which the Christian God can be thought as triune without loss to his unity."[25] Second, "a new ontology is developed: for God to be is to be in communion."[26] What exactly is "new"? Instead of a timeless essence that underlies the three persons (Gunton's summary of Augustine[27]), the *ousia*, or being of God *is* the communion of the three persons. That is, "Hypostases and ousia are conceptually distinct, but inseparable in thought, because they mutually involve one another," and "thought about God cannot proceed in abstraction from the history of salvation because the being of God is thought by means of the concrete revealed threeness of hypostasis."[28] Ultimately, Augustine simply does not understand the Cappadocian construal of *hypostasis* and *ousia*.[29] Gunton contends

---

23. *Promise*, 71–72.
24. Ibid., 39.
25. Ibid.
26. Ibid.
27. Gunton notes that because of Augustine's emphasis on the one essence, there are two possible conclusions: "the being of God will either be unknown in all respects—because it modalistically underlies the being of the persons," or God's being "will be made known other than through the persons, that is to say, the economy of salvation" (ibid., 41).
28. Ibid., 39.
29. Gunton (ibid., 40) refers to *De Trinitate* 5.10 and 7.7. In 5.10 Augustine writes: "The Greeks also have another word, *hypostasis*, but they make a distinction that is rather obscure to me between *ousia* and *hypostasis*. . . . So we say three persons, not in order to say that precisely, but in order not to be reduced to silence." In 7.7 Augustine writes that although the Greeks use the formula, "one *ousia*, three *hypostases*," the Latins intend the same basic idea with "one *being* or *substantia*, three *persons*." Thus, he writes: "And provided one can understand what is said at least in a puzzle, it has been agreed to say it like that, simply in order to be able to say something when asked 'Three what?'" While Gunton contends that Augustine does not understand the Cappadocians, this is less than clear. May not Augustine be interpreted more charitably? Is it possible that Augustine sees little use in quibbling over the exact term, as long as the same *concept* is affirmed? We will pursue these issues further in the chapters devoted to Augustine.

that for the Cappadocians, "the three persons are what they are in their relations, and therefore the relations qualify them ontologically, in terms of what they are." Augustine, on the other hand, "continues to use relation as a logical rather than an ontological predicate," and is thus "precluded from being able to make claims about the being of the *particular persons*, who, because they lack distinguishable identity tend to disappear into the all-embracing oneness of God."[30] Indeed, Gunton writes that "the achievement of the Cappadocians, an achievement Augustine has failed adequately to understand, was to create a new conception of the being of God, in which God's being was seen to consist in personal communion."[31] Thus, for the Cappadocians the *being* of God *is* the communion of the three persons. Gunton laments that for Augustine—despite Augustine's own writings to the contrary—the *being* of God is simply unknown. As Gunton writes, Augustine's position is ultimately "a view of an unknown substance *supporting* the three persons rather than *being constituted* by their relatedness."[32]

To understand this concept of "being in relationship" (or "being as communion"), we must grasp how Gunton (through the Cappadocians) sees the concept of "person" and "relationship." As noted above, the persons themselves are not "relations" (which is how Gunton sees Augustine's position); rather the persons are "concrete particulars in relation to one another,"*and being in relation constitutes what it actually means to be a person*. Or, one might say with the Cappadocians, "relation" is not a predicate which one then "adds" to the concept of "person." Rather, one does not really *have* a "person" without a person who is in relationship, for the person would not be a person if he was not relating. This "relational conception of the person" is a thoroughly Cappadocian construal (particularly Basil), and in such a construal they transformed the concept of person and the doctrine of God.[33] As Gunton sees it, God is now understood in a fresh way which is not hostage to Greek metaphysics, but is now understood "in terms of communion." Quoting Basil, Gunton notes, "God *is* 'a sort of continuous and indivisible community.'"[34]

30. Ibid., 41.
31. Ibid., 53.
32. Ibid., 43.
33. Ibid., 96.
34. Ibid. Gunton is quoting Basil of Caesarea, *Letters* 38, 4 (MPG 32, 332a17f and 333d20).

For Gunton, a flawed understanding of God has led to errors and wrong paths in numerous areas. How we understand God effects how we understand the world, and Gunton holds that in understanding God better we will understand the world better. Indeed, by understanding God better we are on the way, at least hopefully, to overcoming the acidic and destructive tendencies of modernity. For example, in the introduction to *The One, The Three and the Many* Gunton notes that part of his purpose in that volume "is to aid a process of healing the fragmentation which is so much a feature of the world."[35] By failing to appropriate the "better" tradition—i.e., Cappadocian rather than Augustinian—our understanding of the world is confused. Gunton notes, "trinitarian conceptuality enables us to think of our world, in a way made impossible by the traditional choice between Heraclitus and Parmenides, as both, and in different respects, one and many, but also one and many in relation."[36] He can state the thesis of *The One, the Three and the Many* by claiming that "modern disengagement has engendered alienation, and that a renewed thinking and expression of how we belong in the world, of the human habitation of reality, is an urgent requirement."[37] In line with this, we must begin to understand how we are to relate to the world, an understanding which is tied to the doctrine of creation. While having a rightful dominion rooted in the *imago Dei*, we nonetheless a part of *this* world. As Gunton writes, "we shall not understand our place in the world unless we face up to the way in which we are internally related to the rest of the world."[38] A proper (Cappadocian) ontology is the key to understanding God (and virtually everything else) correctly, and we now turn to how this better ontology relates to several key issues in theology. That is, the world itself must be understood in trinitarian categories. It is *this* world which has been created by God through his "hands"—the Son and Spirit—and it is *this* world which God is moving toward its destiny of eschatological perfection. This eschatological perfection is being brought about by the work of Christ and the Spirit.[39] We now turn to how this (Cappadocian) ontology might be a model for anthropology.

---

35. *The One, the Three and the Many*, 7.
36. Ibid.
37. Ibid., 14.
38. Ibid., 15.
39. In calling for a trinitarian understanding of the world Gunton seems rather close to affirming a *type* of vestiges doctrine. That is, the world, in its very being, reflects the

The Being of God as a Model

This "new" ontology is not simply a self-standing doctrine which allows us to grasp the doctrine of God better. Rather, this new ontology is a model or exemplar for much of what it means to be a person. First, this concept of "being in communion" (or in John Zizioulas' words, "being *as* communion"), is a model for anthropology. Indeed, "what we and our institutions are is largely a matter of persons in relationship."[40] Approvingly turning to and summarizing a point made by John Macmurray, Gunton notes, "*As persons we are only what we are in relation to other persons.*"[41] Contra Feuerbach, Gunton wants to argue that our theology leads to anthropology, not vice versa,[42] and ultimately, "A person, we must learn and relearn, can be defined only in terms of his or her relations with other persons, and not in terms of a prior universal or non-personal concept like species-being, evolution or, for that matter, subsistent relation."[43] The failure to understand this relational nature of the person has opened the door for substitute and false conceptions such as individualism and collectivism, and in the emergence of these false conceptions one sees "the disappearance of the one into the many [individualism], or the many into the one [collectivism]."[44]

In the last chapter we outlined Gunton's construal of the doctrine of the image of God. The importance of the *imago Dei* in Gunton's thought is seen when we look at anthropology. Rather than seeing the image as a "static" endowment, such as reason, Gunton contends that the image of God should be construed in relational terms. That is, to be created in the image of God suggests that we relate to God and the rest of the creation in a unique way. The way in which the Trinity is a "model" for anthropology

---

trinitarian being of God. Gunton does not explicitly state this, and neither does he deny it. However, in his affirmation that the world truly reflects the trinitarian being of God, he *does* seem to be rather close to a type of Augustinian vestiges doctrine. In personal conversation (August 6, 1999) Gunton affirmed that he is willing to affirm a type of "vestiges" doctrine. But, Gunton still sees a key weakness in Augustine to be Augustine's discovery of vestiges in the human mind (which for Augustine is construed as non-material), rather than in the good, material world.

40. Ibid., 86.

41. Ibid., 90. Italicizing his. He is referring to John Macmurray, *Persons in Relation*, 213.

42. *Promise*, 93.

43. Ibid., 98.

44. Ibid., 90.

is that for Gunton man must be understood in light of the nature of God, who is at the very center a relational being. Or better said, the being of God *is* the three Persons in relationship, and for Gunton, the relationships of the three Persons should be reflected in who we as human beings are. Indeed, the Trinity *is* reflected in who we are, in that at the very heart of what it means to be humans is our relationality.[45] And Gunton has written, "the doctrine of the image of God represents a relation, primarily to God and secondarily to the other creatures, animate and inanimate alike."[46] Again, Gunton, "Just as Father, Son and Holy Spirit constitute the being of God, so created persons are those who, insofar as they are authentically personal . . . are characterized by subsisting in mutually constitutive relations with one another."[47] Thus, for Gunton the ontology of who God is indeed is reflected in who man is. Shying away from seeing the *imago Dei* as "substantive," and preferring to see it as "relational," Gunton still affirms that we do reflect the being of God. The being of God is a model for anthropology.

Gunton is particularly interested in how the being of God (understood as "being in communion") is, or should be, reflected in the Church. That is, the Church should reflect the fact that God's being *is* "being in relationship." He is explicit at this point: "May not the actual relations of concrete historical persons constitute the sole—or primary—being of the church, just as the hypostases in relation constitute the being of God?"[48] Indeed, the Church should model itself after the reality of the three persons in relationship. As Gunton notes, "the being of the church should echo the dynamic relations between the three persons who together constitute the deity. The church is called to be the kind of reality at a finite level that God is in eternity."[49] If the church is going to "echo" the trinitarian relations of the three persons, this would, for Gunton, exclude

---

45. Some have questioned the whole tendency of seeing God as a "model"? Is this central to Scripture or the Christian tradition? Peter Adam suggests that the emphasis of Scripture is rarely the "model" of the Trinity, but almost always the "message" of the Trinity—i.e., the Gospel. See Peter Adam, "Trinity as Model." The two ("model" and "message") may not be in tension, and we will take up this issue further in our critique of Gunton.

46. *Triune Creator*, 198.

47. Ibid., 208.

48. *Promise*, 75.

49. Ibid., 81.

anything like a hierarchical structure in the church.[50] Rather than anything like a hierarchy, the "perichoretic interrelation" of the three persons is the model for the church's being.[51]

It is clear that Gunton is dependent on Zizioulas when Gunton construes the Church as modeling the Trinity, particularly as seen in Zizioulas' most accessible and well-known volume, *Being as Communion*. The very first line of *Being as Communion* reads, "The Church is not simply an institution. She is a 'mode of existence,' *a way of being*. The mystery of the Church, even in its institutional dimension, is deeply bound to the being of man, to the being of the world and to the very being of God."[52] Zizioulas also wants to find (or reclaim) an ontology that can overcome the weaknesses and limitations of Christendom's Greek philosophical milieu. Whereas Platonic philosophy was always lurking in the background of the Church Father's theological constructions, it was ultimately unsatisfactory, because Greek ontology was essentially monistic. Hence, "it was necessary to find an ontology that avoided the monistic Greek philosophy as much as the 'gulf' between God and the world taught by the gnostic systems—the other great danger of this period." Thus, "The creation of this ontology was perhaps the greatest philosophical achievement of patristic thought."[53] Zizioulas summarizes much of his effort in the following two theses: (1) "There is not true being without communion. Nothing exists as an 'individual,' conceivable in itself. Communion is an ontological category"; (2) "Communion which does not come from a 'hypostasis,' that is, a concrete and free person, and which does not lead to 'hypostases,' that is concrete and free persons, is not an 'image' of the being of God. The persons cannot exist without communion; but every form of communion which denies or suppresses the person, is inadmissible."[54]

---

50. Ibid., 73. This assertion is worth noting. Gunton is generally little interested in "towing" any sort of "modern line." He is resistant to the modern spirit, as is seen all throughout his writings. Thus, it is curious that he so firmly resists the possibility of the legitimacy of hierarchy in human institutions (including the Church). As we will treat in more detail later, it is questionable that Gunton's egalitarianism can be traced to the Cappadocians, particularly with their insistence on the monarchy of the Father in the Godhead.

51. Ibid., 82.

52. Zizioulas, *Being*, 15.

53. Ibid., 16.

54. Ibid., 18.

The question of the One and the Many is always close by as well. Zizioulas brings the One and Many question into relation with God and the Church when he writes that "the mystery of the Church is essentially none other than that of the One who is simultaneously Many—not One who exists first of all as One and *then* as Many, but One and Many at the same time."[55] It should be clear that Gunton's position is, for all intents and purposes, virtually identical to Zizioulas at this point.

To conclude, Gunton wishes to reclaim an ontology which was forged by the Cappadocians and largely lost or squandered by Augustine, and therefore lost, for the most part, in the West. Relationship ontologically constitutes what it means to be a person, and thus there is no such thing as a "person" who is not in relationship. Additionally, the "being" of God is not some sort of essence which underlies the three persons; rather, the communion of the three persons of the Trinity *is* the being of God.

Persons, Substance, and Ontology

Having explored Gunton's view of a truly Christian ontology, one that was advanced by the Cappadocians but largely lost by Augustine, we are in a better position to understand what exactly are Gunton's criticisms of Augustine. But before explicating exactly where Augustine "misses" the Cappadocian doctrine of the Trinity (particularly the "new" ontology of the Cappadocians), we turn to the foundational presuppositions of Augustine's thought, as suggested by Gunton.

At the heart of Augustine's troubles, as Gunton sees it is Augustine's platonic (or neoplatonic) background, and what might be called an "anti-materialism," or aversion to the material world.[56] As much as Augustine will attempt to defend such notions as the possibility of the knowledge of God (as we discuss below), Augustine's platonism keeps getting in the

---

55. Ibid., 112.

56. The *general* charge that Augustine's theology was influenced by Neoplatonism is of course not new nor terribly significant. But as so often is the case, the devil is in the details. The more important question is, whether over time Augustine's thought developed in such a way that as a distinctly Christian thinker he had worked out, or was working out, an appropriately Christian view of things. If such a mature Christian outlook is to be found, most likely it would be found in his later works. We will turn to such a work—*De Trinitate*—in the next chapter. Questions to be dealt with later are (1) the extent to which the Cappadocians were *also* Platonists, and hence (2) if the Cappadocians differ from Augustine in the way in which they were influenced by, or appropriated, platonic thought, *how* do they differ?

way. According to Gunton, Augustine's platonism ultimately undermines many of Augustine's main theological efforts: "The question to Augustine concerns similarly the impact of platonizing doctrines upon his thought. Are they such as to take away with the left hand what had already been given with the right, to undermine the doctrine of God known as triune even while it is being stated."[57]

Augustine's platonism is clearly revealed, according to Gunton, in his anti-materialism, or what Gunton calls his "anti-incarnational platonism." This is seen in three key themes: (1) Augustine's contention that the Old Testament theophanies are *not* pre-Christian "incarnations" or revelations of Christ (they are not Christophanies), but rather the work of angels; (2) Augustine's contention that in Jesus' life, the Holy Spirit did not enter Jesus' life for the first time at baptism, but had been present in Jesus' life since the incarnation;[58] (3) Augustine's effort to find "vestiges" of the Trinity *not* in the physical world but simply in the human mind (which Augustine construed as non-material).[59]

According to Gunton, at the heart of Augustine's theology is an unknowable God. Gunton is aware that this perhaps sounds like an astounding claim to make against a theologian who, perhaps more than anyone in Western theology, wrestled with how it is that we know God. However, as Gunton sees it, what is *really* important are those foundational presuppositions which shape and determine the direction and shape of his thought, and which, despite Augustine's efforts to defend the possibility of knowing God, ultimately undermine true knowledge of God.

This unknowability of God in Augustine is, for Gunton, tied directly to an inadequate construal of the Trinity. Again, the problem is Augustine's

---

57. Ibid., 33.

58. Gunton here points to *De Trinitate* 15.46. When we turn to this passage, Augustine's argument is rather persuasive: is it possible that Christ, the eternal logos and second member of the Trinity could have been somehow *without* the presence of the Spirit? Augustine turns to such biblical texts as Luke 1:15 (Jesus "will be filled with the Holy Spirit even from birth") to show that ultimately the Holy Spirit did not become present with Jesus at his baptism in the sense that the Spirit had been completely absent before this time.

59. Ibid., 35–38. At a later point we will pursue the issue of Augustine's supposed hesitation to find vestiges of the Trinity in the material world, for as Rudolf Alters argues, "the triadic structure [or vestiges of the Trinity], in which he discovers the, be it very faint, resemblance between creature and Creator, is found also in the material world." See his "The Notions of Triad and of Mediation in the Thought of St. Augustine," 499–525 (here, 499).

emphasis on the oneness of God. Ultimately, by beginning with the *one*, the *three* appear to be superfluous. Thus, by emphasizing the one essence of God, and by emphasizing this one essence *apart from* God's triune work in creation and redemption, "The result is that salvation history comes to appear irrelevant to the doctrine of God." Thus, concerning knowledge of God, Gunton writes: "Because the one God is the real God, and known in a different way from the God who is three, God as he is in himself would appear to be, or at least conceivably is, other than the God made known in salvation history." Hence, "The outcome is either a modalistic conception of God, or two competing sources of knowledge which tend to discredit each other."[60] God is not ultimately known in what he does, God's "economy" (i.e., creation and redemption). Rather, the *true* God is the one essence which somehow underlies the three Persons, and this essence is known in some *other* way than through what the three Persons do—if this one essence is known at all.

According to Gunton, Augustine simply does not understand the "new" ontology which the Cappadocians had forged.[61] Gunton contends that "Augustine either did not understand the trinitarian theology of his predecessors, both East and West, or looked at their work with spectacles so strongly tinted with neoplatonic assumptions that they have distorted his work."[62] Indeed, Gunton contends, "When we look at Augustine's treatment of the topic, it becomes evident that he has scarcely if at all understood the central point."[63] Augustine's chief error is that while the Cappadocians use relation to *ontologically* qualify what it means to be a person, Augustine uses relation *logically*.[64] Thus, for the Cappadocians,

60. Ibid., 33. Cf. 41–42.

61. This accusation shows up repeatedly in *Promise*. Gunton can speak of "the Cappadocian development, which Augustine so signally failed to appropriate, is that there is no being anterior to that of the persons" (74).

62. *Promise*, 39.

63. Ibid., 39. It is significant to note a distinction on this point between Gunton and his mentor, Robert W. Jenson. Both Gunton and Jenson lament the tendencies that Augustine introduced into Western thought, and both affirm serious weaknesses in Augustine's doctrine of the Trinity. However, whereas Gunton believes Augustine simply did not understand the Cappadocians, Jenson contends Augustine understood them quite well. That is, Augustine did understand the Cappadocians, but disagreed with certain aspects of their thought. Jenson notes, "Augustine knew what he was doing. He states the Cappadocian doctrine clearly." Ultimately, "Augustine rejected the Cappadocian doctrine for the sake of his simplicity axiom" (119). Cf. Jenson, *Triune Identity*, 114–31.

64. *Promise*, 41.

"the three persons are what they are in their relations, and therefore the relations qualify them *ontologically*, in terms of what they are." On the other hand, Augustine "continues to use relation as a *logical* rather than an ontological predicate," and he is ultimately "precluded from being able to make claims about the being of the *particular* persons, who, because they lack distinguishable identity tend to disappear into the all embracing oneness of God."[65] That is, Augustine is still caught in the "stranglehold of the dualistic ontology which underlies his logic."[66]

Gunton looks to Augustine's *De Trinitate* (5.10 and 7.7) to show that Augustine simply did not understand what kind of distinction Eastern thinkers wished to make between *hypostasis* and *ousia*. In 5.10 Augustine writes,

> The Greeks also have another word, *hypostasis*, but they make a distinction that is rather obscure to me between *ousia* and *hypostasis*, so that most of our people who treat of these matters in Greek are accustomed to say *mia ousia, treis hypostaseis*, which in English is literally one being, three substances.[67]

Gunton takes this section to indicate that Augustine does not understand the Cappadocian construal of the Trinity.

Gunton notes that "Augustine uses the concept of *relation* to designate that which can be predicated of God in the plural but which is yet not accidental."[68] Gunton sees in statements like these Augustine's captivity to a "dualistic ontology."[69] That is, while Augustine does not want to relegate the concept of "relation" to the "accidental," he does not have the conceptual resources by which to affirm, with the Cappadocians, that "relation" actually constitutes the being of the Triune God.

Gunton laments what flows out of Augustine's conception of the persons. Since relationality is not constitutive of the person, the persons are ultimately defined individualistically.[70] Indicative of this individualism is Augustine's attempt to discover analogies for God in the (individual)

---

65. Ibid., 41–42.

66. Ibid., 41.

67. I assume Edmund Hill, the translator of *De Trinitate*, uses "English" here instead of "Latin," since he is translating the work into English, although the use of the term "English" here seems a bit odd. Why not simply say "Latin"?

68. *Promise*, 41.

69. Ibid.

70. Ibid., 96.

human mind. Gunton finds in this individualistic thrust in Augustine a precursor to modernism.[71]

Although we have treated Christology and Pneumatology at some length in the previous chapter, it is worth noting how Augustine's failure to appropriate the new Cappadocian ontology specifically affects his Christology and Pneumatology. In short, Gunton contends that the tendency in the West (again, largely traceable to Augustine) was a Christology which is too "high" and a Pneumatology which is too "low." Much of Gunton's discussion of Christ and Spirit takes place in the context of a discussion of the Church. Gunton's position is summarized as follows:

> The argument stands as follows: that on 'economic' grounds one source of the weakness of the ecclesiological tradition has been identified. An overweighting of the christological as against the pneumatological determinants of ecclesiology together with an overemphasis on the divine over against the human Christ has led to a 'docetic' doctrine of the Church.[72]

What does Gunton seek? In short, Gunton calls for an increased emphasis on Pneumatology. In relation to the Church, this means that Gunton would like to see a reduced emphasis on the Church's *institution* by Christ, and an increased emphasis on the Church's *constitution* by the Spirit. Ultimately, Gunton wants to see Basil's notion of the Spirit as the "perfecting cause" of creation applied to the doctrines of Christology and the Church. Thus, rather than seeing the *Word* as the "motive force" of Jesus' life, more emphasis should be placed on the *Spirit* as the "perfecting cause" and the one

---

71. Ibid., 94. Finding in Augustine a precursor to modernism is not unique to Gunton. See Taylor, *Sources of the Self*, 127–42. On the other hand, Lewis Ayres wishes to strongly challenge any kind of direct link between Augustine's view of the self/knowledge and that of modernism's view (especially Descartes). See his "The Discipline of Self-Knowledge in Augustine's *De trinitate* Book X." Cf. Rowan Williams, "The Paradoxes of Self-Knowledge in the *De trinitate*," in *The Triune God*, 121–34, who also is wary of drawing tight comparisons between Augustine and Descartes. Whereas Descartes sets out "to establish an infallible touchstone for all knowledge, a single foundation," Augustine's goal is to show that "since there are things we know quite independent of *inference*, programmatic scepticism cannot in fact be intelligibly stated" (120). Cf. Mourant, "The *Cogitos*," 27–42; Booth, *Saint Augustine*; O'Daly, *Augustine's Philosophy of Mind*, 162–71; Hanby, *Augustine and Modernity*; Guitton, *Modernity of Saint Augustine*.

72. *Promise*, 71.

"enabling" Jesus' life (including his earthly sinlessness).[73] So Basil is to be preferred to Augustine.

Gunton sees two main streams in Christendom, one positive and one negative. The "bad" stream, which features a weak Pneumatology and is associated with the dualism which Gunton sees in Augustine, has generally lost the eschatological role of the Spirit, while at the same time affirming an *over*realized eschatology, where the Spirit is now reigning infallibly in the institution of the Church. The "good" stream—again Basil is clearly in view—emphasizes that the Church is "the place where the conditions of the life to come may be realised in the here and now."[74] What Gunton is after is an affirmation of the *particular* "agency of the Spirit," rather than a "substance which becomes the possession of the Church."[75] Ultimately, to this end Gunton finds the conceptual help he seeks in the Cappadocians, particularly Basil's notion of the Spirit as the "perfecting cause" of the creation.

Although it has been mentioned above, we devote a separate brief section to the issue of the economy in Augustine's theology as seen by Gunton. Gunton's main complaint against Augustine is that he so emphasizes the one essence that there is really no emphasis given to the three particular persons, which leads to both God being ultimately unknowable, as well as little emphasis being given to the economy of God in creation and redemption.

For Gunton, this search for analogies is driven by Augustine's neoplatonism and hence his aversion to material reality. Tied to these neoplatonist and anti-materialist tendencies is Augustine's overemphasis on the one, which in effect rendered the three—and ultimately the economy—superfluous:

> [T]he problem with the trinitarian analogies as Augustine presents them is that they impose upon the doctrine of the Trinity a conception of the divine threeness which owes more to neoplatonic philosophy than to the triune economy, and that the outcome is, again, a view of an unknown substance *supporting* the three persons than *being constituted* by their relatedness.[76]

---

73. Ibid., 68.
74. Ibid., 65.
75. Ibid.
76. Ibid., 42–43.

Gunton's problem with Augustine is also summarized as follows: "*The crucial analogy for Augustine is between the inner structure of the human mind and the inner being of God, because it is in the former that the latter is made known, this side of eternity at any rate, more really than in the 'outer' economy of grace.*"[77] Thus, by seeking to find analogies of the Trinity in the human mind (which for Augustine is construed as non-physical) we see further evidence that for Augustine's neoplatonism, his overemphasis on the one and denigration of the three, his negligence of the economy, and even the unknowability of God.

Conclusion

In the last two chapters we have examined two of the key themes in Gunton's writings: the centrality of creation and redemption, and the question of ontology. Before moving to an exposition of Augustine, let us briefly summarize what we have found in Gunton's writing on ontology. As we have examined Gunton's thought we have seen that a consistent theme is the significant weaknesses and failures of Augustine, as well as the strengths and successes of the Cappadocians and Irenaeus. In particular we have found the following. First, Gunton has argued that ontology is inescapable, and that the issue must be faced. Additionally, there is the possibility of a truly Christian ontology, and if there is not a Christian ontology, a "foreign" ontology will soon take its place. Second, Gunton contends that the Cappadocians forged a genuinely Christian ontology which was truly trinitarian and faithful to the Christian tradition. This ontology affirmed that relationship was an ontological category, and that "being" is *constituted* by relationship. A "being" is not a "being" unless it is relating. Augustine did not understand this Cappadocian conceptual advance, since he was caught in the "stranglehold" of ontological dualism, and was captive to his platonic and neoplatonic philosophical presuppositions. Augustine saw relationship as a *logical* category (something said "about" the person), but not as something constituting the very being of a person. Augustine ultimately simply did not understand the Cappadocian insight of the centrality of relationship, and thus squandered the Cappadocian inheritance. Third, Augustine's failure to build on the Cappadocians led to

---

77. Ibid., 45. Italicizing his. It is significant that this extended italicization is one of only a few such lengthy italicized phrases in *Promise*. Hence, we can assume Gunton considers it a particularly important statement.

poor theological construals of anthropology, the Church, and ultimately to modernistic individualism (since Augustine saw the individual human mind, not relationships with others, as the place to search for analogies for the Trinity).

These are significant accusations, and Gunton has constructed an impressive critique of the one of the most central thinkers in Western thought. Having examined Gunton, we need to turn to Augustine himself. For only in looking at Augustine himself can we determine the validity of Gunton's criticisms and concerns.

CHAPTER 4

Creation and Redemption in Augustine's *De Trinitate*

THE PURPOSE OF THE fourth and fifth chapters of this monograph is to offer an analysis of key themes in Augustine's *De Trinitate* in light of the criticisms raised by Gunton. We have attempted fairly to exposit Gunton's criticisms, and now we will attempt fairly to expound key themes in Augustine's *De Trinitate* with Gunton's criticisms in view.

It is perhaps appropriate here simply to note the significance of Augustine's *De Trinitate* in relation to his other works. As far as difficulty, *De Trinitate* is more dense than many of Augustine's other writings. Hannah Arendt captures something of the significance of *De Trinitate* in the following remark: Augustine's "treatise *On the Trinity*, a defense of the crucial dogma of the Christian Church, is at the same time the most profound and the most articulated development of his own very original philosophical position."[1] In *De Trinitate* Augustine is a Christian thinker working slowly and thoroughly through a difficult doctrine.

In chapters two and three we have explored the theology of Colin Gunton, particularly as it relates to his largely negative assessment of Augustine. Having done so, we now turn Augustine. Having allowed Gunton to raise the questions that are important to him, we seek to discover what Augustine has to say about these same questions. Therefore, the structure of chapters of four and five will mirror the structure of chapters two and three. Thus, whereas we began chapter two with a discussion of Gunton on "creation and the created order," chapter four begins with a

1. Arendt, *Life of the Mind*, 84–85.

discussion of Augustine on "creation and the created order." By following this general format, we should be able to see clearly the relation between Augustine and Gunton's criticisms of him.

Creation and the Created Order

In our exposition of Gunton we saw that in his doctrine of creation and the created order he emphasized several key themes: the goodness of creation; a christologically mediated creation; a created order which is brought to eschatological perfection by the Holy Spirit; the fundamental and organic continuity between creation and redemption—redemption is the bringing to completion of a *telos* built into the created order. Gunton believes Augustine's positions on these key issues are fundamentally flawed and have contributed negatively to the Western intellectual tradition. Gunton argues the following regarding Augustine's theology: creation is disparaged; the platonic forms have replaced Christ as the mediator of creation; the Holy Spirit's role in creation and the created order is of no particular importance; creation and redemption have been severed. Although *De Trinitate* is not a treatise devoted to creation *per se*, in light of Gunton's critique of creation in the theology of Augustine, it is appropriate to trace out how creation is treated in this key work by Augustine.[2]

It is common to summarize the thought of Augustine by saying that he was a "Christian Platonist." Certainly Augustine had been steeped in neoplatonism, and this is perhaps seen most clearly in his *Confessiones*. However, as A. H. Armstrong has noted, when we speak of Christianity and Platonism, "We are dealing with the interplay of two great traditions, both of which have an inexhaustible capacity for stimulating thought of a great many different kinds."[3] Sometimes the identification of Augustine as a "Christian Platonist" is taken to mean, *ipso facto*, that Augustine saw the material world as inherently bad. While there is little question that Augustine believed that the non-material world is "better," or in some sense "higher" than the material world, we would do well to look at exactly how the material world fares in the thought of Augustine.

---

2. Although we are mostly concerned with *De Trinitate*, we will also make recourse to other works, particularly *De civitate Dei*, *Confessiones*, and *De Genesis ad Litteram*. Cf. O'Toole, *Philosophy of Creation*; Henry, *Augustine on Creation*; Williams, "'Good For Nothing'?," 9–24; Fredericksen, "Vile Bodies," 75–87.

3. Armstrong, "St. Augustine and Christian Platonism," 3.

Creatio Ex Nihilo

Augustine clearly affirmed creation out of nothing. As a Manichee Augustine had been philosophically committed to a type of dualism of good and evil which held that good and evil were eternal forces constantly at war with one another. As he began to think more and more "Christianly" about the created order he came to affirm a thoroughgoing doctrine of *creatio ex nihilo*.[4] This is not explicitly treated in *De Trinitate*, but Augustine's affirmation of *creatio ex nihilo* is seen clearly in *De civitate Dei*,[5] *Confessiones*,[6] *De Natura Boni*,[7] *De Fide et Symbolo*,[8] *De diversis quaestionibus ad Simplicianum*,[9] *Contra Julianum*.[10]

For Augustine it is a changeless and timeless God who creates out of nothing. Indeed, creation out of nothing allows Augustine to affirm that God truly is unchangeable. For if God creates somehow *out of* himself, or *from* himself, it is hard to see how God could remain unchangeable. As Christopher O'Toole has noted, it is at this very point where Augustine differs from Plotinus and the neoplatonists. Whereas Plotinus contends that creation is ultimately a necessity, Augustine attributes the reality and act of creation solely to the will of God. For Augustine God creates because he *wants* to, not because the creative act is somehow a necessity.[11] At the same time, God's will is not, we might say, a "naked" will, but is a will which is an act of God's goodness, for as Augustine writes, "God . . . acts through goodness."[12]

Creation and Trinity

It is also important to note that God's act of creation is a trinitarian act. In *De Vera Religione* Augustine is explicit that creation is an act of the

---

4. O'Toole, *Philosophy of Creation*, 1–9.
5. *De civitate Dei* XII.5.
6. *Confessiones* XII.vii (7); XII.xvii (24); XIII.xxxiii (48).
7. *De Natura Boni* I.3.10.
8. *De Fide et Symbolo* I.2.
9. *De diversis quaestionibus ad Simplicianum* LXXXVIII.I.78.
10. *Contra Julianum* V.31.
11. O'Toole, *Philosophy of Creation*, 11–12. Cf. Plotinus *Enneads* I 8; *De Genesis Contra Manichaeos* I.3, n. 4; *De Genesis ad Litteram* IV.16.
12. *Enarrationes in Psalmos* CXXXIV, n. 10.

Trinity.[13] In *Enchiridion* Augustine writes that all things are created by God "and that there is nothing which either He Himself is not or which does not stem from Him—from Him, the Trinity, the Father, the Son begotten of the Father, and the Holy Spirit proceeding from the same Father, but being the one and the same Spirit of Father and Son."[14] He continues, "by this Trinity supremely, equally, and unchangeably good, all things were created."[15]

Creation and Evil

In coming to terms with the doctrine of creation, Augustine was forced to deal with the question of evil. In one sense, traditional Christianity has made it a bit hard for itself by its thoroughgoing affirmation of *creatio ex nihilo*. While a good/evil dualism might not be *true* on Christian terms, it at least gives one a perhaps palatable solution to the problem of evil. However, Augustine *was* committed to *creatio ex nihilo* and thus he had to deal with the question of the problem of evil. Indeed, Christopher O'Toole suggests that in a Christian doctrine of creation (*ex nihilo*) Augustine finds the *answer* to the problem of evil.[16] All that God creates is good.[17] Since everything that is created is good, evil cannot be relegated or assigned to the material realm. Additionally, since everything is created *ex nihilo* there is in the created order the possibility of reverting or turning back to nothingness.[18] That is, there is the possibility of moving away from God.[19] Thus, Augustine can speak of evil as *privatio boni*, a "privation of good," rather than a "thing" or substance itself.[20] God allows evil,[21] and indeed uses it for good,[22] but He does not create anything evil. With the problem of evil we see a distinct place where Augustine was forced to part

---

13. *De Vera Religione* 18.55.
14. *Enchiridion* 9.
15. Ibid.
16. O'Toole, *Philosophy of Creation*, 6.
17. *De Moribus Ecclesia Catholicae et de Moribus Manichaeorum*, II, 4.
18. Ibid., 6–7.
19. *Contra Julianum*, I, 9.
20. *Contra Secundinum Manichaem*, 15; cf. *De Moribus Ecclesiae Catholicae et de Moribus Manichaeorum*, II, 4; *Contra Epistulam Manichaei*, 33, 35.
21. *Contra Epistulam Manichaei*, 38.
22. Ibid., 41.

ways with the Platonists. Whereas the Platonists traced evil to the body, Augustine affirmed the goodness of the body.[23]

Revelation

In our treatment of Gunton's doctrine of revelation, we found the following key themes: knowledge is not simply a mind-to-mind reality, but entails the whole embodied person; revelation entails knowledge which is always mediated; God has so structured the created order that it has the capacity to reveal God, and does in fact reveal God; knowledge of the supernatural is a real possibility; the Holy Spirit is central in bringing about revelation; the doctrine of revelation is a function of the doctrine of salvation, or of the "divine saving economy," and salvation, or redemption, is ultimately the bringing to completion of God's purpose for creation. Gunton contends that Augustine has mediated unfortunate tendencies into the theological tradition. Augustine's negative contributions are: Augustine's platonic background and tendencies resulted in the preeminence of the platonic forms in his doctrine of revelation and effectively crowded out a distinctly trinitarian—and particularly christological—construal of revelation; the loss of a christological understanding of revelation has led to a construal of revelation which entails unmediated knowledge—in essence the virtual *loss* of a doctrine of revelation. In light of Gunton's criticisms of Augustine we now turn to Augustine himself.

It appears that on one level, we *begin* our quest for knowledge of God by following Paul's words in Rom 1:20: "For his invisible things are discerned by being understood through the things that have been made from the creation of the world."[24] As Augustine reads Paul, we begin with the created order and *then* move *to* a more full knowledge of God.[25] That

---

23. *De civitate Dei* 14, 5. Cf. Stead, *Philosophy in Christian Antiquity*, 223.

24. Does this contradict Augustine's contention at the beginning of *De Trinitate* that one always begins with faith—whether dealing with the Trinity or anything else? In the opening sentence of *De Trinitate* Augustine writes, "The reader of these reflections of mine on the Trinity should bear in mind that my pen is on the watch against the sophistries of those who scorn the starting-point of faith, and allow themselves to be deceived through an unseasonable and misguided love of reason" (I.1). Ultimately, there is no contradiction here. Augustine is clear from the beginning that he accepts the doctrine of the Trinity because it is taught in Scripture and by the Christian Church. Thus, Augustine's analysis or searching of the created order is undertaken against the backdrop of his commitment to the doctrine of the Trinity.

25. Unless otherwise noted, I am working from the following translation of *De Trinitate*: Augustine, *Trinity*.

is, we *begin* with the created order. And when we turn to this created order Augustine is clear that the Trinity is revealed to us. Augustine writes, "So then, as we direct our gaze at the creator by *understanding the things that are made* (Rom 1:20), we should understand him as triad, whose traces appear in creation in a way that is fitting."[26] Augustine later again turns to the first chapter of Romans, and claims again that he is simply following Paul when he is trying to see traces of God in the created order.[27] At the end of *De Trinitate* Augustine is summarizing the volume as a whole, and he writes, "I quote this passage from the book of Wisdom in case any of the faithful should reckon I have been wasting time for nothing in searching creation for signs of the supreme trinity we are looking for when we are looking for God, going step by step through various trinities of different sorts until we eventually arrive at the mind of man."[28] Augustine again alludes to Romans 1 when he writes that we should try and discern God's "invisible things by understanding them through the things that are made, and especially through the rational or intellectual understanding and will that God is a trinity."[29] Augustine offers a type of early affirmation of special and general revelation when he affirms that God is revealed not only in Scripture but in the created order: "It is not, after all, only the authority of the divine books which asserts that God is; the universal nature of things which surrounds us, to which we too belong, proclaims that it has a most excellent founder, who has given us a mind and natural reason by which to see that living beings are to be preferred to non-living, ones endowed with sense to non-sentient ones."[30]

Thus, it would appear, at least *prima facia* that the created order is able to reveal God. However, one does not *stop* there. Rather, the created order is a means to the greater end of the vision of God. This "face to face" vision or contemplation of God is one of the several themes which runs throughout *De Trinitate*. This theme is seen in Augustine's repeated use of 1 Cor 13:12: "Now we see but in a glass darkly, but then we shall see face to face." For example, Augustine writes, "But when the sight comes that is promised us *face to face* (1 Cor 13:12), we shall see this trinity that is

26. *De Trinitate* VI.12.
27. Ibid., XV.3.
28. Ibid.
29. Ibid., XV.39.
30. Ibid., XV.5.

not only incorporeal but also supremely inseparable and truly unchangeable much more clearly and definitely than we now see its image which we ourselves are."[31] Speaking of the human soul Augustine writes, "And therefore if it is with reference to its capacity to use reason and understanding *in order to understand and gaze upon God* that it was made to the image of God, it follows that from the moment this great and wonderful nature begins to be, this image is always there, whether it is so worn away as to be almost nothing, or faint and distorted, or clear and beautiful."[32] Augustine can also argue that the trinity of the mind is only "really the image of God . . . because it is . . . able to remember and understand and love him by whom it was made"—i.e., when it focuses on and thinks on and loves God.[33] When the mind loves God, it is free to love neighbors as itself, for in loving God "it loves itself with a straight, not a twisted love, now that it loves God."[34] Nonetheless, and this is the key point, the created order serves the good purpose of leading us to a fuller contemplation and vision of God.

The importance of the material world is particularly seen in Augustine's doctrine of the sending of the Son. Although we treat this more fully in the following section on "Redemption in *De Trinitate*," it is appropriate to note here that it is through *material* things that we come to see the living and Triune God. Michel R. Barnes states this principle as follows, "The Son has to be(come) *really material* if he is to perform the 'mission' of bringing us to the beatific vision."[35] Barnes continues, "The Homoians claim 'If material, then not divine,' while Augustine wants to assert, 'Material, in order to bring us to the divine.'"[36] Thus, the created order can have a limited goodness, a goodness which is not ultimate, but is still good and points to something better.

Man, Dualism, and Resurrection

Having shown that there is indeed a positive place for the created order in Augustine's thought, it still must be said that there is some sort of dual-

---

31. Ibid., XV.44.
32. Ibid., XIV.9. (emphasis mine).
33. Ibid., XIV.15.
34. Ibid., XIV.18.
35. Barnes, "Exegesis and Polemic," 58.
36. Ibid.

ism between body and soul, and between the material and non-material realms.[37] While Augustine continually forged and worked out a Christian view of man, his neoplatonism seems always to be there to some degree. In 389 Augustine received a letter from a friend, Nebridius, in which the latter wrote: "They speak to me of Christ, of Plato, of Plotinus."[38] Whether the same friend would have stated things similarly some thirty to forty years later is an interesting question. Nonetheless, the soul is in a sense "higher" than the body. Indeed, it is the soul, or mind which is actually made in the image of God, and this is of particular importance.[39] It is the soul or mind which is said to be in the image of God, and if this is so, what can be said for the body? Is it essentially meaningless? Augustine will not say that the body is meaningless, and indeed, he will end up affirming a true resurrection of the body.[40] Margaret Miles has demonstrated that early in his career Augustine affirmed that at death there was an escape from the body.[41] Thus, Augustine could write of the "flight and escape from this body."[42] However, in *Contra Faustum Manicheum*, Augustine argues that God created both the "outer man" and "inner man" good. While the *imago Dei* is to be found in the inner man, man is ultimately one whole being, not two. Sin has plagued both the inner and outer man, but both the inner and outer man will rise again. Augustine writes, "But when that which is sown a natural body shall rise a spiritual body, the outer man too shall attain the dignity of a celestial character."[43]

In his *Retractationes* Augustine will confirm the reality of our own bodily resurrections, which include our fleshly, though transformed bodies. In Augustine's earlier work, *De fide et symbolo*, Augustine had distinguished between a "flesh and blood" and "bodily" resurrection. Augustine argued that "flesh and blood" certainly would not be resurrected, but the

---

37. In this section I am indebted to the work of Margaret Ruth Miles, *Augustine on the Body*.; cf. John M. Rist, "Soul, Body and Personal Identity," chap. in *Augustine: Ancient Thought Baptized*; Vernon J. Bourke, "Body-Soul Relation in Early Augustine," 435–50; George Lawless, "Augustine and Human Embodiment," 167–86.

38. *Epistula* VI.I.

39. The most thorough treatment of Augustine's doctrine of the *imago Dei* is John Edward Sullivan, *Image of God*. Cf. Gilson, *Christian Philosophy of Saint Augustine*, 217–24; Rist, *Augustine*, 92–147 (esp. 145–47).

40. See Miles, *Augustine on the Body*, 99–125; cf. Fredriksen, "Vile Bodies."

41. Miles, *Augustine on the Body*, 106–13.

42. *De Quantitate animae* 76.

43. *Contra Faustum Manichaeum* XXIV.2 .

body would. In *Retractationes* he sought to correct this earlier writing. In Jesus' resurrection Jesus possessed his "members," and we will as well.[44]

Augustine's later thought, such as that just seen in *Retractationes*, is more important to us, since *De Trinitate*—the central text to us here in our endeavors—is also a later work. By the end of his career Augustine is quite adamant about the resurrection of the body, including the flesh. He can write of the state of the resurrected, "The bodies of the saints, then, will rise free from any blemish or deformity." The saints will truly possess *bodies*, not simply spirits. There will be a flesh, of a heavenly type: "Yet with respect to the substance, there will be flesh even then; for even after His resurrection the body of Christ is called flesh."[45] In the same work Augustine admits that while the details of the resurrection are a bit sketchy, he nonetheless is compelled to affirm a bodily resurrection: "This in any case no Christian ought to doubt: that the bodies of all men who have been born and are to be born, and have died and are to die, will rise again."[46]

Is there a dualism in *De Trinitate* between body and soul, or between the material and non-material? Certainly Augustine places the soul higher than the body. However, in light of what we seen in our discussion of Augustine's doctrine of the resurrection of the (*fleshly*) body, it is perhaps wisest to say that Augustine affirms a *limited* dualism in which body and soul are both created and good, but the soul is superior.

Christ

Earlier we expounded Gunton's understanding of the person of Christ. In general, we noted that Gunton's Christology is in many ways very traditional. On the whole, he wants to affirm the intent of Chalcedon without simply engaging in a project of repristination. On the basic affirmation of the full deity and humanity of Christ, Gunton generally agrees with Augustine's orthodox affirmation of Christ's deity and humanity. Gunton's more negative criticisms of Augustine are more evident in the previous section on revelation, in which Gunton criticized Augustine for in effect displacing Christ with the platonic forms, and neglecting the role of the Holy Spirit and Christ in revelation. However, one key negative criticism

---

44. *Retractationes* I.16.
45. *Enchiridion* XCI; cf. *Epistula* CCV 2; see Miles, *Augustine on the Body*, 119.
46. *Enchiridion* 84.

of Augustine is that he mediated to the West (through Descartes and Kant) a dualism between time and eternity, thus making it difficult to construe a christology which fully affirms Christ's *temporal* (i.e., human) and *eternal* (i.e., divine) natures.[47] With Gunton's criticisms in view, let us turn to Augustine.

Augustine writes on Christ against the backdrop of the doctrine of the Trinity. Whereas we discuss the atonement at some length, we limit our discussion here to Augustine's more explicit teaching on the person of Christ.[48] After briefly introducing the reader to his method in the opening sections of *De Trinitate*, Augustine quickly moves to an affirmation of the unity and equality of Father, Son and Holy Spirit.[49] In fact, after consulting the Catholic commentators who have treated the Trinity, Augustine concludes that their united testimony is that

> according to the scriptures Father and Son and Holy Spirit in the inseparable equality of one substance presents a divine unity; and therefore there are not three gods but one God; although indeed the Father has begotten the Son, and therefore he who is the Father is not the Son; and the Son is begotten by the Father, and therefore he who is the Son is not the Father; and the Holy Spirit is neither the Father nor the Son, but only the Spirit of the Father and of the Son, himself coequal to the Father and the Son, and belonging to the threefold unity.[50]

Having affirmed the unity and equality of the three persons, Augustine goes on to broach a difficult issue. If God is one, how is it that some members of the Trinity appear to do different things? Only the Son became incarnate, and only the Father spoke and only the Holy Spirit appeared in the form of a dove at Jesus' baptism. Here Augustine raises a question with which he will wrestle throughout the volume: how can we say that there are really three persons, where the Father is not the Son,

---

47. *Yesterday and Today*, 108–11.

48. It is generally difficult to separate treatments of the person of Christ and the work of Christ, since these topics are so interrelated, as the history of Christian thought testifies. However, we here treat the person of Christ, and we are treating the work of Christ in a separate section. The chief reason for this is I want to later emphasize the particular importance of the work of Christ in *De Trinitate*, and thus the work of Christ is given its own section and treatment.

49. *De Trinitate* I.7.

50. Ibid.

who is not the Holy Spirit, who is not the Father, and *also* say that "the trinity works inseparable in everything that God works."[51]

When turning to Christ, it appears immediately that the Arians are in the background. Augustine speaks of those "who have affirmed that our Lord Jesus Christ is not God, or is not true God, or is not with the Father the one and only God, or is not truly immoral because he is subject to change."[52] Augustine works through a number of key texts in order to defend the full deity and consubstantiality of the Son. From the Prologue to John Augustine can conclude that the Son is "of one and the same substance as the Father. And thus he is not only God, but also true God."[53] Even texts which appear to speak of the Father, can be construed as referring to all three persons. Thus, 1 Timothy 6:16, which speaks of God, "who alone has immortality." Augustine can write, "In these words neither Father nor Son nor Holy Spirit is specifically named, but the blessed and only mighty one, King of kings and Lord of lords, which is the one and only true God, the three."[54] Augustine argues that often when "God" is used in Scripture, the term should be seen as referring to all three persons, and not simply the Father. Augustine's argument is as follows. Romans 11:36 notes, "Since from him and through him and in him are all things, to him be glory forever, and ever," and Augustine takes this as a creation text. But if only the *Father* is in view here, how does one make sense of texts like John 1:2, "All things were made through him?" Are *some* things made by the Father, and others by the Son? Not at all, "But if it is all things through the Father and all through the Son, then it is the same things through the Father as through the Son. So the Son is equal to the Father, and the work of the Father and Son is inseparable."[55] Thus, Augustine contends that Christ "was not made himself, so that with the Father he might make all things that were made."[56]

In attempting to demonstrate the full deity and consubstantiality of Christ, Augustine must deal with those scriptural texts which appear to throw this deity and consubstantiality into doubt. Scripture does,

51. Ibid., I.8.
52. Ibid., I.9.
53. Ibid.
54. Ibid., I.10.
55. Ibid., I.12.
56. Ibid.

Augustine admits, appear to teach at places that the Son is less than the Father (e.g., John 14:28: "The Father is greater than I"). Augustine's interpretive rule is that the Son exists both in "the form of God" (i.e., the Son as eternally God) and in "the form of a servant" (i.e., the Son in his incarnate state). Those scriptures which appear to teach the deity and consubstantiality of the Son are to interpreted in light of the Son existing in "the form of God." Those scriptures which appear to teach that the Son is less than the Father are to be interpreted in light of the Son existing in "the form of a servant." Neither godhead nor creaturehood "turned into" or "changed into" the other in Christ: "neither godhead changed into creature and ceasing to be godhead, nor creature changed into godhead and ceasing to be creature."[57] Augustine summarizes his interpretive rule as follows: "So there need be no hesitation from anyone in taking this to mean that what the Father is greater than is the form of a servant, whereas the Son is his equal in the form of God."[58] This interpretive grid clearly evidences Augustine's commitment to the humanity and deity of Christ. Augustine affirms this commitment as follows, "since the Son of God is both God and man, it is rather the man in the Son that differs in substance, than the Son in the Father."[59]

The person of Christ can never be separated from the work of Christ, and Augustine repeatedly draws attention to the fact that the Son took on flesh for our salvation. The Son's "mission" is to usher believers into the presence of God, where they will see God "face to face," and the Son's role as mediator will have come to an end. Summarizing the teaching of several texts (e.g., John 16:26; Phil 2:7), Augustine paraphrases Jesus' point: "It was not in the form in which I am equal to the Father that I was manifested, but in another guise, namely as less than he in the creature I took on," and "I have shown the form of a servant, which I emptied myself to take (Phil 2:7), even to the eyes of sinners who love this world," and thus, "I am teaching my faithful ones that I can only be fully understood in my equality with the Father."[60] Christ takes on "the form of a servant" so that he can usher believers into "direct vision face to face."[61] But in bringing

---

57. Ibid., I.14.
58. Ibid., I.15.
59. Ibid., I.20.
60. Ibid., I.21.
61. Ibid.

believers to the direct contemplation of God, the Son is not excluded as the object of believer's contemplation: "When he brings the believers to the contemplation of God and the Father, he will assuredly bring them to the contemplation of himself, having said, 'I will show myself to him' (John 14:21)."[62] Thus, as virtually the whole Christian tradition teaches, there is in an organic connection between *who* Jesus is and *what* he has accomplished. The Son has become incarnate, and his mission is to bring believers into the direct presence and contemplation of God.

There is an additional hermeneutical rule or principle which Augustine introduces at the end of Book I which is helpful in understanding his view of the person of Christ. Augustine turns to 1 Cor 2:8, "If they had known, they would have never crucified the Lord of glory." Augustine notes that this text appears at first sight appears to violate his hermeneutical principle that Scripture speaks of the Son as less than the Father in the sense of "Son of Man" (or "form of a servant"), while Scripture speaks of the Son as equal to the Father in the sense of "Son of God" (or "form of God"). However, this text speaks of the *crucifixion* of the *Lord of glory* (and Augustine takes "Lord of glory" to be a "Son of Man" type designation). Given Augustine's hermeneutical rule should not the text have read something like, "... crucified the Son of man"? In response to this apparent conundrum Augustine formulates a type of doctrine of *communicatio idiomatum*. That is, because the one *person* of Christ is at the same time Son of God "in virtue of the form in which he is," as well as the Son of man "in virtue of the form of a servant which he took," Scripture can appropriately speak of the Son in the form of God being crucified. Thus Augustine can write, "It was in the form of a servant that he was crucified, and yet it was the Lord of glory who was crucified." He continues, "it is in virtue of his being God that he glorifies his followers—in virtue, obviously, of his being the Lord of glory; and yet the Lord of glory was crucified, because it is quite correct to talk even of God being crucified."[63] Similarly, argues Augustine, while it is *God* who must judge, Scripture can speak of the Son as *man* who will judge.[64] Augustine here testifies to the unity of the two natures in the one person, Christ. Writing around fifty years before Chalcedon, we see a rather developed Christology which affirms the full

---

62. Ibid., I.18.
63. Ibid., I.28.
64. Ibid.

deity and consubstantiality, as well as humanity of Christ. We also see Augustine's affirmation of the unity of Christ's humanity and divinity in the one person, as evidenced by his affirmation of a type of doctrine of *communicatio idiomatum*.

Holy Spirit

In our treatment of Gunton's doctrine of the Holy Spirit we noted several key themes: the West has given inadequate attention to the Holy Spirit, a tendency which is related to the West's failure to truly affirm the full humanity of Christ; following Basil, the Holy Spirit is the "perfecting cause" of creation, as the Holy Spirit perfects the world—here redemption is construed as the bringing about of the *telos* built in to creation; it is the Holy Spirit who perfected Jesus during his life, sustained him during his suffering and temptation, empowered Jesus' priesthood, and raised Jesus from the dead. In Gunton's view, Augustine made several significant theological missteps: the notion of the Spirit as the "bond" between Father and Son ultimately closes off the Trinity from the created order, an accusation which accords with Gunton's notion that Augustine has severed the Trinity from an ongoing relationship with the particulars of this created world; Augustine's emphasis on the immanent Trinity (evidenced in an emphasis on psychological analogies) mediated to the West a tendency to look away from the economy and towards the epistemological quest (which is centered in the mind); Augustine pays inadequate attention to the Spirit's eschatological role as perfecter of creation and the Holy Spirit's role as the sustainer and perfecter of Christ himself. With Gunton's key criticisms before us, let us turn to Augustine.

As with the doctrine of Christ, Augustine treats the Holy Spirit in the context of his trinitarian concerns. Augustine clearly affirms the unity and equality of the Father, Son and Holy Spirit.[65] While much of Augustine's effort in Book I is spent contending for the deity and consubstantiality of the Son, attention is given to the Holy Spirit, and later in the volume more attention is directed to the Holy Spirit. Like the Son, the Holy Spirit "too is God and not a creature."[66] The Holy Spirit is "absolutely equal to the Father and the Son, and consubstantial and co-eternal in the oneness

---

65. Ibid., I.7.
66. Ibid., I.13.

of the three."⁶⁷ The Holy Spirit is indissolubly connected to the Father and the Son, so that "he cannot be separated from the Father and the Son."⁶⁸ In short, the Holy Spirit is absolutely equal to the Father and Son, being fully divine and being consubstantial with the Father and the Son.

In *De Trinitate* Augustine is wrestling with the question of the best and truest way to speak about God. The person of the Holy Spirit provides a particularly difficult challenge here. As we will see in chapter five below, the concept of "relationship" becomes particularly important for Augustine in speaking of the Trinity. That is, while there is only one God, only one substance, there are nonetheless three persons. How do the persons differ? On Augustine's understanding, the three persons differ "relationship-wise," but not "substance-wise." They differ in terms of their relationship to the other members of the Trinity. This way of construing the differences of the persons is rather easily understandable when speaking of the Father and the Son: The Father is father of the Son, and the Son is son of the Father. But how do we speak of the Holy Spirit? The Holy Spirit *is* the Holy Spirit of the Father, but the Father is *not* the father of the Holy Spirit. Likewise, the Holy Spirit *is* the Holy Spirit of the Son, but the Son is *not* the son of the Holy Spirit. Thus, while "relationship" is a central term by which Augustine tries to construe the differences of the person, he struggles with how the Holy Spirit figures into such an understanding.⁶⁹ Additionally, Augustine also notes that while *the* Holy Spirit is a person, and only the Holy Spirit should be called "Holy Spirit" as a particular title (neither the Father nor Son is *the* Holy Spirit), it is appropriate to call the Father and the Son both "holy" and "spirit," since clearly these general terms do describe Father and Son as well.⁷⁰

Eventually Augustine suggests that we refer to the Holy Spirit as "gift" (*donum*).⁷¹ Augustine is unable to find a better "relational" word, and so settles with "gift." He picks up "the gift of God" from Acts 8:20 and John 4:10, and contends that since the Holy Spirit is the gift of *both* the Father and the Son, that it is fitting to call the Holy Spirit "gift."⁷² For Augustine

---

67. Ibid.
68. Ibid., I.18.
69. Ibid., V.13.
70. Ibid., V.12.
71. This theme shows up throughout *De Trinitate*. See IV.29; XV.29, 33–36, and others we will discuss below.
72. Ibid., V.12.

this notion of gift is organically connected to the double procession of the Spirit. Thus, he notes that "gift" is an appropriate word for the Spirit because, quoting John 15:26, the Spirit "proceeds from the Father." But the Spirit also proceeds from the Son, contends Augustine, pointing to Rom 8:9, "Whoever does not have the Spirit of Christ is not one of his." The notions of "gift" and double procession lead directly into Augustine's suggestion that the Holy Spirit is the "bond" between Father and Son. He writes, "So the Holy Spirit is a kind of inexpressible communion or fellowship of Father and Son."[73]

The term "gift" raises an interesting question. If the Holy Spirit is "gift," was he "gift" before he was "given" (i.e., to the world). Or more potentially troubling, does the Holy Spirit only begin to *be* when he is given?[74] Augustine concludes that it is wisest to affirm that the Holy Spirit does not begin to be only when he is given, but that the Holy Spirit "always proceeds and proceeds from eternity." Additionally, it is legitimate to refer to the Holy Spirit as "gift" before he was given, since "because he so proceeds as to be giveable, he was already gift even before there was anyone to give him to."[75]

There is also a certain uniqueness to the Holy Spirit if he is properly called "gift." Since the Holy Spirit is "given" *by* someone *to* someone, the Holy Spirit is somehow both the Spirit of the one giving and the Spirit of the one receiving. That is, the Spirit is both the Spirit of the Father and the Son, and our Spirit. As Augustine writes, "the Holy Spirit is not only called the Spirit of the Father and the Son who gave him, but also our Spirit who received him." Augustine suggests there is analogy with salvation: "It is like salvation, which is called the salvation of the Lord who gives salvation, and also our salvation because we receive it."[76]

Augustine then makes a point which is crucial to his trinitarian theology, and which we will develop more fully later. Augustine argues that the one who *gives* the Spirit is also the *origin* of the Spirit. That is, since the Holy Spirit is *given* by the Father and the Son, then the Father and the

---

73. Ibid.

74. Ibid., V.16.

75. Ibid. Augustine will qualify this and say that the Holy Spirit is "gift" (*donum*) from eternity, but only "donation" (*donatum*) in time (i.e., when he is actually given in time). "Donation" in Latin is *donatum*, a perfect passive participle—"that which has been given"—a definition which more clearly makes Augustine's point. Cf. ibid., V.17.

76. Ibid., V.15.

Son are the *origin* of the Holy Spirit. Since Augustine sees in Scripture that the Father and Son send the Holy Spirit (e.g., John 15:26), he concludes that the Father and Son are therefore the origin of the Holy Spirit. In other words, the *mission* of the Holy Spirit (i.e., "sending") in time reflects the *procession* of the Holy Spirit in eternity.[77]

Having settled to his own satisfaction the consubstantiality and equality and unity of the Holy Spirit with Father and Son, as well as the eternal procession of the Spirit from the Father and the Son, much of Augustine's treatment of the Holy Spirit throughout the rest of *De Trinitate* is a variation on the theme of the Holy Spirit as the bond between the Father and the Son. The Holy Spirit is "that by which the two are joined each to the other, by which the begotten is loved by the one who begets him and in turn loves the begetter."[78] The Holy Spirit is "something common to Father and Son, whatever it is, or is their very commonness or communion, consubstantial and coeternal." The best word to describe this commonness or communion is simply love.[79] In the Trinity there is "one loving him who is from him, and one loving him from whom he is, and love itself."[80] It is interesting to note that while the Holy Spirit is this bond of love between the Father and the Son, this bond of love also moves "out" of the Trinity into the world. Augustine can write, "it is the Holy Spirit in the triad, not begotten, but the sweetness of begetter and begotten pervading all creatures according to their capacity with its vast generosity and fruitfulness, that they might all keep their right order and rest in their right places."[81]

We will not work through in detail all the analogies which Augustine deals with in *De Trinitate*, but we will point to certain commonalities related to the Holy Spirit which run through many of these analogies. A few key questions appear to drive Augustine's quest related to the Holy Spirit as he discusses possible analogies of the Trinity. First, if the Holy Spirit proceeds from the Father, as the Son proceeds, why is the Holy Spirit not *also* called the Son? Second, and flowing from the first, if the Holy Spirit proceeds from the Father, as the Son proceeds, what is the *difference*

---

77. Ibid.
78. Ibid., VI.7.
79. Ibid.
80. Ibid.
81. Ibid., VI.11.

between the Son and the Spirit. A partial answer to both these questions is to argue, as we have mentioned above, for the double procession of the Holy Spirit. This provides a distinction between the Father and the Son. But the double procession only goes part way to answering the first question, of why the Spirit should not *also* be called Son. The *role* which the Holy Spirit plays in most of the analogies provides a further answer to this question, as the Spirit's *activity* is different from the Son's.

A third crucial question or issue is the question of how we are to know God. Augustine posits two theses which open up a conundrum for him: (1) we must love God in order to see him; and (2) we must know God in order to love him.[82] To perhaps express the apparent dilemma a little more clearly, let us substitute "know" for "see" in the first sentence (the meaning of which is Augustine's intention). Now the dilemma would be: (1) we must love God in order to know him; and (2) we must know God in order to love him. But how can this be accomplished? We must love in order to know, and we must know in order to love. How do we even get started. In light of this apparent dilemma, Augustine argues that ultimately we already *do* know God, if obliquely. By seeing love we *do* "see" God. Augustine writes, "Oh but you do see a trinity if you see charity."[83] Indeed, argues Augustine, "because God is love the man who loves love certainly loves God; and the man who loves his brother must love."[84]

Having set the stage with the centrality of love, Augustine moves to the *mens* (mind) in order to find the Trinity somehow reflected in the human mind. He can speak of "mind," "the mind's knowledge of itself," and "the mind's love of itself" (*mens, notitia sui, amor sui*).[85] This knowledge of itself is a kind of "word" or "image" "that we beget by uttering inwardly, and that does not depart from us when it is born."[86] This knowledge is joined with the mind by love: "So love, like something in the middle, joins together our word and the mind it is begotten from, and binds itself in with them as a third element in a non-bodily embrace, without any confusion."[87] Here, as so often throughout *De Trinitate*, this third

82. Ibid., VIII.6.
83. Ibid., VIII.12.
84. Ibid.
85. Ibid., IX.2
86. Ibid., IX.12.
87. Ibid., IX.13.

member, the Holy Spirit, is that which joins together the first two members, Father and Son.

But a question arises. If the knowledge can be construed as a word, or image, or begotten, why cannot love *also* be construed as word, image, or begotten? Augustine's answer is not particularly persuasive. Augustine argues that the reason the Holy Spirit is not word, image, nor begotten is that *knowledge* is a sort of "finding out what is said to be brought forth to light." Augustine suggests that there is an inquisitiveness or an "appetite for finding out," and this is roughly compared to the Holy Spirit. This appetite in a sense elicits the knowledge of self. This "appetite" "becomes love of the thing known when it holds and embraces the acceptable offspring, that is knowledge, and joins it to its begetter."[88] Thus, the Holy Spirit is construed (or at least this third member of the trinitarian vestige in the mind is construed) not as an offspring, but as that which brings the mind and offspring (i.e., knowledge) together.

Augustine works with another key analogy: mind, memory and will. Again, the "third member"—the will—is that which brings memory and understanding together.[89] Well into Book XIV Augustine will contend that it is in *this* trinity in the mind that we are to look for the image of God in man.[90] In this analogy, as with all the key analogies for the Trinity in *De Trinitate*, it is imperative to recognize that the analogies are dealing with *acts* and not simply *faculties*. That is, we are dealing with remembering, understanding and willing as *activities* and not simply as *faculties*. Thus, while it is fine to speak of psychological analogies, to speak of psychological *activities* might better preserve Augustine's intention.

The last main or central analogy with which Augustine works is memory of God, understanding of God and love of God.[91] This analogy is in a sense an "advance" upon the previous analogy of mind, memory and will. Whereas the last analogy dealt with the mind remembering itself, understanding itself, and loving *itself*, the focus now shifts outward and upward to God: the mind remembering, knowing and loving *God*. Augustine writes: "This trinity of mind is not really the image of God

---

88. Ibid., IX.18.

89. Ibid., X.17–19. By Book XIV this trinity is modified just a bit and becomes: the mind remembering itself, understanding itself and loving itself (*memoria, intelligentia, voluntas sui*).

90. For example, see ibid., XIV.13.

91. Ibid., XIV.2ff.

because the mind remembers and understands and loves itself, but because it is also able to remember and understand and love him by whom it was made."[92] Augustine's point is that the image of God in man is only fully realized when the minds is engaged in the *activity* of focusing on God, worshipping God, looking to God, etc. (i.e., remembering God, knowing God, loving God). This image of God in man has been tainted but not obliterated by sin, and the transformation of this image into what it should be takes place over a lifetime.[93] For those who turn to the Lord, "the image begins to be reformed by him who formed it in the first place."[94] This image is only perfected when we see God "face to face." Quoting 1 Cor 13:12, "We see now through a puzzling reflection in a mirror, but then it will be face to face," Augustine writes, "For only when it comes to the perfect vision of God will this image bear God's perfect likeness."[95] Indeed, "the image of God will achieve its full likeness of him when it attains to the full vision of him."[96]

Toward the end of *De Trinitate* Augustine is struggling with the ability of the trinitarian image of God in man to point us to the Trinity. There is certainly a pessimistic emphasis at points, Augustine arguing that *any* trinitarian reality reflected in the image of God in the mind is so shadowy and enigmatic as to be of limited value in helping us to understand the actual Trinity.[97] There is such a radical unlikeness between the trinity in the mind and the actual Trinity that Augustine suggests it is extremely difficult to move from the former to the latter.[98] However, the trinity reflected in the image of God in man can still serve the purpose of helping us focus our minds on God. A direct understanding of the Trinity by means of the created order (cf. Rom 1:20) is rejected, and Augustine also argues that an indirect vision of God (i.e., 1 Cor 13:12—"seeing in a glass darkly") is extremely problematic.[99] In treating 1 Cor 13:12, Augustine is again treating the "mirror" or "glass" as the image of God in man—i.e., the mind. However, regarding the image of God in man, it *is* possible to dis-

92. Ibid., XIV.15.
93. Ibid., XIV.22–26.
94. Ibid., XIV.22.
95. Ibid., XIV.23.
96. Ibid., XIV.24.
97. This theme is expounded throughout virtually all of Book XV.
98. Ibid., XV.21ff.
99. Ibid.

cern *some* likeness between the image of God in man and the Triune God. Augustine can write, "those who do see through this mirror and in this puzzle, as much as it is granted to see in this life, are not those who merely observe in their own minds what we have discussed and suggested, but those who see it precisely as an image, so that they can in some fashion refer what they see to that of which it is an image, and also see that other by inference through its image which they see by observation, since the cannot see it face to face."[100]

One of the reasons it is difficult to move from the image of God in man (i.e., the mind) to the Trinity helps us to understand Augustine's doctrine of the Holy Spirit. Augustine contends that even though he has suggested such analogies as memory, understanding and will/love, and that he has correlated these to the different persons of the Trinity—Father to memory, Son to understanding, and Holy Spirit to will/love—he nonetheless argues that all three parts of the analogy truly can be predicated of *each person* of the Trinity. Thus, the Father remembers, understands, loves, the Son remembers, understands, loves, and the Holy Spirit remembers, understands, loves. Thus, when we think about remembering we do not simply see a reflection of the Father, but of the "undifferentiated" Godhead, for Father, Son and Spirit *each* "remember," or can be correlated with remembering. Interestingly, though, Augustine still wants to argue that it is particularly appropriate to call the Holy Spirit "charity." The Father and Son are also loving, but the Holy Spirit has special rights to this title. As Augustine writes: "while in that supremely simple nature substance is not one thing and charity another, but substance is charity and charity is substance, whether in the Father or in the Son or in the Holy Spirit, yet all the same the Holy Spirit is distinctively named charity."[101] And this unique "right" of the Holy Spirit is linked to Augustine's doctrine of the double procession of the Holy Spirit: "Because [the Holy Spirit] is common to them both, he is called distinctively what they are called in common."[102]

In conclusion, the Holy Spirit in Augustine's view is fully divine and fully equal to and consubstantial with the Father and Son. The Holy Spirit proceeds from both the Father and the Son a (although principally from the Father). While all the members of the Trinity are loving, the Holy Spirit

---

100. Ibid., XV.44.
101. Ibid., XV.29.
102. Ibid., XV.37.

has unique right to this title, since he is the love which is common to both Father and Son. The Holy Spirit is the bond between Father and Son, "a kind of inexpressible communion or fellowship of Father and Son."[103]

Redemption

In our earlier treatment of Gunton, we noted that one of Gunton's key themes is that redemption (broadly considered) is really the bringing to completion of the *telos* built into creation. That is, redemption is not simply the rescue of a world gone bad, an "intervention" into a fallen world. Rather, redemption is the *completion* of God's work which began with creation. Interestingly, in Gunton's writing on the work of Christ, he spends little time engaging the thought of Augustine. Gunton's chief concern—that redemption should be seen as the bringing to completion of the *telos* built into creation—is affirmed, and we learn *elsewhere* in Gunton's writing that the West's failure to so construe redemption is to be traced to Augustine. But in Gunton's specific treatment of the atonement there is no effort to link Augustine to a failure to construe redemption in the way Gunton favors. With Gunton's criticism before us, let us turn to Augustine.

As we look at *De Trinitate* we will look both at the nature of the work of Christ and how it functions in *De Trinitate*. That is, we will ask how Augustine's construes the atonement in this work, and we will also ask how Augustine's doctrine of the atonement functions within the work *De Trinitate* itself. We first look at the key components of Augustine's doctrine of the work of Christ, followed by a discussion of possible functions of that doctrine as part of the whole volume.

Augustine's Doctrine of the Work of Christ

Trinitarian Concerns

Perhaps the first thing that must be said about the work of Christ in Augustine's thought, particularly as seen in De Trinitate, is the fact that the work of Christ is part of the trinitarian life of God. That is, Christ, in dying for sinners, reveals something about the Triune God. The whole Trinity is involved in redemption, although of course it is only the Son who actually bleeds and dies on the cross. Augustine writes: "Thus the

103. Ibid., V.12.

Father and the Son and the Spirit of them both work all things together and equally and in concord. Yet the fact remains that we have been justified in the blood of Christ and reconciled to God through the death of his Son, and how that was done I shall explain here too as best I can and as fully as seems necessary."[104] That is, it is God as a Trinity who redeems sinners, although we cannot help but recognize that there is some differentiation of the particular acts that bring this about.

Redemption, Missions, and Processions

But perhaps most important for our concerns is the larger question of the relation between what God does in history, or time, and who God is in eternity. That is, what kind of connection can we make between God as he acts in creation and redemption (the "economic" Trinity), and God as he is in Himself in eternity (the "immanent" or "transcendent" Trinity)? Augustine holds that what God does in time reveals who God is in eternity. To this extent, he is in complete agreement with Rahner's contention that the "economic Trinity is the immanent Trinity." Augustine lays out his position in his discussion of missions and processions. The "missions" or "sendings" are temporal and reveal the "processions" which are eternal. That is, what God does in time reveals who God truly is in eternity. Thus, what God does in history and in time genuinely and faithfully reflect the triune being of God. Edmund Hill has written, "The sendings of the Son and the Holy Spirit reveal their eternal processions from the Father (and the Holy Spirit's procession from the Son as well), and thus reveal the inner trinitarian mystery of God."[105] Augustine explicitly makes this point toward the end of Book IV. The key biblical text is Gal 4:4: "When therefore the fullness of time had come, God sent his Son made of woman, made under the law." Thus, the Son is sent at a certain point in history, but what of the Son's relation to the Father before the sending? This relation is one of "proceeding."[106] Augustine can write, "And just as being born means

---

104. *De Trinitate* XIII.15.

105. Hill, *Mystery of the Trinity*, 89.

106. A note of clarification. In *De Trinitate* the word "procession" can be used in two main ways. (1) In the most general sense, "procession" denotes the eternal procession of the Son from the Father, and the Holy Spirit from the Father and Son. (2) In the more particular sense, "procession" denotes the relation of the Spirit to Father and Son, while "generation" is the term which denotes the relation of the Son to the Father. When I speak of eternal *processions* and temporal *missions* I (with Augustine) am using the first, general sense above.

for the Son his being from the Father, so his being sent means his being known to be from him. And just as for the Holy Spirit his being the gift of God means proceeding from the Father, so his being sent means his being known to proceed from him."[107] That is, both Son and Spirit proceed from the Father eternally but are sent in time. This principle is crucial for understanding Augustine's doctrine of the work of Christ. Because, if what God does in time reveals who God is in eternity, then the cross of Christ (or the "economy") is not really divorced from who God is in his being. Rather, the sending of Christ (the mission of Christ) reveals the proceeding of the Son from eternity (the procession of Christ). Hill makes this point nicely, "And so this mystery of God's being is organically linked to the economy of salvation, above all to the mystery of the incarnation and of the saving death and resurrection of Jesus Christ. As St Paul's text, just quoted [i.e., Gal 4:4], shows us, to be saved is to enter in some way into the divine relationships of the three persons."[108]

Christ came to earth to elicit faith. He came from eternity and returns to eternity, and his purpose in coming is to elicit faith: "Everything that has taken place in time in 'originated' matters which have been produced from the eternal and reduced back to the eternal, and has been designed to elicit the faith we must be purified by in order to contemplate the truth, has either been testimony to this mission or has been the actual mission of the Son of God."[109] Why was the Son sent? The purpose of sending the Son was "that the Word might become flesh, that is, become man."[110]

Like the Son, the Holy Spirit is also sent in time, and this mission of the Spirit in *time* reveals the procession of the Spirit from Father and Son in *eternity*.[111] Augustine is clear that the fact that the Son and the Spirit are sent does not imply that they are unequal to the Father. Speaking of the Son as one who flows from the Father, Augustine writes, "But in this case what flows out and what it flows out from are of one and the same substance."[112] He was sent because he was the *Son* not because he was *less* than the Father: "For he was not sent in virtue of some disparity of power

---

107. *De Trinitate* IV.29. Cf. IV.28, where Augustine writes, "But that he is sent means that he is known by somebody in time."
108. Hill, *Mystery of the Trinity*, 90.
109. *De Trinitate* IV.25.
110. Ibid., IV.27.
111. Ibid., IV.29.
112. Ibid., IV.27.

or substance or anything in him that was not equal to the Father, but in virtue of the Son being from the Father, not the Father being from the Son."[113] Likewise, the Holy Spirit is consubstantial with the Father and the Son.[114]

Thus, in *De Trinitate* Augustine's construal of the missions and processions help us to see that for him the cross of Christ, indeed the whole reality of the "missions" of the Son and Spirit are ultimately reflective of the life of the eternal Triune God. The temporal *missions* reveal the eternal *processions*. Indeed, it is in this principle that the West will claim a key argument for the *filioque* clause. For, since the Son claimed that he would send the Spirit (John 15:26), and what God does in *time* reveals who God is in *eternity*, then the Spirit must *eternally* be "sent," or more precisely "proceed." What is crucial here, though, is the simple recognition that Augustine wishes to confirm that God's actions in history are part of an "organic whole" with who God is in eternity. We now turn to the initial sending of the Son, the incarnation.

Sin and Incarnation

For Augustine the *purpose* of the incarnation is redemption. He can write that the incarnation took place "for the sake of restoring us to health."[115] The need for redemption, and hence the incarnation, is sin. While our goal is to "participate in the Word," we cannot because we are "absolutely incapable of such participation and quite unfit for it, so unclean were we through sin, so we had to be cleansed."[116] On the radical nature of human sin Augustine writes, "Each thing of ours, that is, both soul and body, was in need of healing and resurrection, in order to renew for the better what had changed for the worse."[117] And it is only Christ who can heal this sin: "the only thing to cleanse the wicked and the proud is the blood of the just man and the humility of God; to contemplate God, which by nature we are not, we would have to be cleansed by him who became what by nature we are and what by sin we are not. By nature we are not God; by

---

113. Ibid.
114. Ibid., IV.30.
115. Ibid., I.14.
116. Ibid., IV.4.
117. Ibid., IV.5.

nature we are men; by sin we are not just."[118] Thus, against this backdrop of human sin and need, Augustine discusses the reality of the incarnation and atonement.

It was necessary that Christ assume our humanity. Augustine writes that we could not "pass from being among the things that originated to eternal things, unless the eternal allied himself to us in our originated condition, and so provided us with a bridge to his eternity."[119] Augustine has an eloquent way of stating the reality and necessity of the incarnation: "The sinner did not match the just, but *the man did match man*. So he applied to us the similarity of his humanity to take away the dissimilarity of our iniquity, and becoming a partaker of our mortality he made us partakers of his divinity."[120] Thus, Christ truly assumed our human nature, since this was the way to lead us to God.

CENTRALITY OF DEATH AND RESURRECTION

In outlining Augustine's "theory" of the atonement it becomes clear that Augustine's doctrine of the atonement does not fit nicely under one or more of the rubrics of historical and systematic theology. Rather, his doctrine of Christ's death and resurrection is constituted by a number of interlocking themes and concerns, including such broad themes as victory, substitution, satisfaction and ransom. It has even been suggested that it is wrong to trace the "satisfaction" model to Anselm, since this theme is clearly in Augustine.[121] What is at the heart of the death of Christ in *De Trinitate*? Augustine contends that the death and resurrection of Christ are central. Christ's death and resurrection indeed both serve as a sacrament and model for us. That is, Christ's death and resurrection is a *model*

---

118. Ibid., IV.4.
119. Ibid., IV.24.
120. Ibid., IV.4 (emphasis mine).
121. For example, see Portalie, *Guide to the Thought of Saint Augustine*, 165. Portalie contends that while it has long been fashionable "to maintain the Anselmian theory of satisfaction was inspired by the principles of German law," the "best Protestant critics, the ones furthest removed from dogmatic presuppositions, have shown all the incongruous elements in an assertion which adduces the German custom of *wergild* as the origin for a belief long before studied by St. Augustine and even formulated earlier by such Fathers as Tertullian and Cyprian." Portalie's volume is a helpful summary of Augustine's doctrine of the work of Christ. Portalie basically summarizes the work of Christ under four key themes: (1) mediator, (2) sacrifice, (3) deliverance from Satan, and (4) moral influence of Jesus.

for the "outer" man and a *sacrament* for the "inner" man. Specifically, Christ's *death* is both (1) the *model* of the death of our "outer" man (i.e., our physical self) and (2) the *sacrament* of the death of our "inner" man (i.e., our spiritual/inner man). On the other hand, Christ's *resurrection* is both (1) the *model* of the resurrection of our "outer" man and (2) the *sacrament* of the resurrection of our "inner" man.[122] It appears that the point Augustine is wanting to make by his use of the terms "model" and "sacrament" is that Christ's death and resurrection are efficacious both in terms of our physical and spiritual existence and needs, as well as our temporal and eternal needs. There are "two deaths" (physical and spiritual), and in the death and resurrection of Christ a solution is found by which both of these deaths might be conquered. The *physical* man really does die (Christ's death is a model for the death of the outer man), but in Christ the physical man is truly resurrected (Christ's resurrection is a model for resurrection of the outer man). Also, the believer has spiritually died to death and sin (Christ's death is a sacrament of the death of the inner man), and in Christ is being renewed in the inner man (Christ's resurrection is a sacrament of the renewing of the inner man).

Christ as Mediator

Christ is the mediator between God and men. The devil is the false mediator while Christ is the true mediator. Augustine writes: "The devil grew high and mighty, he fell, and pulled down man who consented to him; the Christ came humble and lowly, he rose, and raised up man who believed in him."[123] A key weakness in the devil's scheme, as Augustine sees it, is the devil's "determined preference for power over justice." Augustine, on the other hand, will prefer justice over power, and this preference for justice is meted out in terms of his view of the atonement. That is, the reality that justice must be met is central to the atonement in Augustine's view.[124]

In the early sections of Book IV one is struck by how Augustine speaks at length on the devil and on justice. Whereas the traditional "theories" of the atonement are often presented as distinct and perhaps

---

122. *De Trinitate*, IV.6.
123. Ibid., IV.13.
124. If I am right here, then Portalie's suggestion above that it is an error simply to trace the "satisfaction" theory of the atonement to Anselm and his legal background would receive some justification.

contradictory options, Augustine intertwines his discussion of the devil and the question of justice. The devil is the false mediator who deceives sinners. Indeed, he deceived Adam in the beginning.[125] While God was not the cause of sin, he did "impose a wholly just death on the sinner as retribution."[126] Indeed, "We came to death by sin, he [Christ] came by justice; and so while our death is the punishment of sin, his death became a sacrifice for sin."[127] Christ's death was a payment offered for "our sakes." Christ "wished" to die, in that nothing external to himself forced him.[128] Although Augustine does speak of payment, and he speaks of the devil being destroyed by the cross, he rarely speaks of anything like payment *to* the devil. For example, "By his death he offered for us the one truest possible sacrifice, and thereby purged, abolished, and destroyed whatever there was of guilt, for which the principalities and powers had a right to hold us bound to payment of the penalty."[129] Here the principalities had a "right" of "payment" over us. Augustine can also say that the devil had "full property rights over" sinners.[130] How then does the cross of Christ deal with this dilemma? For Augustine it is in terms of justice. Augustine writes, "Yet in being slain in his innocence by the wicked one, who was acting against as it were with just rights [note a possible hesitation here—"*as it were* with just rights"], he won the case against him with the justest of all rights, and thus *led captive the captivity* (Eph 4:8; Ps 68:19) that was instituted for sin, and delivered us from the captivity we justly endured for sin, and by his just blood unjustly shed *cancelled the I.O.U.* (Col 2:14) of death, and justified and redeemed sinners."[131] Here Christ does not pay anything *to* the devil, but rather "won the case" against the evil one, since Christ was unjustly slain by the devil. It appears that Augustine's logic is that in killing Jesus the devil had perpetrated an injustice, and in this act forfeited any possible just reign he had over sinners.

The sacrifice of Christ truly reconciles us to God.[132] We also see a hint of the doctrine of union with Christ. Augustine can argue that Christ

125. *De Trinitate* IV.14.
126. Ibid.
127. Ibid., IV.15.
128. Ibid., IV.17.
129. Ibid.
130. Ibid.
131. Ibid., IV.18.
132. Ibid., IV.19.

is one with God, and those who are in Christ are also in the presence of God: "And this one true mediator, in reconciling us to God by his sacrifice of peace, would remain one with him to whom he offered it, and make one in himself those for whom he offered it, and be himself who offered it one and the same as what he offered."[133]

The Enemies of the Work of Christ

Augustine works out his view of the mission of Christ against the backdrop of those who despise or mock the cross. These opponents are certain philosophers, in particular the platonists. He speaks of "some people who think they can purify themselves for contemplating God and cleaving to him by their own power and strength of character."[134] Augustine suggests that some persons *have* been able to "direct the keen gaze of their intellects" in such a way as to achieve at least a small glimpse of "the light of unchanging truth," but that many find they cannot achieve such a task. What of it? Should the Christian place himself on the side of the few who can achieve such a daunting task? Not at all. Augustine writes, "But what good does it do a man who is so proud that he is ashamed to climb aboard the wood, what good does it do him to gaze afar on the home country across the sea?" He continues, "And what harm does it do a humble man if he cannot see it from such a distance, but is coming to it nonetheless on the wood the other disdains to be carried by?"[135] In short, there is no shame in admitting one's weaknesses and embracing the cross. Indeed, why "gaze from afar" when the "wood" (the cross) is the only way by which one can reach the "home country?" Augustine's analogy is worth pondering. Even the man of keen mind does not really "make it" to the homeland. Even he can only see the homeland from "afar." That is, the option is not between (1) having a keen mind which allows one to be in the presence of the One, or God and (2) not having a keen mind and thus needing the cross. Rather, the *only* way to reach the homeland is through the cross, and the keenest of minds will at most gaze from afar on the homeland of the presence of God.

Augustine is clear that while the vision of God is our goal, our current state impedes such a goal. He writes, "To sum up them: we were incapable

133. Ibid.
134. Ibid., IV.20.
135. Ibid.

of grasping eternal things, and weighed down by the accumulated dirt of our sins, which we had collected by our love of temporal things, and which had become almost a natural growth on our mortal stock; so we needed purifying."[136] While the love of "temporal things" keeps us from grasping eternal things, it is *only* through "temporal things" that we can be led to eternal things. That is, it is the central "temporal thing" of the work of Christ which leads us to eternal things. Only through Christ can we be purified, and be led to eternal things. Augustine writes that it would not be appropriate to "pass from being among the things that originated to eternal things, unless the eternal allied himself to us in our originated condition, and so provided us with a bridge to his eternity."[137] Thus, the Word becomes flesh for our salvation, and through this fleshly Word we are led to see the eternal Word: "But there he was, manifest before their eyes; surely then it can only mean that he was offering the flesh which the Word had been made in the fullness of time as the object to receive our faith; but that the Word itself, *through whom all things had been made* (Jn. 1:3), was being kept for the contemplation in eternity of minds now purified through faith."[138]

But what role does faith play? Faith must look to Christ, a "temporal thing" in order to be led to eternal things. As Augustine writes, "So now we accord faith to the things done in time for our sakes, and are purified by it; in order that when we come to sight and truth succeeds to faith, eternity might likewise succeed to mortality."[139] That is, there is a *telos* to faith. Faith looks to what Christ has done, a "temporal thing," which leads in the end to "truth," which is ultimately an eternal thing. In the end faith *becomes* truth, when we no longer have to trust things done in the past (i.e., the cross), but we rather see God: "therefore when our faith becomes truth by seeing, our mortality will be transformed into a fixed and firm eternity."[140] Ultimately, our faith "follows" Jesus to his ascended position in heaven. And just as Jesus has ascended, so will those who trust Christ. As Augustine writes, "our faith has now in some sense followed him in whom we have believed to where he has ascended," and since Jesus has

---

136. Ibid., IV.24.
137. Ibid.
138. Ibid., IV.26.
139. Ibid., IV.24.
140. Ibid.

been "raised to life" and "taken up," "we can justly hope that they are going to happen to us."[141]

Central Images of Redemption

Augustine emphasizes faith as central to redemption. While each believer has "faith," there is in a sense a common faith which has been impressed upon believers from "one single teaching."[142] Augustine suggests that as there is a type of common faith, there is also a common will. While only believers have faith, all persons share a common will, the desire to be happy: "all men have one common will to obtain and retain happiness."[143] The one who is happy "has everything he wants, and wants nothing wrongly."[144] Augustine states it similarly when he writes that only that man is truly happy who (1) "has the good things he wants," and (2) "does not want any bad things."[145]

Ultimately, true happiness requires immortality, and immortality requires faith. Hence, we see that faith is indispensable to a happy life.[146] Augustine writes, "They cannot be happy unless they are alive; therefore they do not want their being alive to cease."[147] Our faith must be placed in Christ, for it is through being in Christ that we participate in immortality: "for it is in him alone and thanks to him alone that they can be happy, by sharing in his immortality."[148]

We noted earlier that Augustine can affirm a number of different metaphors of the atonement. As Augustine examines the incarnation and death of Jesus in Book XIII, he affirms that Christ's death was truly a demonstration of God's love for us.[149] However, it is the question of justice which appears most important for Augustine. After raising a possible theological conundrum by pointing to texts that appear simultaneously to point to (1) the Father's *anger* towards us and the Son's sacrifice (Rom

---

141. Ibid.
142. Ibid., XIII.5.
143. Ibid., XIII.7.
144. Ibid., XIII.8.
145. Ibid., XIII.9.
146. Ibid., XIII.10.
147. Ibid., XIII.11.
148. Ibid., XIII.12.
149. Ibid., XIII.13.

5:8, 10) and (2) the Father's being *for* us (Rom 8:13), Augustine works through his view of justice and the atonement.

As descendants of the "first parents" we are all handed over to the Devil by "a kind of divine justice."[150] All persons following Adam and Eve are "bent by sin, not as created straight in the beginning."[151] Thus, persons find themselves, by God's permission, subjected to the devil.[152] At this point we must stress again Augustine's point that in God's dealings *justice* precedes *power*. This principle will be worked out in a different sphere in *De civitate Dei*, where in the city of man justice must precede power as well. And here in *De Trinitate* Augustine contends that the devil's error was in loving power more than justice: "The essential flaw of the devil's perversion made him a lover of power and a deserter and assailant of justice, which means that men imitate him all the more thoroughly the more they neglect or even detest justice and studiously devote themselves to power, rejoicing at the possession of it or inflamed with the desire for it."[153] Thus, God defeats the devil in terms of *justice*. As Augustine writes, "So it pleased God to deliver man from the devil's authority by beating him at the justice game, not the power game, so that men too might imitate Christ by seeking to beat the devil at the justice game, not the power game."[154] But how is this so? We noted earlier that while Augustine says clearly that Christ paid our debts, the idea of payment *to* the devil is not prominent. Rather, payment appears to fit under the rubric of justice. Augustine asks, "What then is the justice that overpowered the devil?" His answer: "The justice of Jesus Christ—what else?"[155] It is hard to avoid the impression that Augustine is affirming something like penal substitution, even if he does not use that exact terminology. For how does this "justice of Jesus Christ" work? He notes that the devil "found nothing in him deserving of death and yet he killed him." Thus, it "is therefore perfectly just that he should let the debtors he held go free, who believe in the on whom he killed without his being in his debt."[156] Likewise, he paid "for us

---

150. Ibid., XIII.16.
151. Ibid.
152. Ibid.
153. Ibid., XIII.17.
154. Ibid.
155. Ibid., XIII.18.
156. Ibid.

debtors the debt he did not owe himself."[157] While justice precedes power, Augustine contends that power is present as well. Thus, *justice* is brought about by Christ's *death*, while *power* is brought about by Christ's *resurrection*.[158] As Augustine writes, "So he overcame the devil with justice first and power second, with justice because *he had no sin* (2 Cor 5:21; 1 Peter 2:22) and was most unjustly killed by him; with power because dead he came back to life never to die thereafter."[159]

Augustine summarizes how Christ's blood defeated the devil in terms of justice as follows: "That is when this blood of his, of one who had no sin at all, was shed for the remission of our sins, and the devil, who once held us deservedly under the sentence of death as we were guilty of sin, was deservedly obliged to give us up through him he had most undeservedly condemned to death, though guilty of no sin."[160]

There appears to be only one place in *De Trinitate* where Augustine speaks of Christ's blood being a price paid *to* the devil. He writes that in "this act of redemption the blood of Christ was given for us as a kind of price, and when the devil took it he was not enriched by it but caught and bound by it, so that we might be disentangled from his toils."[161]

In justly defeating the devil we are now reconciled to God through Christ's death. While we were God's enemies, only "in the sense that sins are the enemies of justice," now we are reconciled, for when sins "are forgiven such hostilities come to an end, and those whom he himself justifies are reconciled to the just one."[162]

Augustine can freely speak of Christ paying our debts. Christ is the second Adam" who is not only man but also God, and who pays for us a debt he did not owe, with the result that we have been set free from debts, both ancestral ones and our own personal ones, which we do owe."[163]

Although "example" or "demonstration" are not the key components of Augustine's doctrine of the work of Christ, Augustine does see the incarnation as serving as a type of example or demonstration. First, the fact

---

157. Ibid.
158. Ibid.
159. Ibid.
160. Ibid., XIII.19.
161. Ibid.
162. Ibid., XIII.21.
163. Ibid.

that Christ took on *human* nature demonstrates that false mediators (i.e., demons) need have no pride in the fact that they claim to mediate God and man while being without flesh.[164] Second, the incarnation should be a model of humility in the sense that the Word became flesh, and that the human nature was joined to deity not by any merits of the human nature, since from the very beginning the human nature was *already* filled with deity.[165] Third, and similar to what has just been mentioned, the incarnation is a example of humility, since it was God Himself who humbled Himself and took on human nature, and the incarnation reminds man of the depths of his sin, when he contemplates how far the Son has come for us.[166] Fourth, the incarnation is also an example of obedience, when we consider that Christ's obedience was obedience to death, "even death on a cross."[167] Fifth, we see a demonstration of God's justice and goodness when we see that the devil "should be outdone by the same rational creature as he congratulated himself on outdoing, and outdone by one man issuing from that race, which he had held the whole of in his power because its origin had been vitiated by one man."[168]

Augustine is clear that for this justice to be brought about, it required a sinless sacrifice, born of a virgin.[169] God hypothetically *could* have accomplished redemption in some different way (i.e., without the incarnation), but "God judged it better" to redeem by means of the incarnation.[170] The virginal conception teaches us that there was "no desire of flesh involved," "so that what was there born of the stock of the first man would only derive from him a racial not a criminal origin."[171] It is this incarnate savior, the "second Adam" who conquers the "first Adam": "Here we have

164. Ibid., XIII.22.

165. I believe Augustine's point is one that is tied up with the doctrine of *anhypostasia*, the doctrine that the human nature of Christ did not really have any true personal identity *until* the hypostatic union, i.e., until the human and divine natures were joined. Thus, Augustine's argument is that even with the incarnate Christ, the human nature did not have the "opportunity" to achieve any merit, for the human nature of Christ had *always* been joined to deity—a joining which by its very reality excludes the need of merit (Christ was God).

166. *De Trinitate* XIII.22.

167. Ibid.

168. Ibid., XIII.22.

169. Ibid., XIII.23.

170. Ibid.

171. Ibid.

the conqueror of the first Adam, holding the human race in his power, conquered by the second Adam and losing the Christian race, a part of the human race set free from human crime by one who was not involved in the crime though sprung from the race; thus that deceiver could be conquered by the race which he had conquered by his crime."[172] Thus, the second Adam, being human but without sin, is able to conquer the devil, who is now conquered by one who is truly part of the race which the devil originally conquered.

Redemption, Wisdom, and Knowledge

Augustine closes Book XIII by relating redemption to "wisdom" and "knowledge." As we have mentioned, in Augustine's view "wisdom" is higher than "knowledge." As Augustine sees it, it is appropriate to refer *truth* to *wisdom* and to refer *grace* to *knowledge*.[173] That is, *grace* is the means by which we obtain the *truth*, and since grace leads to truth, Augustine can construe "truth" (and its concomitant, "wisdom") as "higher" than "grace" (and its concomitant, "knowledge"). Augustine construes Christ as the locus of both "wisdom" and "knowledge" in the following way: "Our knowledge therefore is of Christ, and our wisdom is the same Christ. It is he who plants faith in us about temporal things, he who presents us with the truth about eternal things. Through him we go straight toward him, through knowledge toward wisdom, without ever turning aside from one and the same Christ."[174] Thus, the Christian moves through "knowledge" before moving higher to "wisdom."

This move from "knowledge" to "wisdom" helps constitute what it means to live a redeemed life. What is important for our concerns is that this redeemed life in no way is possible without the death of Christ. This redeemed life, which is rooted in the cross, also brings about the restoration of the image of God in man, and this whole question brings us back to the issue of the Trinity. For Augustine, the restoration of the image of God in man is not simply a loosely-defined side-effect of the sanctifying work of the Spirit in the believer's life. Rather, the image of God in man is a *trinitarian* image, and this image is only complete when it is truly

---

172. Ibid.
173. Ibid., XIII.24.
174. Ibid.

focused on God. And the only path to the restoration of the trinitarian image, and hence, the vision of God, is through the death of Christ.

Purpose, Rhetoric, and Polemic in *De Trinitate*

It is appropriate to pause at this point and ask a fundamental question of how the work of Christ functions in *De Trinitate*. We need to ask how our discussion of the work of Christ might relate to Augustine's larger purpose(s) in writing *De Trinitate*. That is, was Augustine doing more than simply laying out his doctrine of the work of Christ, as well as of other doctrines? Was Augustine hoping to accomplish something by his exposition besides simply a presentation of Christian doctrine?

Much has been written about the purpose of *De Trinitate*, and about Augustine's intent in writing the volume. First, it is asked whether *De Trinitate* is philosophy or theology. While some have argued that *De Trinitate* is largely philosophy, and some theology, it is probably wiser to say, with R. D. Crouse, that in Augustine's world such a dichotomy simply did not exist. Indeed, such a dichotomy is more a modern than an ancient phenomenon. As Crouse has noted, "The distinction according to which theology has to do with revelation, while philosophy has to do with human reflection, is after all a relatively modern one, and certainly quite foreign to the thought of St. Augustine."[175] Indeed, it is best to simply set aside the distinction between philosophy and theology when one approaches *De Trinitate*. Again Crouse notes, "Whatever one might think in general about the usefulness of these modern categories and distinctions, at least the direct application of them in the interpretation of the *De Trinitate* must be a highly suspect procedure."[176] Ultimately Augustine's way of doing things is thoroughly unmodern, in that for Augustine philosophical thought, when done properly, should find its natural end in things divine. As Crouse notes, "the question as to whether *De trinitate* is philosophical or theological can easily be answered by saying that it is philosophical in the highest sense; that is to say, it is theological, seeking an ascent from the level of belief to a rational and intellectual understanding of the Divine Nature."[177] For our purposes, we will be content to affirm that for Augustine there is no radical dichotomy between philosophy and theol-

---

175. Crouse, "St. Augustine's *De Trinitate*: Philosophical Method," 502.
176. Ibid.
177. Ibid., 503.

ogy, and that in the thought of Augustine we find a rigorous mind being applied to the central question of the doctrine of God.

A key issue in interpreting *De Trinitate* is the question of Augustine's rhetorical and polemical intentions. Rhetoric and polemic are particularly important for our interests, for it may be that in ferreting out Augustine's intentions in *De Trinitate* we will be better able to see if Gunton's criticism of Augustine can withstand scrutiny. That is, by determining Augustine's rhetorical and polemical intentions we are better able to understand the work itself, and better able to deal with Gunton's charges.

In *De Trinitate* is Augustine engaged in irenics or polemics? In a helpful summary of the many criticisms that have been leveled against Augustine, George Lawless suggests that *De Trinitate* is ultimately an irenical work: "*The Trinity*, as a matter of fact, is an essentially irenic and exploratory work."[178] Roland Kany, on the other hand, considers *De Trinitate* to be thoroughly polemical: "one vast polemic against all theologies which do not proceed from Christian faith at the very beginning."[179]

If Augustine is engaged in polemics, who are his enemies? Kany's above definition is attractive: Augustine is combating all those who deviate from the historic Christian faith. Certainly Augustine is eager to defend the deity of the Son, and this is quite appropriate in a work devoted to expounding the Trinity. The Church had experienced the Council at Nicaea several generations prior to *De Trinitate*, and it is certainly the case that the issue of Son and the Spirit, and their relation to the Father, was by no means a settled issue. As Augustine fervently sets out to prove the deity of the Son, it seems clear that at least *one* set of opponents are those who deny the deity of the Son. These most likely would be Arians or at least those who would generally affirm some form of *homoian* theology.[180] Michel René Barnes has argued that "Latin Homoianism" was Augustine's polemical target in *De Trinitate* and that indeed *De Trinitate* provided an opportunity for Augustine to hone his own appropriation of Nicene theology. Barnes writes, "Like his polemical predecessors [i.e., Hilary, Victorinus, and Ambrose], Augustine found that the refutation of Latin Homoianism provided the perfect opportunity to develop his

---

178. Lawless, "Augustine of Hippo and His Critics," 7.
179. Kany, "'Fidei Contemnentes Initium,'" 327.
180. See Barnes, "Arians of Book V," 185-95; idem, "Exegesis and Polemic," 43-59.

own account of the Nicene faith."[181] Over against those who argue that *De Trinitate* is free from polemics, which is argued by H. Paissac, A. Malet and M. J. Le Guillou, Barnes contends that Augustine follows his Western predecessors such as Hilary, Victorinus and Ambrose in eloquently arguing for the deity of Christ against the "Arian" Latin Homoians.[182] Barnes concludes, "Not only is *de Trinitate* a polemical work, but many of its central themes—regularly described by some scholars as non-polemical 'speculation'—are in fact shaped within and by that polemical engagement."[183] Indeed, the person of the Son is crucial to the ultimate goal of *De Trinitate*, which is concomitant with the goal of the Christian life—the vision of God. Augustine's goal in *De Trinitate* is to explore how we come to see God. Ultimately, we only see God because the Son leads, or brings us, to such a state. The Son's "mission" is to become incarnate for us, to unite us to him, and ultimately to lead us to the vision of God. He thus must be truly human (or else he was never truly incarnate), as well as truly divine (for the Son Himself leads us into the presence of God). As Barnes notes, "The Homoians claim 'If material, then not divine,' while Augustine wants to assert 'Material, in order to bring us to the divine.'"[184] Thus, Augustine's arguments for the deity of the Son are intrinsically and organically related to his overall quest to explore and expound how we see God and what it means to see God.

John Cavadini also argues for the polemical nature of *De Trinitate*, contending that in holding forth the centrality of the work of Christ, Augustine is making a not-so-subtle move against neoplatonism.[185] Similarly Earl C. Muller points to the centrality of the cross in *De Trinitate* as revealing Augustine's polemical and rhetorical intent. While Augustine opens *De Trinitate* by pointing to the necessity the "starting-point of faith," and throughout the volume is pointing the reader to the contemplation

---

181. Barnes, "Arians of Book V," 195. Barnes is arguing against the weight of much Augustine scholarship, which often sees Augustine's christological opponents in the Eunomians. As such Barnes is arguing against the following scholars: Schmaus, *Die Psychologische Trinitätslehre*, 143; Schwindler, *Wort und Analogie in Augustine Trinitätslehre*, 151–53; du Roy, *L'Intellegence de la Foi en la Trinité Selon Saint Augustin*, 458.

182. Barnes, "Arians of Book V," 193–95.

183. Barnes, "Exegesis and Polemic," 58.

184. Ibid.

185. Cavadini, "Structure and Intent of Augustine's *De Trinitate*," 103–23.

of God, Muller argues that such contemplation is not even *possible* apart from the death of Christ, which is the key redemptive work which leads to the purification of the mind.[186]

The issue of rhetorical or polemical intent is particularly important when we come to the work of Christ, for if the work of Christ as it is portrayed in *De Trinitate* serves in some way as a means to an end—i.e., as a means to defeat opposition, then Augustine is putting a high premium on the death of Christ. And *this* fact is important, for in the death of Christ we come up against that aspect of Christianity which is particularly *not* dualistic or "neoplatonic," for in the death of Christ we are dealing not with an esoteric realm to be reached by the vigilant soul, but with the body and blood of this material realm. Ultimately, then, if Augustine's goal in *De Trinitate* is to chart a way to the vision of God, and if this way is *only* found through a crucified, earthly, physical man, might this not serve as an anti-neoplatonic polemic?

This is the general argument of Cavadini, who contends that in *De Trinitate* Augustine pushes the neoplatonic contemplative quest outside the usual 'noetic' realm into the area of the physical—the body of and blood of Christ on the cross. He writes, "the *De trinitate* uses the Neoplatonic soteriology of ascent only to impress it into the service of a thoroughgoing critique of its claim to raise the inductee to the contemplation of God, a critique which, more generally, becomes a declaration of the futility of any attempt to come to any saving knowledge of God apart from Christ."[187] While Cavadini does not stress here as much the *death* of Christ, as we are suggesting might be central, his insight is similar to ours, in that the goal of seeing God is never found outside of Christ.

E. C. Muller makes a similar point when he stresses the centrality of the death of Christ as necessary to the vision of God. Muller writes, "This then is the key theological point which governs the rhetorical structure of the *De Trinitate*: *there can be no intellectus* [understanding] *apart from the concrete sacrificial act of Christ*."[188] This *is* the issue I wish to raise: the centrality of the death of Christ in the structure and intent of *De Trinitate*. Hence, as Augustine is laboring to lead the reader to a vision of God, he suddenly, in book XIII launches into a discussion of the death of Christ.

186. Muller, "Rhetorical and Theological Issues," 356–63.
187. Cavadini, "Structure and Intention," 106.
188. Muller, "Rhetorical and Theological Issues," 359.

But why? If Augustine is trying to lead the reader up to a vision of the Triune God, why revert to the more material and earthly reality of the death of Christ? Most likely, Augustine is trying to show that in order to be in the presence of God—in order to see God—one must go through the cross. As Muller argues, the reason Augustine seemingly "reverts" to a discussion of the death of Christ is because "*he refuses to deal with anything above the human mind without first purifying his mind in the sacrifice of Christ, the only way for sinful humans to obtain the eternal.*"[189] Muller goes as far as to argue that the death of Christ is virtually *the* key issue in the work, for what Augustine intended *De Trinitate* to be was "*an act of worship grounded in the one sacrifice of Christ.*"[190]

Edmund Hill offers a similar suggestion when he states that Augustine was explicitly criticizing neoplatonists Plotinus and Porphyry. Hill writes that while the neoplatonists believed that one could achieve purification by their "unaided powers," Augustine "argues for the necessity of purification by faith, faith precisely in the temporal and physical reality of the incarnation and in the death and resurrection of Christ."[191]

Edward Booth sees both anti-Arian and anti-neoplatonic polemic in *De Trinitate*.[192] Augustine's arguments for three hypostases, yet one *ousia* were directed against both Arian subordinationism and the neoplatonist conception of triad, a conception which was the philosophical backdrop for Arianism.[193] But what of neoplatonist terminology found in *De Trinitate*? Booth suggests, "Even the place of scriptural quotations can be read as having in mind Porphyry, who had claimed that the Christian scriptures were a mass of contradictions: from them was deduced a philosophical system which showed up the inadequacies of neoplatonism, even while it used its ideas."[194] Why have many not seen or affirmed an anti-neoplatonic polemic in *De Trinitate*? Booth contends, "The anti-neo-Platonist apologetic of the *De Trinitate*, with its persuasively established relationships within the tradition of philosophical eclecticism, was so stylistically like the rest of his writings that generations of readers have

---

189. Ibid., 362.
190. Ibid., 363.
191. Hill, "Introductory Essay on Book IV," 150.
192. Booth, "St. Augustine's *notitia sui*," (1977): 70–132, 364–401; 28 (1978): 183–221, 29 (1979): 97–124.
193. Booth, "St. Augustine's *Notitia Sui*," 27 (1977): 103.
194. Ibid., 103–4.

overlooked not only the difference in its contents and orientation but also the immediate significance of the distinction he frequently made in the work between faith and knowledge, and his implication that parts, at least, were written for non-believers."[195]

Augustine is clear that while the vision of God is our goal, our current state impedes such a goal. He writes, "To sum up then: we were incapable of grasping eternal things, and weighed down by the accumulated dirt of our sins, which we had collected by our love of temporal things, and which had become almost a natural growth on our mortal stock; so we needed purifying."[196] And the means of this purification is the person and work of Christ. Augustine writes that it would not be appropriate to "pass from being among the things that originated to eternal things, unless the eternal allied himself to us in our originated condition, and so provided us with a bridge to his eternity."[197] Thus, the Word becomes flesh for our salvation, and through this fleshly Word we are led to see the eternal Word: "But there he was, manifest before their eyes; surely then it can only mean that he was offering the flesh which the Word had been made in the fullness of time as the object to receive our faith; but that the Word itself, *through whom all things had been made* (John 1:3), was being kept for the contemplation in eternity of minds now purified through faith."[198]

Church

In our exposition of Gunton we noted the following central themes: the Church is the *locus* where the work of Christ is made real in people's lives, since the life of the Church is rooted in the atonement; the Church is the temporal embodiment of the life of the Trinity—i.e., the Trinity is to be a model for the Church, which is an "echo" of the life of the Trinity. On Gunton's view, Augustine erred gravely in his understanding of the Church. Augustine's chief error is a trinitarian error, because Augustine does not have a conception of the Spirit as the one who realizes future blessings now through the creation of community (i.e., the Church). For Augustine the Church is an institution which mediates grace to the indi-

---

195. Ibid., 104.
196. *De Trinitate* IV.24.
197. Ibid.
198. Ibid., IV.26.

vidual, not a community which echoes the trinitarian being of God. With Gunton's criticisms in view, let us turn to Augustine.

As important as the doctrine of the Church in Augustine's theology as a whole, he does not make much explicit use of the doctrine in *De Trinitate*. He sets his work in *De Trinitate* against the backdrop of "all the Catholic commentators I have been able to read," and these commentators are treated as authorities.[199] He can speak briefly about the Church as the body of Christ.[200] At the end of *De Trinitate* Augustine can speak of the Church as that house which is built after Jesus conquers the devil.[201] More closely related to the issues raised in this paper, Augustine contends that the Church is the locus of the work of the Holy Spirit. Augustine notes that at Jesus' baptism the Holy Spirit in the form of a dove alights on Jesus and anoints Jesus. This prefigured the life of the Church, which is the place where the anointing of the Holy Spirit takes place in the lives of believers.[202]

Eschatology

As we have mentioned at length earlier, eschatology is central to Gunton's theology. The key eschatological themes in his thought are: following Irenaeus, redemption is the bringing to completion of the *telos* built into redemption, not the "intervention" of God into a world gone bad; following Basil, the Holy Spirit is the "perfecting cause of creation," and the Holy Spirit helps realize future eschatological blessings now; eschatology is thoroughly christological, in that Christ is not only the creator, but also the means of the re-establishment of the image of God in humanity; the death, resurrection and ascension are eschatological in that these events are representative of the future renewing and transformation of the whole created order. Augustine's key weaknesses related to eschatology are: creation has been severed from redemption; the role of the Holy Spirit, particularly his role as the one who realizes eschatological blessings now, has been minimized, in part due to the fact that attention has been diverted from the economy, and placed on the immanent Trinity. With Gunton's criticisms in view, let us turn to Augustine.

199. Ibid., I.7.
200. Ibid., IV.12.
201. Ibid., XV.34.
202. Ibid., XV.46.

Like the best of theologians, Augustine is ultimately a theologian who affirms the centrality of eschatology. History is moving towards a *telos*, and the best is yet to come. Along these lines it is evident that Augustine sees a type of eschatology in the created order. That is, creation has a purpose. For example in *Enchiridion*, in his discussion of the resurrection of the body, Augustine says some intriguing things about the resurrection of aborted fetuses. He asks if there is anyone who would deny "that the act of resurrection would fill out whatever was lacking to the form?" (of the aborted fetuses). This would be appropriate, and parallels in a sense the resurrection state of the average, scarred, aged, person. Thus, "Nature, then would not be defrauded of anything fitting and harmonious which the passage of days was to bring nor be disfigured by anything of an opposite kind which passage of days had added, but rather that which was not yet complete would be completed, just as that which had suffered blemish will be renewed."[203]

We simply note that in this discussion of the aborted fetus there is a type of eschatology built-in to the created order. Or perhaps better put, the resurrection is God's means by which he completes and perfects the imperfections found in the created order—even in the unborn.

Rowan Williams also draws attention to the purposefulness of creation. Williams rejects the notion that Augustine should be read as "inventing or reinforcing a simple matter-spirit dualism."[204] Indeed, Williams sees in Augustine's view of creation much of what Gunton sees as *lacking* in Augustine's view. Whereas Gunton sees Augustine as severing creation and redemption, as ignoring the *telos* or goal which is built in, or intrinsic to creation, as seeing creation as solely the result of the stark will of God, Williams sees a different picture. He writes that for Augustine, in creation "God wills that there be reality quite other than God, and that this entails the positing of a reality that can change: if so, it entails also the dialectic of the possible and the actual, it entails a world of purposive fluidity, things becoming themselves, organising themselves more successfully or economically over time."[205] He continues: "Creation, then, is the realm in which good or beauty or stability, the condition in which everything is most freely and harmoniously itself in balance with everything else, is

---

203. *Enchiridion* 85.
204. R. Williams, "'Good For Nothing?,'" 11.
205. Ibid., 17.

being sought and *being* formed." Indeed, the road to heaven takes time, because "we must *grow* into new life."[206] Thus, if we want to know God, "we must follow the course of the incarnate Word, not look for a timeless penetration of God's mind."[207] The heart of Williams' concern is that for Augustine God does not "need" creation. God, as Triune Being is completely "satisfied," and has no need unmet. Then why does God create? Following Augustine Williams suggests that God creates us out of love. Loving can either be instrumental or contemplative, or using and enjoying. The idea that God "enjoys" us or contemplates us in the sense that we "enjoy" or contemplate God is problematic, in that it implies that God needs us. Thus Williams suggests that perhaps God loves us "instrumentally" or "uses" us. He concludes, "So we must say that God 'uses' us for the sake of our greatest good, which is, of course, loving God: God loves us so that we may come to *our* highest good, not so that *God's* good may be served."[208] He continues, "God's love is instrumental for our good, and so is wholly selfless, since my enjoyment of God is the greatest possible bliss for me, but adds nothing to the endless bliss of God."[209] Thus, for Williams creation is purposeful, in that creation is the means by which God brings about love for himself, which in fact is the very thing that gives human creatures the greatest bliss and joy.

It would appear that in Augustine the created order is good, although not ultimate, and that there is a limited dualism between the material and non-material realms. The created order is a means by which the human mind can begin to contemplate God, but this effort of contemplation does not end with the created order. Rather, the created order is a means to an end: the contemplation, or vision of God. This role for the created order does not violate the starting point of faith in Augustine's thought, for the quest for contemplation of, or the vision of God is always set against the backdrop of the acceptance of the truthfulness of Scripture and Church teaching.

---

206. Ibid., 18.
207. Ibid.
208. Ibid., 20.
209. Ibid.

Conclusion

In this chapter we have attempted to outline the theme of creation and redemption as found in Augustine's *De Trinitate*. We have done this in part because Colin Gunton contends that in Augustine—and in the West following the Bishop of Hippo—creation and redemption have been effectively severed. We have sought to exposit the themes of creation and redemption in *De Trinitate* in order to determine if Gunton's criticisms can withstand scrutiny. We conclude the following. Augustine was an ardent proponent of *creatio ex nihilo*, that God created a God world out of nothing. *Creatio ex nihilo* ultimately provides a sound and legitimate response to the problem of evil. Creation was ultimately a trinitarian act, and there are vestiges of the Trinity in the created world. While Augustine does affirm a type of matter-spirit dualism, we have argued that it is important to see that for Augustine this is a *limited* dualism. Both matter *and* spirit are good, although Augustine sees the spiritual as superior. The created order is ultimately a means of revelation, and it is through the created order that we are led to a knowledge and vision of the eternal. Resurrection includes the material world (Augustine is not a gnostic), and there is an eschatological element to creation—redemption is not simply the rescue of creation, but in some sense the proper end of creation. Redemption is ultimately trinitarian, and the point of the incarnation was the redemption of sinners. Christ is the one true mediator between God and sinners, and we have seen that Augustine brings together various historical "theories" of the atonement into an impressive doctrine which simultaneously emphasizes justice, satisfaction, victory, sacrifice and example. Of particular importance is Augustine's contention that Christ's work is often seen in terms of justice. Lastly, we suggested that there is indeed a polemical and rhetorical thrust to *De Trinitate*. Certainly some sort of "Arian" heresy is in view, for Augustine's pro-Nicene argument for the consubstantiality of the Son and the Spirit is crystal clear in the volume. Also, Augustine is arguing against some sort of speculative neoplatonist tendency which would downplay the centrality of the cross in the process of redemption. Augustine's thorough emphasis on the centrality of the cross as the sole means of redemption, as the sole means of ever obtaining a vision of God, demonstrates that for Augustine a neoplatonic ascent to the One (apart from the cross) was simply an impossibility. The only way to the vision of God is through a bloody, human body. The only reason one can ascend to God is because he has descended to us. This argument is important, because it shows that for Augustine the material, temporal world, although in some sense "less" than the spiritual is the means God has chosen by which eternal life is achieved. *This* world is a good world, and God uses material, temporal things as good means to a better, spiritual end. It does appear clear that Augustine is issuing a challenge to the neoplatonists. He speaks of "some people who think they can purify themselves for contemplating God and cleaving to him by their own power and strength of character."[210] Augustine suggests that some persons *have* been able to "direct the keen gaze of their intellects" in such a way as to achieve at least a small glimpse of "the light of unchanging truth," but ultimately these persons do not see God. Whatever the strengths of the neoplatonic system, it cannot deliver. Augustine's repeated emphasis on a real incarnation and the necessity of the cross as the only means to arrive at a vision of God appears to serve as a polemic against those persons—the neoplatonists—who deny the necessity of the incarnation and cross of Christ. Augustine presents the death of the incarnate Word as the only means to move from this physical existence to the presence of God, where all we can simply do is gaze upon God. What is central to our concern is that we have seen in this chapter that for Augustine the temporal missions reveal the eternal processions. Stated a little differently, what God does in time reveals who He is in eternity. And according to Augustine, one of the *chief* things God does is send his Son, who dies for sinners. Thus, if our reading of Augustine is correct, we would be forced seriously to reconsider a significant amount of Gunton's reading of Augustine. For example, we would have to question Gunton's contention that Augustine somehow severs the "one" God from the "many" particulars of the created order. We would also have to question the notion that somehow the one, timeless essence is made superfluous, and that this one essence is not intrinsically and organically related to the work of the Son and Spirit. Indeed, if we are right in our understanding of Augustine, the *chief* way we come to know God is through the work of at least one of Irenaeus' "hands" of God, the Son. For, in the Son's redemptive work, he truly reveals the transcendent, immanent Trinity.

---

210. Ibid., IV.20.

CHAPTER 5

Being and Ontology in Augustine's *De Trinitate*

CENTRAL TO *DE TRINITATE* is the question of how one is to speak about God, and Augustine deliberates at length as to what are the language and terms which are appropriate when speaking and thinking about God. Augustine spends a good deal of time wrestling with how one can speak of the Triune God. Augustine's deliberations take him through a discussion of the Latin terms *substantia, essentia, persona*, and the Greek terms οὐσία and ὑπόστασις (and briefly, φυσίς). Augustine has had numerous detractors regarding his construal of the Trinity, and we should begin by noting that Gunton is not a maverick or a loose cannon when he voices his consternation with Augustine. Many others have expressed similar concerns. G. L. Prestige, among others, contends that the Cappadocians had a fundamentally different metaphysic from that of Augustine, and this difference is seen in their respective construals of the Trinity. Prestige writes, for example, "Neither the Latin language, nor the ordinary Latin intellect, was capable of the subtlety of the conception which approved itself to the Greek theologians."[1] Eugene Webb also posits a dichotomy between East and West. Webb contends that "Greek trinitarian thinking, of which Augustine was largely ignorant" opened up the possibility for human understanding of the Triune God, which is mediated through participating in the life of the Son and Spirit.[2] However, for Augustine, such knowledge of God was impossible, and Augustine could simply offer that

1. Cf. Prestige, *God in Patristic Thought*, 235 (see also 157–78).
2. Webb, "Augustine's new Trinity," 191–212.

"one can only speculate abstractly about the meaning of the trinitarian doctrine," and one can believe in the Triune on the sole basis of church tradition.[3] Webb also contends that Augustine's metaphors for the Trinity simply did not work, and this failure was a nagging source of anxiety for Augustine.[4] Webb even suggests that the religious persecution and coercion in the West might be traced to this "anxiety" which Augustine's trinitarian metaphors bequeathed to the West.[5]

T. R. Martland likewise wishes to affirm a significant theological chasm between East and West, in particular between the Cappadocians and Augustine.[6] In a sentence which could serve as a perfect summary of the general trend to drive a wedge between the Cappadocians and Augustine Martland writes, "Augustine's doctrine of the Trinity contributed to a fuller understanding of what the Christian means when he asserts that God is one, but the cost of this contribution was a failure to take seriously the Christian assertion that God of His nature is a multiple."[7] Augustine's "trinitarian thought introduced the West to the primary concern with unity."[8] Summarizing the key difference between Augustine and the Cappadocians, Martland writes, "Whereas the Cappadocians knew God as three persons before they knew Him as one God, Augustine knows Him as one God before he knows Him as three persons."[9] Martland's concerns are very similar to those of Gunton's, particularly with Martland's concerns that Augustine ultimately makes the Trinity superfluous: "Augustine's strong defense of the unity of God and of the absolute equality of the persons tends to reduce the doctrine of the Trinity to an irrelevancy and to unintelligibility."[10] Indeed, Augustine's "preoccupation with the unity of God has reduced the doctrine of the Trinity to a meaningless dogma which is accepted solely on the grounds of authority."[11] Martland laments that with Augustine, it "is as if the Western church knowingly and

---

3. Ibid., 204.

4. Ibid., 206–8.

5. Ibid., 208.

6. Martland, "Study of Cappadocian and Augustinian Trinitarian Methodology," 252–63.

7. Ibid., 252.

8. Ibid., 256.

9. Ibid.

10. Ibid., 257.

11. Ibid., 262–63.

willingly turned from an understanding of the doctrine as a necessary formula to capture the implications of empirical Christian encounters, to an understanding of the doctrine as a dogma, a *mysterious nonsense* (beyond-sense?), acceptance of which marks the faithful off from the unfaithful."[12] Ultimately, concludes Martland, the Western Church chose authority over reason.[13]

Others are more skeptical of affirming thoroughly different conceptions between East and West. Michel René Barnes, for example, summarizes the common conception of an East/West dichotomy as follows: "Greek theology begins with the reality of the distinct persons while Latin theology begins with the reality of the divine nature."[14] However, Barnes contends that this way of construing the differences between East and West is relatively new. Indeed, "only theologians of the last one hundred years have ever thought it was true," and this is due largely to the influence of Theodore de Régnon's *Études de théologie positive sur la Sainte Trinité*.[15] Barnes contends that "it is de Regnon who invented the Greek/Latin paradigm, geometrical diagrams and all."[16] According to Barnes, the systematician's penchant for "grand, architectonic narrative forms," combined with reduced attention to primary texts and a love for the centrality of *ideas*, not *doctrines*, in history, has led to a thorough misreading and misunderstanding of Augustine's trinitarian theology.[17]

Rowan Williams warns that this tendency to characterize Augustine as emphasizing the one timeless essence to the detriment of the three persons is misguided.[18] Williams contends that a full understanding of what Augustine is doing in *De Trinitate* would help commentators avoid picturing Augustine as committed to one, timeless, abstract essence. Williams writes, "What should be particularly noted is that Augustine, so far from separating the divine substance from the life of the divine persons, defines that substance in such a way that God cannot be other than relational, trinitarian."[19] As Williams sees it, "The divine essence is

---

12. Ibid., 263.
13. Ibid.
14. Barnes, "Augustine in Contemporary Trinitarian Theology," 237.
15. Ibid. De Régnon, *Études de théologie positive sur la Sainte Trinité*.
16. Barnes, " Augustine, Trinity, and Contemporary Theology," 238.
17. Ibid., 237–50.
18. Williams, "*Sapientia* and the Trinity," 317–32.
19. Ibid., 325.

not an abstract principle of unity, nor a 'causal' factor over and above the hypostases; to be God at all is to be desirious of and active in *giving* the divine life." He continues, "That is the essence, the definition of God for our purposes; there is no 'divinity' not constituted by the act of *caritas*, and thus no divinity that can adequately be conceived apart from the trinity of persons."[20] Williams also contends that it is simply inaccurate to say that in Augustine the divine essence somehow is anterior to, or underlies the three persons. Williams writes, "we have noted that the divine persons do not 'possess' the divine essence, but are what it is."[21] Williams is adamant that the three persons are *not* subordinated to the divine essence in *De Trinitate*. He notes, "There can therefore be no question of any subordination of trinitarian plurality to a unity of essence."[22]

Lewis Ayres is also skeptical of construals of Augustine which summarize his trinitarian thought by saying that Augustine emphasized unity over plurality. On the idea that Augustine posited a divine "essence" which undergird the three persons, Ayres writes, "Whatever faults one finds theologically with Augustine's thought it really is time that ascribing such a simplistic style of doctrine to Augustine ceased."[23] Ayres argues that Augustine's use of such terminology as *essentia* and *substantia* is more complicated than is often admitted, and this complexity is rarely taken into account by those construals which simply contend that Augustine "emphasized" the unity of God over against the plurality.[24]

Edmund Hill, who is generally quite favorable to Augustine's construal of the Trinity, also posits that the simple divide between "East" and "West" is an inaccurate and unhelpful schema. He writes, "Augustine and Ambrose wrote in Latin, Athanasius and Basil and John Chrysostom in Greek. But to cast over them the shadow of this modern stereotype is simply to overlook the fact which was of paramount importance in the fourth and fifth centuries—that Athanasius stood in the Alexandrian or Egyptian tradition, Ambrose in the North Italian, Augustine in the African, Basil in the Cappadocian and John Chrysostom in the Syrian." He continues, "It

---

20. Ibid.
21. Ibid., 328.
22. Ibid., 330.
23. Ayres, "Augustine, the Trinity and Modernity," 130. Cf. idem, "Fundamental Grammar of Augustine's Trinitarian Theology"; idem, "Augustine on the Unity of the Triune God."
24. Ibid.

was these *local* traditions that counted then, not the later crude divide between Greek and Latin, East and West. They influenced each other, of course, but not just the Greek-speaking Churches on one side and the Latin on the other."[25] Interestingly, Edmund Hill, who argues persuasively for the basic legitimacy and coherency of Augustine's trinitarian theology, nonetheless argues that the West after Augustine does show certain tendencies which are inimical to a sound doctrine of the Trinity. Hill contrasts two groups: "economic" theologians and "transcendental" theologians (Hill uses "transcendental" instead of "immanent"—although he considers them to be synonyms—because "immanent" in other contexts means something like "close" or "near," which is not what is intended by immanent in a trinitarian context). Economic theologians emphasized the Trinity in its relation to creation and redemption (the economy) (e.g., Justin, Irenaeus, Tertullian and Novatian). Transcendental theologians emphasized who God is apart from creation and redemption, as in God in his eternal relations "in and of himself" (e.g., the Cappadocians and Augustine). The tendency which Hill laments is an inference which is often drawn from Augustine's axiom that the outward works of the Trinity are undivided (*opera Trinitatis ad extra sunt indivisa*). The inference is that if the outward works of the Trinity are undivided, then we human creatures do not actually relate to the *persons* of the Trinity, but simply to the one undifferentiated God. Hill concedes how one could make the inference, but contends that it is an unnecessary, and ultimately harmful inference, because it really does sever the Triune God from real relationships with human creatures.[26]

Having surveyed key options in contemporary reflection on Augustine, particularly related to the question of ontology, we turn to Augustine himself to exposit his own writings on these issues. With particular attention to *De Trinitate*, we will seek to come to terms with Augustine's own position on the question of ontology. What is Augustine's teaching, especially in *De Trinitate* on key concepts such as substance, essence, persons and relations? Gunton contends that Augustine falls short of the theological sophistication and advances of the Cappadocians, and as we have mentioned above, Gunton is not alone in this claim. Others such as Robert Jenson and John Zizioulas are equally displeased with

---

25. Hill, *Mystery of the Trinity*, 116.
26. Ibid., 95–96.

Augustine and pleased with the Cappadocians. As we approach the theme of ontology, we should note that this chapter will not attempt to be a full-fledged treatment of the metaphysics of Augustine. Such an effort deserves a monograph of its own, and others have attempted such a task.[27] Rather, we will concentrate on the doctrine of God, particularly the questions of essence, substance, persons and relations, as seen in *De Trinitate*.

Ontology and Relationship

In our exposition of Gunton we saw that Gunton believes that Augustine failed to articulate a truly Christian ontology. The Cappadocians saw relationship as that which *constitutes* being, while Augustine saw relationship as something which is *predicated* about being. Additionally, Gunton contends that the Cappadocians gave full weight to three real persons, while Augustine failed, due to his overemphasis on unity, to give full weight to the reality of the three persons. Augustine errs gravely in failing to appropriate the Cappadocians' ontology. With Gunton's main criticisms in view, let us turn to Augustine.

Edmund Hill offers a helpful introduction to our theme. Hill correctly points to the difficulty of speaking of one and three. He writes, "The trouble is, once again—the absolute simplicity of God. God does not have distinct and distinguishable attributes; he *is* all his attributes, and his attributes, and his attributes *are* the divine substance or being. Thus in God these attributes are not really distinct from one another; they are only distinct in our minds, in our manner of thinking and talking about God."[28]

As we have seen in our exposition of Gunton, Gunton contends that Augustine emphasizes the one, timeless essence of God to the detriment of the three persons. The one essence or being or nature is so emphasized that the three persons ultimately become superfluous.

It is appropriate for us to plumb Augustine's thought on the being or nature of God. If Augustine's theology could be summarized in one word (a perilous attempt), a possible contender would be "theocentric." Vernon J. Bourke notes, "No reader of the *Soliloquies* and the *Confessiones* will have to be reminded that Augustine's thought is completely theocentric. Whatever may be his other interests, Augustine's chief concern is about

---

27. Cf. Anderson, *St. Augustine and Being*; Bourke, *Augustine's View of Reality*.
28. Hill, *Mystery of the Trinity*, 61.

God."[29] Augustine's theology is radically God-centered, and thus it is no surprise that Augustine expends great effort in *De Trinitate* trying grapple with the nature of God. To grapple with the nature of God is ultimately to engage in metaphysics, and it is little wonder that in Joseph Stephen O'Leary's attempt to "overcome metaphysics," he devotes an entire chapter to "overcoming Augustine."[30] Vernon Bourke could note in 1964 that there was no thorough study of the metaphysics of Augustine, and this lacuna exists somewhat still today.[31] This chapter will not fill this gap, but it is hoped that we will at least contribute to an understanding the basic metaphysical structure which informed Augustine's thought on the being of God as found in *De Trinitate*.

Vernon Bourke points out that for Augustine "metaphysics" has a thoroughly theocentric focus. Augustine's metaphysics is of a different type from Aristotle's. As Bourke notes, "In the cognitive sense, Augustinian *ratio* has little to do with discursive and demonstrative reasoning in the Aristotelian sense. Reason is the gaze of the mind upon its appropriate objects.[32] This concept of reason is essential to an understanding of *De Trinitate*, for in *De Trinitate* Augustine's purpose is to plumb how it is that we human sinners can ever come to gaze upon God. Our ultimate goal is simply to gaze upon God, and this gazing is a "higher" act than all the "discursive and demonstrative reasoning" which leads up to the point when the believer gazes upon God.

Augustine and Aristotle

In discussing Augustine's metaphysics, we should note, with Vernon Bourke, that "Augustine was much limited by the nature of his education

---

29. Bourke, *Augustine's Question of Wisdom*, 203.

30. Cf. the chapter, "Overcoming Augustine" in Joseph Stephen O'Leary's *Questioning Back*, 165–202. O'Leary posits that genuine Christian faith, if it is to remain so must overcome metaphysics. Following Derrida, O'Leary calls for a rejection of logocentricism and metaphysics in general. O'Leary writes (225), "As faith builds on these latter foundations [i.e., of "peace, justice, and freedom"] it must reshape the meaning of tradition in accord with them, in a counter-metaphysical reading which frees faith from the morose, introspective provincialism characteristic of the metaphysical theology which is still dominant." Anything less will fail to bring about "the integral liberation of faith from its imprisonment in representations which have become idolatrous."

31. Bourke, *Augustine's View of Reality*, x.

32. Ibid., 2.

and by the conditions of the Latin language in his time."³³ However, the fact that Augustine was not well versed in the niceties of the discipline of metaphysics should not be taken to mean that Augustine somehow did not think or reason in terms of metaphysics. What is particularly interesting to us is the extent to which Augustine proffered a trinitarian metaphysic, or what might be called a trinitarianly informed metaphysic.³⁴

It is also important to take a brief look at possible precursors to Augustine's own metaphysics. Since Gunton contends that Augustine is caught in the stranglehold or Aristotelian logic, it is worth looking, at least briefly, at Aristotle, and attempt to ask if Augustine is indeed "Aristotelian" in his metaphysics.³⁵ Augustine was familiar with Aristotle's *Categories*, as Augustine makes clear in the *Confessiones*.³⁶ Augustine says about Aristotle's *Categories*, "The book seemed to me an extremely clear statement about substances, such as man, and what are in them, such as a man's shape, what is his quality of stature, how many feet, and his relatedness."³⁷ Augustine also writes that he tried to speak of and construe God in terms of the ten categories: "Thinking that absolutely everything that exists is comprehended under the ten categories, I tried to conceive you also, my God, wonderfully simple and immutable, as if you too were a subject of

33. Ibid., 14.

34. Ibid., 20ff.

35. Edward Booth's doctoral dissertation traces out Augustine's doctrine of "knowledge of oneself" as it relates to Aristotle and neo-Platonism. Booth's work has been published in a lengthy series of articles titled: "St. Augustine's *notitia sui* Related to Aristotle and the Early Platonists." Particularly helpful for our purposes here is the section "From Aristotle to Augustine," in *Augustiniana* 27, 70–104. Booth is more sympathetic to seeing certain continuities, rather than discontinuities, between Aristotle and Augustine. Booth, 82, writes, "if there is some truth in the statement that 'Aristotle and Augustine are both rivals who contend with each other in the learning and mentality of the following centuries,' it was because their followers did not perceive what they had in common." Booth is quoting Adolf Harnack, *Lehrbuch der Dogmengeschichte*, 4th ed. (Tübingen, 1910), 106.

36. Cf. *Confessiones* IV.16.28, where Augustine writes, "What good did it do me that at about the age of twenty there came into my hands a work of Aristotle which they call the *Ten Categories*? My teacher in rhetoric at Carthage, and others too who were reputed to be learned men, used to speak of this work with their cheeks puffed out with conceit, and at the very name I gasped with suspense as if about to read something great and divine. Yet I read it without any expositor and understood it." Marius Victorinus had translated *Categories* into Latin, and this is likely what Augustine had read. See Henry Chadwick's comment in his translation of *Confessiones* (Oxford: Oxford University Press, 1991), 69 n. 33.

37. *Confessiones* IV.16.28.

which magnitude and beauty are attributes. I thought them to be in you as if in a subject, as in the case of a physical body, whereas you yourself are your own magnitude and your own beauty. By contrast a body is not great and beautiful by being body; if it were less great or less beautiful, it would nevertheless still be body."[38] However, Augustine repudiates this understanding, and concludes that this Aristotelian scheme was simply a lie: "My conception of you was a lie, not truth, the figments of my misery, not the permanent solidity of your supreme bliss. You had commanded and it so came about in me, that the soil would bring forth thorns and brambles for me, and that with toil I should gain my bread (Gen 3:18)."[39] Augustine's familiarity with Aristotle's categories is also seen in *De Trinitate*, where he quickly runs through all the categories.[40] We will look at Augustine's teaching on substance and essence below, and only then will we be able to determine the extent to which Augustine was Aristotelian.

We are introduced to Aristotle's metaphysics in *Categories*, but other key works are *Metaphysics* and *On Interpretation*. We will not offer an exhaustive treatment of Aristotle's metaphysics. Rather, we simply outline key themes in Aristotle, particularly those key themes which relate in some way to our treatment of Augustine. Aristotle contended that there were ten categories which can be used to signify things: substance, quantity, quality, relation, place, time, position, state, action, affection.[41] At times Aristotle mentions other categories, or slightly changes this list, but this list is representative of Aristotle's scheme. These categories refer to *things* themselves, and not simply terms or signs for things.[42] They are, in Lloyd's words, "the ultimate classes into which whatever exists or is real may be said to fall."[43] These categories are not "universals" in the platonic sense, for Plato's doctrine of forms appears to be the foil in the background of Aristotle's categories. Lloyd writes that for Plato "the particular objects of the world of everyday experience certainly 'share' in the Forms and are not totally non-existent: but what is 'really real' is the Form in its pure state." However, for Aristotle in the *Categories*, "'substance' is a term applied pri-

38. Ibid., IV.16.29.

39. Ibid.

40. *De Trinitate* V. 7, 8.

41. Besides Aristotle's *Categories* themselves, helpful secondary literature is Lloyd, *Aristotle*, 111–32; Stead, *Philosophy in Christian Antiquity*, 31–39.

42. Cf. Stead, *Divine Substance*, 57; Lloyd, *Aristotle*, 113.

43. Lloyd, *Aristotle*, 114.

marily to the concrete individual object, the complex of form and matter, this table, this chair, Socrates, this specimen of dogfish and so on."[44] The categories are concrete realities, not atemporal or eternal forms.[45] Thus, as Lloyd summarizes, "qualities . . . cannot exist by themselves, that is apart from the individual substances that have the qualities."[46]

In his *Categories* Aristotle distinguishes between "primary" and "secondary" substances. A "primary substance" (πρώτη οὐσία) or in Stead's words, "*what is most properly called ousia,*" is this particular man, or that particular man. On the other hand, "secondary substances" (δεύτεραι οὐσίαι) are the species "man," or the broader genus "animal."[47] Thus, the particular man himself is οὐσία in a primary sense, whereas more general groupings like "man" (species) or "animal" (genus) are only οὐσία in a secondary sense. Stead helpfully summarizes this point: "individuals *exist* in their own right whereas universals in some sense depend upon them; or even that the individual exists in the true sense of the word, whereas ὁ ἄνθρωπος, Man, exists only in the secondary sense that instances of it exist."[48]

On the question of "being" Aristotle's position is that "'being' is used with reference to one thing and to a single nature. . . . '[B]eing' is used with reference to a single thing."[49] While Aristotle affirms that "the term 'being' (τὸ ὄν) is used in various senses," he still contends that it is used "with reference to one central idea (φύσιν) and one definite characteristic, and not as merely a common epithet."[50] A few lines later Aristotle can write that "'being' (τὸ ὄν) is used in various senses, but always with reference to one principle (ἀρχήν)."[51] Of the ten categories listed above, "being" is most often used with the category of "substance," although it can be used of other categories as well.[52] Aristotle writes, "Now of all these senses which 'being' (ὄντος) has, the primary sense is clearly the 'what,' (τί ἐστιν) which

---

44. Ibid., 52.
45. Ibid., 114–15.
46. Ibid., 115.
47. *Categories*, 5; cf. Stead, *Divine Substance*, 57.
48. Stead, *Divine Substance*, 61.
49. Ibid., 128.
50. Aristotle, *Metaphysics* 1003a, 34ff.
51. Ibid., 1003b, 5–6.
52. Ibid., 1028a 10ff.

denotes the substance (οὐσίαν)."[53] Ultimately, notes Lloyd, "the root idea of substance is 'the what it is to be a thing' or the form."[54]

One of Aristotle's chief concerns in *Metaphysics* is the question of "being." It is curious that Aristotle has seemingly dropped the question of "primary substance" and "secondary substance" discussed in *Categories*. We see in *Metaphysics* Aristotle's doctrine of matter and form, and we encounter key terms such as οὐσία, ὑποκείμενον, and εἶδος. Matter is generally the physical "stuff," whereas form is that which makes something what it is, what gives something this, rather than that shape. Οὐσία can refer to the concrete whole (form and matter), or form, but is less often used to refer to matter. Ὑποκείμενον, on the other hand is often used for the concrete whole (form and matter) and matter, but rarely is used to refer to the form.[55] The term εἶδος, one of Aristotle's "principal legacies from Platonism," is particularly difficult to grasp, for while the term might seem to denote an affirmation of universals, Aristotle rejected the teaching of universals espoused by his former teacher.[56] Stead suggests that the primary understanding of εἶδος is "a geometrical shape or configuration."[57] For Aristotle εἶδος can also mean "species," although this is the less common meaning. Additionally, Aristotle seems to imply that εἶδος means something like "the shape or form characteristic of a species," a conception which seems rather close to Plato's conception of independent universals.[58]

We should note at this point the important work by Michael Durrant on Aristotle's doctrine of substance, and its possible influences on theological traditions both East and West.[59] Durrant presupposes in his study that "the doctrine that God is three persons in one substance"

53. Ibid., 1028a, 14ff.
54. Lloyd, *Aristotle*, 131.
55. Stead, *Divine Substance*, 72–73.
56. Ibid., 73.
57. Ibid., 74.
58. Indeed, Stead, *Divine Substance*, 76, concludes, "It is in the end impossible to give a consistent account of Aristotle's views on the relationship of the εἶδος and the universal."
59. Durrant, *Theology and Intelligibility*. Durrant's work contains a short summary statement on the title page (although this does not appear to be a subtitle): "An examination of the proposition that God is the last end of rational creatures and the doctrine that God is Three Persons in one Substance (The Doctrine of the Holy Trinity)."

is a fair statement of the orthodox, historic doctrine of the Trinity.[60] Durrant concludes that this "Trinitarian formula is an impossible one and hence that the doctrine of the Trinity is an impossible one."[61] Durrant argues that the Greek Fathers fundamentally misunderstood the notion of οὐσία that they received. Certain scholars in this field have made things worse, for they have introduced "a misguided, indeed impossible concept of 'substance' in their appreciation of those writings of the Greek Fathers which they regard as central to the doctrine of the Trinity."[62] Durrant appears to presuppose that if later thinkers use οὐσία in a way different from Aristotle, such thinkers have erred.[63] Durrant also argues that "scholars in this field are also open to the charge of perpetrating an unintelligible concept of ὑπόστασις."[64] Ultimately, by the time of Augustine such key terms and concepts as οὐσία and ὑπόστασις have been so thoroughly muddled that Durrant can conclude the following: "the backcloth against which St. Augustine's discussion of God as substance and his subsequent discussions of correlative notions is set is a patchwork of confusion."[65] Augustine's use of such terms as *substantia* and *essentia*, as well as his use of terminology like "of the same substance," "in the same substance," "in one substance," and Augustine's construal of the three *persons* of the Trinity all fail.[66] Particularly important for us here is Durrant's contention that Augustine's use of "substance" as applied to God is nonsensical.[67] Augustine, like the Greek Fathers, muddles and confuses Aristotle's notion of substance. Durrant contends that a proper Aristotelian notion of substance *entails* accidents—i.e., a substance is not a substance without concomitant accidents. However, as Durrant correctly notes, Augustine claims that since God is unchangeable and simple, he has no accidents. Thus, Durrant claims that since for Augustine God has no accidents, he cannot be substance.[68] Indeed, notes Durrant, "The idea of an unchangeable substance, that is the idea

60. Ibid., x.
61. Ibid.
62. Ibid., xvi.
63. Ibid.
64. Ibid., xvii.
65. Ibid.
66. Ibid.
67. Ibid., 112–25.
68. Ibid., 121–22.

of a substance which cannot sensibly be spoken of as being subject to change ... is a nonsensical one, hence to say that God is an unchangeable substance is itself nonsensical. I thus contend that, far from it being the case that St. Augustine has established an important truth, he has engrossed himself in a nonsense."[69] Durrant appears to push his argument a bit hard and fails to deal adequately with the following objections: (1) it is irrelevant whether Augustine (or the Greek Fathers for that matter) use substance in an Aristotelian way. Augustine is under no mandate to do so, and what really matters is how he adopts and uses such terminology/concepts to his own ends and purposes; (2) Augustine is exploring how terms and concepts such as substance might apply to God, and as such Augustine is under no restriction to use the term in the same way it is used when being applied to the created order.

Let us state in summary the chief components of Aristotle's ontology which concern us as we turn to Augustine. As we have seen, Aristotle deals at length with the concept of substance. Although we would like to find in Aristotle one, simple, consistent answer, Aristotle's own position is not quite so easily ascertained. Nonetheless, it is appropriate to try and locate the key themes in Aristotle (or at least in his successors) which may have influenced Augustine. First, Aristotle held that being or substance was unchanging. In his more explicitly theological writings this theme would show up in his contention that God is the unmoved mover. Second, although Aristotle ultimately rejected his master's (Plato's) conception of Forms, Aristotle still affirmed that everything has an οὐσία (an "essence" or "substance"), and such "accidents" as quantities, qualities and relations attach to "substances." While a "substance" does not (indeed cannot) change, without a thing ceasing to be that thing, "accidents," such as quantities, qualities and relations can change. Christopher Stead notes, "Aristotle develops a distinction between a thing's substance, namely what belongs to it in virtue of its definition, and 'accidents', or predicates which do not necessarily and always attach to it."[70] It is this ontology which Gunton sees in Augustine, and it is this ontological tradition which did not allow Augustine to appropriate the ontological advance and contribution of the Cappadocian Fathers. Thus, we must seek to determine more exactly Augustine's relation to this Aristotelian tradition.

---

69. Ibid., 122.
70. Stead, *Philosophy in Christian Antiquity*, 36.

Augustine begins to deal seriously with "metaphysics" in Book V. Augustine begins Book V with a disclaimer, admitting to the trepidation with which one ventures to speak of the nature or being of God: "From now on I will be attempting to say things that cannot altogether be said as they are thought by a man—or at least as they are thought by me."[71] Indeed, as Augustine continues: "In any case, when we think about God the trinity we are aware that our thoughts are quite inadequate to their object, and incapable of grasping him as he is; even by men of the calibre of the apostle Paul he can only be seen, as it says, *like a puzzling reflection in a mirror* (1 Cor 13:12)."[72] It is appropriate to pause at this point. In these opening lines from Book V we see at least two key points. First, the quest for analogies must be seen against the backdrop of Augustine's trepidation and reticence in trying to speak about God. He realizes that the quest for adequate construals and conceptions of God is fraught with difficulty, and the analogies which Augustine will soon be discussing should be seen against such trepidation and reticence.[73] Second, Augustine here refers to 1 Cor 13:12, and this verse serves as a type of paradigmatic verse for Augustine's quest as a whole in *De Trinitate*. Our construals and conceptions of God are always thoroughly limited and impartial (although not necessarily "wrong"), and we must concede that we will only see God truly when we see him face to face when we depart for the direct presence of God. Unless both (1) Augustine's trepidation and reticence, as well as (2) the eschatological nature of our vision of God are kept in mind, Augustine's analogies and quest for knowledge of God are likely to be misunderstood.

There is indeed nothing wrong in wanting to know God rightly and speak of Him rightly. As Augustine writes, "there is no effrontery in burning to know, out of faithful piety, the divine and inexpressible truth that is above us, provided the mind is fired by the grace of our creator and savior,

---

71. *De Trinitate* V.1.

72. Ibid.

73. A similar sentiment is expressed near the beginning of *De Doctrina Christiana* (I.5). Augustine writes, "Have I said anything, solemnly uttered anything that is worthy of God? On the contrary, all I feel I have done is to wish to say something; but if I have said anything, it is not what I wished to say." While Augustine expresses his own humility about speaking about God, he can still write, "And yet, while nothing really worthy of God can be said about him, he has accepted the homage of human voices, and has wished us to rejoice in praising him with our words." Thus, while our words are extremely limited, we are nonetheless to attempt to speak truly about God.

and not inflated by arrogant confidence in its own powers."[74] Augustine writes, "God is a substance (*substantia*), or perhaps a better word would be being (*essentia*); at any rate what the Greeks call *ousia* (οὐσία)."[75] Augustine writes that "just as we get the word 'wisdom' from 'wise,' and 'knowledge' from 'know,' so we have the word 'being' (*essentia*) from 'be' (*esse*)."[76] While other things are also called "beings" (*essentiae*) or (*substantiae*), all such things (besides) "admit of modifications (*accidentiae*)."[77]

Augustine contends that when speaking of most things, one can speak of *substance*—what a thing truly is, and one can speak according to *accident*—non-substantial characteristics which can be added, removed, increased or diminished, without changing what a thing is. Thus, there is the *substance* of a man, what a man truly is. Black hair or red hair are simply according to *accident*. Hair color can change without changing the *substance* of a man. But, things are different when we speak of God. Since God is both immutable and simple, ultimately *nothing* can truly be said of God according to *accident*. While a man may be good or not, and good here would be considered an accident, to say that God is *good* is to say something about the substance of God. God does not simply "have" goodness, He *is* his goodness. Whereas "goodness" is an accident with man, it is substance with God. As Roland Teske has remarked, "Since there can be no accident in God, what seems to be said of God according to accident must be understood to be said of him according to substance, that is, must be understood to signify or designate the substance of God."[78]

Augustine is wrestling with how to speak and think about God, and the backdrop for his concerns is at least in part the challenges from the Arians.[79] Augustine summarizes the Arian argument as follows: "Whatever is said or understood about God is said substance-wise, not modification-wise. Therefore the Father is unbegotten substance-wise, and the Son is begotten substance-wise. But being unbegotten is different from being begotten; therefore the Father's substance is different from the

---

74. *De Trinitate* V.1.
75. Ibid., V.3.
76. Ibid.
77. Ibid.
78. Teske, "Augustine's Use of '*Substantia*,'" 149; cf. idem, "Properties of God," 1–19.
79. In *De Trinitate* V.3 Augustine, in setting up his discussion of substance/essence, can speak of "the many objections which the Arians are in the habit of leveling against the Catholic faith."

Son's."[80] This challenge of the Arians provides Augustine a springboard from which to try to explore how one speaks and thinks of God correctly. He has already argued that God cannot be modified in any way, "and therefore the substance or being which is God is alone unchangeable, and therefore it pertains to it most truly and supremely to be, from which comes the name 'being.'"[81] Indeed, "there is no modification in God because there is nothing in him that can be changed or lost."[82] Thus, according to Augustine God cannot be modified—he cannot change. But, if what is said of God is always said "substance-wise," and if "unbegotten" applies to the Father, and "begotten" to the Son, does this mean that the Father and the Son are of different substances?

Augustine will spend books V–VII wrestling with the issue of what it means to speak of God according to substance, and of how to know when one is doing this or not. He argues that while with created things, they are spoken of either substance-wise or modification-wise, for whatever is not said substance-wise is said modification-wise.[83] However, Augustine suggests that with God, nothing is said modification-wise (for God cannot be modified), but that not everything is said substance-wise. And here we are introduced into what it means to call God "Father" and "Son," for it is terms like "Father" and "Son" which are spoken neither substance-wise nor modification-wise, but which "are said with reference to something else, like Father with reference to son and Son with reference to Father."[84] Augustine continues: "Therefore, although being Father is different from being Son, there is no difference of substance, because they are not called these things substance-wise but relationship-wise; and yet this relationship is not a modification, because it is not changeable."[85] Augustine argues that both "Father" and "Son" are neither spoken substance-wise nor modification-wise, but rather "relationship-wise," and that begotten is virtually equivalent to "son," while unbegotten is virtually equivalent to "father."[86] Augustine summarizes his position thus far as follows: "The

80. Ibid.
81. Ibid.
82. Ibid., V.5.
83. Ibid., V.6.
84. Ibid.
85. Ibid.
86. Ibid., V.8.

chief point then that we must maintain is that whatever that supreme and divine majesty is called with reference to itself is said substance-wise; whatever it is called with reference to another is said not substance- but relationship-wise; and that such is the force of the expression 'of the same substance' in Father and Son and Holy Spirit, that whatever is said with reference to self about each of them is to be taken as adding up in all three to a singular and not to a plural."[87] Augustine's central point here is that Father and Son can be in some sense different without being of different substance. To demonstrate this, Augustine is laboring to show that "Father" and "Son," though different words, do not denote different substances. Why? Because the words/titles denote different *relationships* without denoting different substances. The difficulty which lurks in the background, and which Augustine will face below, is how can some words be spoken of God substance-wise and some not?

Augustine proceeds to speak of the Holy Spirit, and it is clear that "making sense" of the Holy Spirit is a bit more difficult.[88] To speak of "father" and "son" as terms of relation seems rather normal, but to speak of "Holy Spirit" as a relationship term seems a bit awkward. The Father is the Father of the Son, and the Son is the Son of the Father. But, while the Holy Spirit is the Holy Spirit of the Father, the Father is not the "Father" of the Holy Spirit. Augustine will struggle with the proper name for, and place of, the Holy Spirit virtually through the end of *De Trinitate*.[89] But in Book V Augustine suggests why it is that the Son is born while the Holy Spirit proceeds, and why it is that the Holy Spirit is not *also* a son. Augustine suggests that perhaps it is the case that the Holy Spirit proceeds, not in the sense of being "born," but in the sense of being "given" because while the Son is not *our* Son, the Holy Spirit *is* in a sense *our* Spirit. As Augustine writes, "what has been given [i.e., the Holy Spirit] is referred both to him who gave and to those it was given to; and so the Holy Spirit is not only

---

87. Ibid., V.9.

88. Ibid., V.13.

89. Within the last few pages of *De Trinitate* (XV.48; 51 is the last section) Augustine is still asking how one can distinguish the *generation* from *procession*, and why the Son is *generated* while the Spirit *proceeds*. He answers his own question from quoting from one of his own previous sermons on John (XV.49; quoting *Homilies on the Gospel of John* 99, 8–9).

called the Spirit of the Father and the Son who gave him, but also our Spirit who received him."[90]

At the end of Book V Augustine briefly discusses the question of God's relationship to time, and whether God can be "lord" before there is something over which to be lord. And if it is the case the case that there was a time when God "became" lord, are we forced to say, after all, that something *is* said of God by way of modification?[91] Augustine suggests that again we are dealing with terms of relationship. Nothing in God's nature has changed when there became a created order over which he was Lord. Creation has come into being, but God has not changed: "Thus when he is called something with reference to creation, while indeed he begins to be called it in time, we should understand that this does not involve anything happening to God's own substance, but only to the created thing to which the relationship predicated of him refers."[92] Augustine continues, "anything that can begin to be said about God in time which was not said about him before is said by way of relationship, and yet not by way of a modification of God, as though something has modified him."[93]

Augustine begins book VI by looking at a biblical text which appears to complicate his goal of speaking and thinking about God correctly. The text is 1 Cor 1:24: "Christ the power and wisdom of God." Augustine states the apparent problem: "Equality seems to be lacking here, since the Father is not himself, according to this text, power and wisdom, but the begetter of power and wisdom."[94] Augustine wonders if this text, where God apparently is not *himself* power and wisdom, but apparently the *begetter* of power and wisdom, shows that virtually all substance words are really a type of relative predication. That is, should we say that God himself is not power, but only the begetter of the power by which he is powerful? Augustine is not willing to follow this line of argument, and ultimately concludes that it is necessary to affirm that the Father is not simply the begetter of power and wisdom, but is power and wisdom himself. That is, such words as power and wisdom are substance words, and not just words of relationship. As Augustine writes, "But for God it is the same thing to

90. Ibid., V.15.
91. Ibid., V.17.
92. Ibid.
93. Ibid.
94. Ibid., VI.1.

be as to be powerful or just or wise or anything else that can be said about his simple multiplicity or multiple simplicity to signify his substance."[95] Augustine also concludes that it is necessary that all substance words be applicable to both Father and Son: "that the Son is in no way equal to the Father, if he is found in any way that has to do with signifying his substance to be unequal."[96] Augustine then includes the Holy Spirit in his discussion and contends that substance words must be applicable to the Holy Spirit as well. He writes, "But just as it [i.e., the Holy Spirit] is substance together with the Father and the Son, so is it great together and good together and holy together with them and whatever else is said with reference to self, because with God it is not a different thing to be, and to be great or good etc."[97] The equality of the Holy Spirit with the other members of the Trinity is ultimately grounded in the simplicity of God: "the Holy Spirit is equal too, and if equal, equal in every respect, on account of the total simplicity which belongs to that substance."[98]

Toward the end of Book VI Augustine notes that the question he is exploring needs further attention, but he feels confident in stating some justifiable conclusions. He writes, "we have demonstrated as briefly as we could the equality of the triad and its one identical substance. So whatever may be the solution of this question, which we have put off for more searching examination, there is nothing now to prevent us from acknowledging the supreme equality of Father, Son, and Holy Spirit."[99]

Being of God as a Model

In our exposition of Gunton we saw that ontology has important applications. For Gunton, the being of God should serve as a model for life in this world. Specifically, the being of God serves as a model for anthropology and the Church. Thus, God as a community of persons, engaged in loving, reciprocal relationships should be reflected both in anthropology and the Church. Gunton contends Augustine is inadequate here because relationship is only a *logical*, and not an *ontological* concern—for Augustine relationship does *not* define what it means "to be." Augustine's

95. Ibid., VI.6.
96. Ibid.
97. Ibid., VI.7.
98. Ibid.
99. Ibid., VI.10.

failure to understand the being of God *as* the three persons in relationship keeps Augustine from affirming the being of God as a model for anthropology and the Church. With Gunton's criticism in view, let us turn to Augustine.

Gunton's criticisms are interesting at this point, for one way of reading *De Trinitate* is as a long exploration for how man (particularly the mind) models, or reflects the Trinity. However, Gunton would at this point reply that the very *nature* of Augustine's exploration is troubling, for Augustine looks in the *mind* (considered by Augustine to be basically *non*-material), rather than in the economy or in the rest of the created order (besides simply the human mind). Interestingly, at several points in *De Trinitate* Augustine does teach that the Trinity serves as a type of model. For example, in a discussion of the Holy Spirit, Augustine contends that the Holy Spirit is "that by which the two are joined each to the other, by which the begotten is loved by the one who begets him and in turn loves the begetter."[100] Augustine adds that this "mutuality," this closeness of the three persons of the Trinity is not found "in virtue of participation but of their very own being, not by gift of some superior but by their own gift."[101] What Augustine appears to be saying here is that somehow the intimate relations of the three persons constitute the being of God. And this mutuality is one Christians are to imitate: "We are bidden to imitate this mutuality by grace, both with reference to God and to each other, in the two precepts on which *the whole law and the prophets depend* (Matt 22:40)." Indeed, "In this way those three are one, only, great, wise, holy, and blessed god. But we find our blessedness *from him and through him and in him* (Rom 11:36), because it is by his gift that we are one with each other; with him we are one spirit (1 Cor 6:17), because our *soul is glued on behind him* (Ps 63:8)."[102]

While the Trinity as model does not appear to be central theme for Augustine, it is at least worth noting that Augustine scholars have at times found a similar emphasis in Augustine himself. Mary T. Clark, in her 1969 Saint Augustine Lecture, "Augustinian Personalism," speaks of "The Trinity, Archetype of Community."[103] Clark suggests that "Augustine

---

100. *De Trinitate* VI.7.
101. Ibid.
102. Ibid.
103. Clark, *Augustinian Personalism*.

looks to the ontological relationships within the Godhead for the clue as to the world's relation to God and particularly as pertaining to human vocation."[104] Clark can also suggest that Augustine's trinitarian thought was never simply abstract and removed from everyday life. Rather, the doctrine of the Trinity has direct implications for everyday, common life: "Thus, for Augustine, Trinitarian dogma was never merely a declarative statement about God's interior life; it was an ethical imperative for man."[105] Ultimately, with Augustine's emphasis on the relations within the Godhead, and we image that relating God, Clark contends that "the real relations within the Trinity became the paradigm for Christian moral life."[106] These trinitarian relations provide the "archetype of human community."[107]

On the whole, though, Augustine does not make a lot of use of the Trinity as "model." Augustine's goal in *De Trinitate* is to try to think and speak truthfully about God. The ultimate goal of the Christian life is to see God "face to face." The starts and fits which belabor Augustine in this volume is in trying to discern whether and to what extent the Triune God is somehow seen in creation and in the *imago Dei* in man. Although we have noted a key text where the Trinity *is* a model for Christians, the idea of the Trinity as model does not appear to be prime concern for Augustine in *De Trinitate*.

Persons, Substance, and Ontology

In our earlier treatment of Gunton we looked at some length at his suggestions for a distinctively Christian ontology, and the ways in which he sees Augustine to have failed in this area. Augustine fails largely because of his anti-incarnational platonism, and because Augustine, in looking to the human mind and *not* creation and redemption, renders God virtually unknowable. Gunton's chief criticism, though, is twofold: (1) Augustine simply did not understand the Cappadocian ontology of "being in relationship"; and (2) that Augustine embraces a non-Christian ontology which does not see "relationship" as constituting being, but as that which somehow is predicated of, or attaches to, being. With Gunton's key criticisms before us, let us turn to Augustine.

104. Ibid., 16.
105. Ibid., 18.
106. Ibid., 19.
107. Ibid., 20.

In Book VII Augustine deals in depth with a key question which has been raised and partially dealt with in Books V and VI, and in this book he most clearly synthesizes and approaches a solution to the various ontological and linguistic questions he has raised thus far. Augustine states the question as follows: "whether we can predicate of each person in the trinity by himself, and not just together with the other two, such names as God and great and wise and true and omnipotent and just and anything that can be said of God with reference to self as distinct from by way of relationship; or whether these names can only be predicated when the trinity or triad is meant."[108]

The difficulties posed by the text, "Christ the power of God and the wisdom of God" (1 Cor 1:24) are what brought this issue to the fore, and Augustine reduces the question to the following: "So the question is whether the Father taken singly is wise and is indeed his own wisdom, or whether he is wise in the same way as he is uttering."[109] That is, is the Father wise in himself, or he is wise by means of the wisdom (or here "Word"—thus the "uttering") he begets (i.e., the Son)? Augustine concludes that to say the Father is wise by means of the wisdom he begets leads to ludicrous conclusions. This is because in such a scheme the Son ends up the being of the Father; that is, the Son is not simply *of* the being of the Father, but the Son *is* the being of the Father, in that the Father does not have his being "in and of himself," but only by means of the Son. If the Father is only wise *by means of* the wisdom he begets, then the Father indeed is *not* wise in himself. And Augustine sees "wisdom" and "power" on an equal plane with all other like words. Since for Augustine "it is not one thing that makes him great and another that makes him God," words like "wisdom" and "power" are on a plane with "being." Thus, if the Father is wise and powerful by means of the wisdom and power he begets, then the Father also has "being" by the being he begets—which ultimately means the Father does not have being in and of himself.

Ultimately, to say that the Father is wise by means of the wisdom he begets logically entails that the Father cannot be said to have Being by himself, because Being also becomes a relationship word. Augustine writes, "in the case we are considering, if being is predicated by way of

---

108. Ibid., VII.1.
109. Ibid.

relationship, then being is not being."¹¹⁰ Augustine's position is that "every being that is called something by way of relationship is also something besides the relationship."¹¹¹ Thus, Augustine concludes that certainly the Father has being in and of himself, and one is required to affirm that the Father is wise and powerful in himself, and not simply in relation to, or by means of the Son he begets. He writes, "So if the Father is not also something with reference to himself, there is absolutely nothing there to be talked of with reference to something else."¹¹²

Augustine outlines his conclusion as follows: "With God to be is the same as to be wise. If then in this case to be is the same as to be wise, it follows that the Father is not wise with the wisdom he has begotten; otherwise he did not beget it, but it begot him."¹¹³ Ultimately, words like "wisdom" and "power" are substance, not relationship words. Augustine contends, "So Father and son are together one wisdom because they are one being, and one by one they are wisdom from wisdom as they are being from being. And therefore it does not follow that because the Father is not the Son nor the Son the Father, or one is unbegotten, the other begotten, that therefore they are not one being; for these names only declare their relationships. But both together are one wisdom and one being, where to be is the same as to be wise; they are not however both together Word or Son, because it is not the same here to be as to be Word or Son, since as we have quite sufficiently shown, these are terms of relationship."¹¹⁴ Finally, Augustine can write, "the Father is wisdom, the Son is wisdom, the Holy Spirit is wisdom; and together they are not three wisdoms but one wisdom; and because in their case to be is the same as to be wise, Father and Son and Holy Spirit are one being."¹¹⁵

At the heart of Augustine's whole discussion has been his belief in the immutability and simplicity of God. The Arians also affirmed the simplicity of God, and their radical insistence on this theological axiom ultimately drove them to deny the deity of the Son. Augustine had to figure out a way to affirm both the simplicity of God *and* the full deity

---

110. Ibid., VII.2.
111. Ibid.
112. Ibid.
113. Ibid.
114. Ibid., VII.3.
115. Ibid., VII.6.

of the Son. To do this he had to affirm the simplicity of God, God's one essence, the Son's (and Spirit's) consubstantiality with the Father, *and* the reality of three ... somethings! Thus, Augustine affirmed the simplicity of God and the idea that all apparent accidental predicates are actually either substantive or relative predicates. Thus, nothing in God "changes" or is complex, but there are nonetheless things that can be said of God, without being said according to substance (*substantialiter*). Thus, when we speak of "Father" and "Son" we are speaking in terms of relation, or what can be called relative predications. Edmund Hill summarizes Augustine as follows: "God is one in respect of substantive predications, yet three in virtue of certain relative predications which, following the scriptural revelation, we make of him."[116]

Augustine continues in Book VII with a rather rigorous investigation of the terms "persons" and "substance." It is again important to notice Augustine's reticence in speaking about God. He begins section seven by writing, "And so, for the sake of talking about inexpressible matters, that we may somehow express what we are completely unable to express..."[117] He also contends that "the total transcendence of the godhead quite surpasses the capacity of ordinary speech. God can be thought about more truly than he can be talked about, and he is more truly than he can be thought about."[118] We should also recognize, with Christopher Stead, the somewhat complex nature of such words as οὐσία, ὑπόστασις, *essentia* and *substantia*. For example, Stead has convincingly argued that οὐσία and ὑπόστασις had a number of possible meanings, and that while *most* of the possible meanings for οὐσία could be "matched" by the possible meanings for ὑπόστασις, the words can very often be distinguished as well.[119] Additionally, while οὐσία, ὑπόστασις, *essentia* and *substantia* have their own pre-Christian and Pre-Augustinian history, we must pay attention to how Augustine and the history of trinitarian reflection which precedes him uses such terms. We must allow for the possibility that in seeking to speak about God Augustine not only uses this or that term, but

---

116. Hill, *Mystery of the Trinity*, 100.

117. *De Trinitate* VII.7.

118. Ibid.

119. See Stead, *Divine Substance*, 131–222; idem, *Philosophy in Christian Antiquity*, 148–86.

uses a term in his own unique way, and his usage may have both continuity and discontinuity with past usage.[120]

Augustine suggests that the Greek and Latin theologians are in basic agreement about the Trinity. Different words are used, but they are nonetheless saying the same basic thing. Greek theologians speak of one being οὐσία, three substances ὑπόστασις, while Latin theologians speak of one being (*essentia*) or substance (*substantia*), three persons (*personae*). Augustine notes that in Latin the equivalents of the Greek "being" (οὐσία) and "substance" (ὑπόστασις) are virtually identical, so Latin theologians instead speak of one "substance" (*substantia*) and three "persons" (*personae*).[121]

How important are these actual terms? Augustine's conclusion is that these particular terms are not as important as the concepts themselves, and that these particular terms were developed out of necessity. He writes, "Perhaps we just have to admit that these various usages were developed by the sheer necessity of saying something, when the fullest possible argument was called for against the traps or the errors of the heretics."[122] Indeed, "Human inadequacy was trying by speech to bring to the notice of men what it held about the Lord God its creator, according to its capacity, in the inner sanctum of the mind, whether this was held by devout faith or by the least amount of understanding."[123] We should note two things. First, we see again Augustine's contention that humans are limited beings, and that our statements about God are by necessity limited, but that speaking about God is nonetheless a good thing. Second, we see that part of the motivation for speaking correctly about God is to be able to speak *against* heretical movements. Augustine is clear that he wants to

---

120. We should note that one of Gunton's central points, as we have discussed earlier, is that the Cappadocians essentially forged a new Christian ontology. In so doing, they used *ousia* and *hypostasis* in such a way that in the effort to speak of the Triune God a new Christian ontology was formed. Cf. Gunton, *Promise*, 71–81.

121. I am simply summarizing, and not criticizing Augustine at this point. The terms οὐσία and ὑπόστασις are not easily summarized, and simply to say they are synonymous would be a bit misleading. As Christopher Stead, in his *Divine Substance*, 131, has written, "The usage of οὐσία in the early Christian centuries presents more problems than is commonly supposed." See Stead, "The Word *Ousia* in Late Antiquity" and "God's Substance in Theological Tradition," both in *Divine Substance*, 131–56, 157–89. Cf. idem, "The Concept of Divine Substance," in *Substance and Illusion*, 1–14; idem, *Philosophy in Christian Antiquity*, 143–86.

122. *De Trinitate* VII.9.

123. Ibid.

avoid both tritheism and modalism. On the danger of tritheism, he writes that we should not say "three beings, in case it should be taken as meaning any diversity in that supreme and ultimate equality."[124] On modalism, he writes, "On the other hand it could not say that there are not three somethings, because Sabellius fell into heresy by saying precisely that." Thus, our statements about God must seek to guard against both the tendencies toward tritheism and modalism, and "human inadequacy searched for a word to express three what, and it said substances or persons."[125] Later in the book Augustine will reiterate his desire to avoid both tritheistic and modalistic tendencies. At the end of Book VII he writes, "There must be neither confusion or mixing up of the persons, nor such distinction of them as may imply any disparity."[126] Augustine concludes, "By these names it did not wish to give any idea of diversity, but it wished to avoid any idea of singleness; so that as well as understanding unity in God, whereby there is said to be one being, we might also understand trinity, whereby there are also said to be three substances or persons" (although Augustine will end up saying that ultimately we should not say three "substances," but rather simply three "persons").[127]

Augustine will ultimately argue that "essence" (*essentia*) is a better word than "substance" (*substantia*) when describing God. Augustine's reasoning seems to run as follows. He states that "we get substance from to subsist."[128] Augustine contends that technically speaking if we say that God subsists, and can be called substance, we are saying that "something is in him as in its underlying subject, and he is not simple." That is, to say God subsists is to sever God from his attributes. For example, regarding "goodness," to say God subsists is to say that God somehow "underlies" his goodness. Augustine writes, "But it is impious to say that God subsists to and underlies his goodness, and that goodness is not his substance, or rather his being, nor is God his goodness, but it is in him as in an underlying subject."[129] But Augustine is willing to be flexible with the terms, as long as the concepts are maintained. And the key idea he wishes to affirm

124. Ibid.
125. Ibid.
126. Ibid., VII.12.
127. Ibid., VII.9.
128. Ibid.
129. Ibid., VII.10.

is that whether substance or being is used, it must be affirmed that whatever is said regarding substance or being is said regarding God (i.e., the entire Godhead), and not simply regarding one or other of the persons. As Augustine writes, "But in any case, whether he is called being, which he is called properly, or substance which he is called improperly, either word is predicated with reference to self, not by way of relationship with reference to something else. So for God to be is the same as to subsist, and therefore if the trinity is one being, it is also one substance."[130]

If one does not want to say three "substances," and Augustine does not, perhaps it is best to say three "persons." Just as it is one and the same thing for God to be and to be wise, so for Augustine it is one and the same thing for God to be and to be person. But this takes us back to a familiar conundrum. It is one and the same thing for God to be and to be person. But if this is so, since we say three persons, why can we not say three beings? Or, on the other hand, since we say one being, why can we not say simply one person? Augustine's answer is a bit startling: "So the only reason, it seems, why we do not call these three together one person, as we call them one being and one God, but say three persons while we never say three Gods or three beings, is that we want to keep at least one word for signifying what we mean by trinity, so that we are not simply reduced to silence when we are asked three what, after we have confessed that there are three."[131] Augustine explores this question, playing with the idea that perhaps we can speak of God in terms of genus and species. That is, "being" might be a genus word, and "substance" (in the Greek/Eastern sense) or "person" might be species words. For example, "man" could be a genus word, while Abraham, Isaac and Jacob are species words. But we are up against a familiar problem. We would not say one "man," three "persons," but three men, three persons, with men denoting the genus, and persons denoting the species. And this certainly could not be applied analogously to God, for God *is* three persons, but *not* three beings.[132]

It is true that Augustine's doctrine of the Trinity differs from many of his predecessors, particularly those of the East (e.g., the Cappadocian Fathers), but also in certain ways from some in the West (e.g., Tertullian). One key difference from certain predecessors is the issue of the origin

130. Ibid.
131. Ibid., VII.11.
132. Ibid.

of the second and third persons of the Trinity. The Cappadocians held that the Son and the Spirit had their origin in the Father, and as such, derive their deity from the Father. Augustine was more interested in affirming that the three members of the Trinity ultimately possessed a common deity, without confessing that this deity was "from" the Father. But this Augustinian theme, interestingly, might be used to buttress and affirm the reality and importance of the three persons. Augustine wants to argue that *each* person of the Trinity ultimately possesses "full" deity, and this "possession" of deity is not because they derive this deity from a person "higher up" (i.e., the Father). Thus, it might be argued that in an Augustinian view an importance is placed on the full, eternal deity of each of the persons, a deity which is not derived from another person, but which is rightfully and "naturally" the possession of each person.[133]

It is important to note that with Augustine, the persons are centrally important. We have noted above that there is not an abstract essence undergirding the three persons. Indeed, "that triad is what this nature is."[134] Also, "there is nothing else, of course, of this being besides this triad."[135] That is, according to Augustine there *is* nothing else besides the three persons.

We should also note that while a type of *perichoresis* is often found in the Cappadocians (and more fully in John of Damascus), at least a trace of the concept can be found in *De Trinitate*. Augustine here is concerned to affirm the simplicity of God as well as the individuality of the three persons and their intimate relationship with one another. He writes, "Nor because he is three must we think of him as triple, or three by multiplication; otherwise the Father alone or the Son alone would be less than the Father and the Son together."[136] But while there are three persons, their unity must not be forfeited: "admittedly it is not easy to see how you can talk of the father alone or the Son alone, since the Father is always and inseparably with the Son and the Son with the Father." And *perichoresis* is seen in what follows: "not that both are Father or both Son, but that they are always in each other and neither is alone."[137] A type of *perichoresis* is

---

133. Cf. Wolfson, *Philosophy of the Church Fathers*, 353.
134. *De Trinitate* XV.43.
135. Ibid., VII.11.
136. Ibid., VI.9.
137. Ibid.

also seen in Augustine's discussion of how traces of the trinity can even be seen in the created order. Augustine writes, "In that supreme triad is the source of all things, and the most perfect beauty, and wholly blissful delight." He continues, "Those three seem both to be bounded or determined by each other, and yet in themselves to be unbounded or infinite... . So they are each in each and all in each, and each in all and all in all, and all are one."[138] In short, Augustine wishes to affirm both the essential unity of the one Triune God, while also affirming the reality of three persons in intimate and inseparable relation to one another.

At this point Augustine suggests that perhaps we should speak in terms of *nature* (φύσις).[139] He notes that this term was used before "substance" and "being" were common terms, and perhaps "nature" would be helpful in speaking about God. Thus, the issue would be on "common material." Augustine uses an example of gold and three gold statues. Instead of speaking in terms of genus and species, the example works in terms of three things with "a common material" (and of course Augustine is no longer using a biological example). However, Augustine concludes that this example ultimately is also unhelpful. The Trinity, unlike the three gold statues, is not "three things consisting of one material." Also, with the Trinity we do not speak of "three persons out of the same being, as though what being is were one thing and what persons is another, as we can talk about three statues out of the same gold."[140] With the gold statues "being gold is one thing, being the statutes another," but this is not the case with the Trinity. The "man"/"three men" example is also problematic, because whereas with men, it is always possible for another man (and another and another) to emerge out of that nature, such is not possible with the Triune God. Additionally, Augustine notes that with both the gold statues and man/three men examples there is a sort of math problem when compared to the Triune God. With gold statues and men, the higher number of statues or men increases the amount of gold or "menness." With the Trinity this is not the case, since Father and Son combined are not more being than the Father alone or the Son alone. Augustine writes, "those three substances or persons together, if that is what they must be

---

138. Ibid., VI.12.
139. Ibid., VII.11.
140. Ibid.

called, are equal to each one singly," and this truth is not perceived by the sensual man.[141]

Augustine closes Book VII by returning to a brief discussion of the image of God, which has been introduced briefly in Book VII, and will occupy much of the rest of *De Trinitate*. Having struggled to discern how to speak of the Trinity thus far, Augustine now encourages his readers to "go" inside and seek to discover the trinitarian image of God in man. In the midst of this discussion he briefly discusses the way some words refer to the "self" of God, while other words are spoken in terms of relationship. Thus, with "I and the Father are one" (John 10:30), "one" is spoken in terms of being, while "are" is spoken in terms of the relationship between Father and Son. Some texts do not even contain "being" words, although the oneness of God is understood. For example, John 14:23 says, "We will come to him, I and the Father, and will dwell with him." Augustine concludes, "'We will come and dwell' is in the plural, because the subject is 'I and the Father,' that is, the Son and the Father which signify mutual relationships."[142] Similarly, on Gen 1:26, "Let *us* make man in our image," Augustine writes, "'Let us make' and 'our' are in the plural, and must be understood in terms of relationships."[143]

Augustine's extended search for the right way to speak and think about God in Books V–VII ends with the definite sense that Augustine knows he has not truly reached a satisfactory statement or understanding. Books VIII and following will turn "inward" into man and seek to discover some sort of trace of the Trinity in the image of God in man. For now, Augustine ends with the following encouragement. Speaking of the need in one's articulation of the Trinity to at least avoid both tritheism and modalism, Augustine writes, "If this cannot be grasped by understanding, let it be held by faith, until he shines in our minds who said through the prophet, *Unless you believe, you will not understand* (Isaiah 7:9)."[144]

In attempting to draw some conclusions regarding Augustine's position in *De Trinitate* on substance, essence, persons and relations, we need to consider the notion that Augustine may be influenced by Aristotelian tendencies, but shapes these influences such that he uses them for his own

---

141. Ibid. Augustine here quotes 1 Cor 2:14.
142. Ibid., VII.12.
143. Ibid.
144. Ibid..

ends. One scholar who argues along these general lines is Ronald J. Teske.[145] Teske suggests, "Augustine uses '*substantia*' and '*essentia*' in speaking of God in a fashion that would seem to indicate that he means to say that God is an Aristotelian substance, albeit an Aristotelian substance unlike any other."[146] With Teske we should note that Augustine suggests that we use *substantia* of God in an "improper" sense, and that ultimately *essentia* is the more "proper" term.[147] Thus, the primacy given to *essentia* is an "un-Aristotelian" move. However, this move by Augustine is not necessarily unique, since, as Teske notes, "this combination of the Aristotelian and Platonic traditions is not a concoction original with Augustine. Rather in the '*libri platonicorum*' with which Augustine came into contact in the year before his baptism in Milan, he found ready-made this transformation of the Aristotelian '*ousia*' into the intelligible, immutable, and eternal being of the Neoplatonists." And Augustine drew a connection between this Neoplatonist conception and the *ego sum qui sum* in Exodus 3:14.[148]

Teske's summary of Augustine on the Aristotelian themes of substance and accident is accurate and helpful: "Since there can be no accident in God, what seems to be said of God according to accident must be understood to be said of him according to substance, that is must be understood to signify or designate the substance of God."[149]

In another article, Ronald Teske attempts to defend Augustine's position that affirms both that (1) there are no accidents in God, *and* (2)

---

145. Specifically, Teske, "Properties of God," 1–19; idem, "Augustine's Use of '*Substantia*,'" 147–63; Durrant, *Theology and Intelligibility*. Cf. La Croix, "Augustine on the Simplicity of God," 468–69; Wainwright, "Augustine on God's Simplicity," 118–23; La Croix, "Wainwright, Augustine and God's Simplicity," 124–27.

146. Teske, "Augustine's Use of '*Substantia*,'" 159.

147. Ibid.

148. Ibid. Cf. Booth, "St. Augustine's *notitia sui*," 70–104; idem, "St. Augustine's *de Trinitate*." Booth's concerns are a bit outside of our interests here. Booth argues that Augustine's emphasis on knowledge of self is not simply a result of platonic or neo-platonic influence. He argues that Augustine's interest in self-knowledge should be traced to Aristotle's notion of *noesis noeseos* found in *Metaphysics* Book V. Booth's main point is captured in the following quote (Booth, "St. Augustine's *notitia sui*," 102): "The hermeneutically developed Aristotelian conception of self-thinking alongside the Aristotelian notions of beatitude and contemplation and the Platonist conception of gradations of reality—the results of the mutations by style of commentary and the spirit of Romanitas—were the objects to which Augustine applied his mind particularly when he wrote his *De Trinitate*."

149. Teske, "Augustine's Use of *Substantia*," 149.

there are contingent predications about God.[150] Teske argues, in my view persuasively, that Augustine's argument that God can be immutable, but can still "possess" relative properties is coherent. That is, God can be both unchangeable, and can be said to "begin" to be something at a certain point in time. For example, we can say (1) God is unchangeable and (2) God began to be Lord of Israel at a certain point in history. How? In short, God has not changed, but a nation—Israel—was called into being at a certain point in history. Thus, nothing in God's being has changed; rather, something in the created order has come into existence, or changed. God has not changed, the change is in that to which he relates.[151] Teske summarizes Augustine's position nicely: "Since the being that God is is utterly unchangeable, the change requisite for the truth of the statement must be in the creature with respect to which God is said to be relatively."[152] God can also be said to be my refuge, and the same principle would apply. Teske writes, "when God begins to be said to be my refuge, the new relative property ascribed to God need not signify a change in God. Indeed, given his immutability, it cannot. The change requisite for the truth of the proposition rather lies in me who take (*sic*) refuge in him."[153] Teske intentionally forgoes discussing Augustine's actual doctrine of the Trinity, preferring to limit the discussion simply to a discussion of the logical coherency of both affirming immutability (as well as simplicity) and attributing relative properties to God.

Conclusion

Let us draw together Augustine's general position on essence/substance, nature, persons and relations. There is little doubt that Augustine *does* emphasize the oneness of God. For example, in the first book of *De Trinitate* Augustine summarizes Catholic commentary on Scripture as follows: "Father and Son and Holy Spirit in the inseparable equality of one substance present a divine unity; and therefore there are not three gods but one God."[154] Augustine contends that such texts as 1 Tim 6:16, which

---

150. Teske, "Properties of God."
151. Ibid., 11–16.
152. Ibid., 14.
153. Ibid., 14. Presumably, the sentence should either read: (1) "... lies in *we* who take ..."; or (2) "... lies in *me* who *takes* ..."
154. *De Trinitate* I.7.

speaks of "God alone" dwelling in immortality, does "not refer to the Father alone but to the one and only God which the trinity is."[155] However, all these quotations come from the opening book of *De Trinitate*, where Augustine's point is not really simply to affirm the oneness of substance, but rather to affirm the full and complete unity and equality of the three persons. The background to Augustine's concerns, and we have dealt with this above, is most likely some sort of "Arian" challenge, which denies the deity of Christ.[156] Augustine can write of certain persons: "Those who have affirmed that our Lord Jesus Christ is not God, or is not true God, or is not with the Father the one and only God, or is not truly immortal because he is subject to change."[157] In light of this challenge, Augustine will argue at length for the deity of Christ, contending that the Son and the Father are of the same substance.[158]

However, it must also be said that Augustine is not simply emphasizing the one timeless essence of God. For example, Augustine at times wants to stress that the being of God does not somehow underlie the three persons. He writes, "And yet we do talk of the three persons of the same being, or three persons one being; but we do not talk about three persons out of the same being, as though what being is were one thing and what persons is another, as we can talk about three statues out of the same gold."[159] That is, Augustine here wants to stress that the being of God is not anterior to the three persons, nor does the being of God underlie the three persons. For indeed, the being and persons in one sense are *not* two different things which can be separated in any way. What Augustine appears to want to affirm is that ultimately the three persons are the one

---

155. Ibid., I.10.

156. Michel René Barnes suggests that Augustine's opponents in book I are Eunomians, who were basically "Arians" during Augustine's time. See Barnes, "Exegesis and Polemic in Augustine's *De Trinitate* I." However, Edmund Hill suggests that Augustine has no *particular* heresy in mind, but rather a general attitude: "What he [Augustine] is on the defensive against is not so much particular heresies or errors, as a certain attitude of mind." Hill suggests that in book I Augustine's polemic is directed against "intellectual roughness and impatience which demands cut-and-dried solutions to problems, and quickly." See Hill's note in his translation of *De Trinitate*, 91 n. 14.

157. *De Trinitate* I.8.

158. Cf. ibid., I.9, where Augustine argues, that since "all things were made through him [i.e., Christ]; therefore he is of one and the same substance as the Father. And thus he is not only God, but also true God." Cf. also V.6, where Augustine writes, "although being Father is different from being son, there is no difference of substance."

159. *De Trinitate* VII.11

God. Augustine writes: "In the nature of divinity, or of the deity if you prefer it, *that triad is what this nature is*, and is unchangeable and always equal within itself; nor was it some time not or some time different."[160] Similarly, Augustine in Book VII also contends that, in the end, all there is is the three persons. There is not some essence undergirding the three persons. Augustine writes that we do not "talk about the trinity as being three persons or substances, one being and one God, as thought they were three things consisting of one material, even if whatever that material might be it were wholly used up in these three." Indeed, "for there is nothing else, of course, of this being besides the triad."[161] Augustine here seems to say that the three persons *are* the nature of God, which seems to be very similar to the conception Gunton sees, and favors in the Cappadocians.

We have seen that essence (*essentia*) is ultimately to be preferred to substance (*substantia*), since substance is prone to being understood as that which is "under" the thing itself, rather than simply the thing itself. However, Augustine is also clear that essence and substance *language* is a secondary concern to the *concepts* and *realities* themselves. Augustine does not argue that these terms must be used, but admits that a main impetus for trying to speak truthfully about God are the twin errors of tritheism and modalism. Augustine thus wishes to fend off error, and he is quite happy to concede that his construals and efforts are impartial and limited, and necessarily so, given the nature of the subject of discussion: the Triune God. Ὑπόστασις and *persona* similarly are words that the Christian tradition has appropriated, and that the more important issue is the actual concept which is being considered. We have noted that when Augustine finally discusses what is actually meant by "persons" (*personae*), his answer appears to be less than satisfactory. He notes that we use the word "person" so that we are not reduced to silence when asked, "three *what*?" Gunton and others have argued that this text in particular points to serious weaknesses in Augustine's doctrine of the Trinity. If Augustine's position/logic leads him to such a conclusion, surely something must be wrong with Augustine's fundamental understanding of the Trinity. Perhaps this is true, but in fairness to Augustine we should note that on Augustine's own terms, and given his own presuppositions, Augustine's position generally makes sense. As we have noted, Augustine contends

---

160. Ibid., XV.43. (emphasis mine).
161. Ibid., VII.11.

that the words we use in describing the Trinity (particularly *personae*) have been appropriated, at least in part, in order to demarcate the bounds of proper belief—to ward off heresy. While we also want to speak *positively* about God, Augustine concedes that our best efforts are rather limited (although not useless), and that while *personae* serves a certain purpose, it does not really allow us to penetrate the mystery of the Trinity in a thoroughgoing way. Whether other persons or traditions can make a better case for this or that word is a question we will not deal with here, but given Augustine's own concerns and presuppositions, his use of *persons* is generally satisfying.

CHAPTER 6

A Critique of Colin Gunton

THE LAST FOUR CHAPTERS have been devoted to exposition; chapters two and three centered on Gunton, and chapters four and five centered on Augustine. By doing this we have been able to lay out before us the key issues and arguments. We have seen that throughout Gunton's writings appear the recurring themes of the One and the Many, the continuity between creation and redemption, and the necessity of a Christian trinitarian ontology. Throughout his writings we have seen that Gunton's ancient mentors are primarily Irenaeus and the Cappadocian Fathers. We have also seen that if Irenaeus and the Cappadocians are his theological friends, Augustine is a theological foe. Augustine shows up repeatedly in Gunton's writings, and virtually always in a negative way. Augustine, with his emphases on the unity and oneness of God, his platonic and anti-material bias, his diminishing of particularity, and his forfeiture of Cappadocian insights, has been more of a bane than blessing in the history of Western thought. Indeed, Gunton can trace modernity to Augustine.

This is a significant reconstruction of the history of Western thought, and deserves attention. Having engaged in exposition, it is time to turn to criticism. In our criticisms we will be looking at Gunton's theology as a whole, but we will also be directing our attention especially to his generally anti-Augustinian tendency which we have shown to pervade his work.

My criticisms will proceed as follows. I will basically follow the structure of chapters two through five. After a brief section on the usefulness of Gunton's schema of the One and the Many, I will offer criticisms under the broad categories of Creation and Redemption, and Ontology.

The One and the Many

I have suggested that one of the overarching themes in Gunton's work is the theme of the One and the Many. This theme is most explicitly seen in *The One, the Three and the Many*, where it functions as *the* paradigm against which Gunton unpacks his historical reconstruction of Western thought. Gunton can write, "The question of the one and many takes us to the very beginnings of philosophy and theology."[1] As Gunton sees it, the history of thought is in one sense the ongoing battle between heirs of Parmenides on the one hand, and Heraclitus on the other.[2] He writes that Parmenides and Heraclitus "present to later thought what are often considered to be exhaustive possibilities for an approach to the question of the one and the many. In variations between the two can be seen to lie one of the continuities linking the thought of every age since their time, so that the dialectic of the one and the many has provided the framework for most subsequent thinking about many of the basic topics of thought."[3]

The centrality of the schema of the One and the Many as a backdrop to the history of Western thought is important in Gunton's system, because it serves, in a true sense, as the "problem" for which the Trinity is the "answer." That is, after showing that the One and the Many is a perennial issue in the history of thought, and then showing that the twin tendencies towards "oneness" or "manyness" always lead to various problems, Gunton can argue that the only true answer to the dilemma is the doctrine of the Trinity, where the One and the Many are joined in perfect harmony. And on Gunton's terms this makes sense. If a flawed understanding of God leads to the plethora of problems we see today, surely a true understanding of God is at least a key step in putting us in the right direction. Since, in Gunton's view cultures have almost always affirmed that God in some way "may be conceived to constitute or to undergird the unity of things," it follows that one's view of God is going to shape one's view of everything else.[4] One's view of the world is rooted in one's view of God: "from the

---

1. *One, the Three and the Many*, 17.
2. Ibid.
3. Ibid., 18.
4. Ibid., 24.

beginning of Western thought the concept of God, or its equivalent, has served to provide a focus for the unity of the world."[5]

At least two things, one positive and one negative, can be said about this way of viewing the history of Western thought. Positively, it should be said that Gunton is certainly correct in thinking *theologically* about the past, and about the history of Western thought in particular. That is, Gunton's schema is a thoroughly theological construal, and he is to be lauded for attempting to understand the history of thought in relation to the reality of God. On Christian terms this is certainly important. Many analyses will give attention to the secularization of the West, or some similar notion, and many older historians portray the history of thought in explicitly theological terms, noting that God is sovereign over history, and rules over history as its sovereign Lord. However, in the contemporary academy to read a history of Western thought which posits the Triune God at the center is a unique experience. Any critique of Western thought which seeks to be faithful to historic Christianity must follow, on the whole, Gunton's emphasis on the centrality of a culture's view of God. Rather than simply point to the rise of autonomous reason, or to the ideological, philosophical or other cultural shifts, a full-orbed Christian critique *does* need to probe into how a culture views God. On biblical grounds, God is sovereign over all of history (Acts 17:26). He raises and brings down nations (Job 12:23; Ps 22:28). Gunton is engaged in a view of history which takes seriously the Teacher's words, "What has been will be again, what has been done will be done again; there is nothing new under the sun" (Eccl 1:9). Gunton is concerned to ask, how do certain ideas show up repeatedly in history, and how do different ideas yield different social, cultural and political consequences. Given texts like Eccl 1:9, this is the right question. A Christian view of history should certainly take the "long view," and ask how current trends are a reflection of, or a reworking of, very old ideas or tendencies in human history.

On a negative side, while Gunton is to be praised for his general approach, it is worth asking whether his specific schema is helpful. That is, is the grid of the One and the Many the most helpful for understanding the history of Western thought? One does not have to accept David Cunningham's suggestion that Gunton has accepted a Hegelian notion of thesis and antithesis to ask if the scheme of the One and the Many

---

5. Ibid., 22.

is helpful.⁶ Does it generate the kind of insights necessary for a proper understanding of where we are and where we have been? One might ask, is the scheme of the One and the Many the best way of construing the history of Western thought? On Christian and biblical grounds might there not be other contenders? For example, would a better schema perhaps be something like Belief and Unbelief.⁷ From Genesis to Revelation, the schema which Scripture seems both to affirm and at times implicitly presuppose (cf. Gen 3:15ff.; Deut 28) is that of belief and unbelief.⁸ For example, in Romans 1 it is clear that a lack of recognition of, and obedience to the one true God elicits the judgment of God. In Rom 1:21 Paul can write, "For although they knew God, they neither glorified him as God nor gave thanks to him, but their thinking became futile and their foolish hearts were darkened. Although they claimed to be wise, they became fools and exchanged the glory of the immortal God for images made to look like mortal man and birds and animals and reptiles" (1:21–23). The judgment of God is seen in the next verse (1:24), where God "gave them over" to various forms of sexual immorality, because of their failure to glorify God and give thanks to Him. Texts like these seem to show that in the Christian tradition there *is* a connection between a people's relation to God and the shape of that culture. However, the connection or relationship is not primarily rooted in their *ideas* of God *per se*, but in whether the people glorify and thank God. It is dangerous to oppose "heart" and "head," but it is important to note that according to Paul's logic, the failure to glorify God and thank him *lead to* false thinking about God. That is, "futile" thinking appears to be the *result* of failing to glorify God and give thanks to Him.

It may be that Gunton's historical reconstruction is here incomplete. What I am trying to argue is that in the Christian tradition, especially in its most central text, Scripture, there *is* a connection between a culture's situation and its view of God. However, Gunton's schema appears to give inadequate attention to the central importance of belief and unbelief, and

---

6. Cunningham, *These Three Are One*, 39, writes: Gunton "reads the history of thought through a Hegelian scheme of thesis and antithesis."

7. For a criticism along somewhat similar lines, see S. Williams, *Revelation and Reconciliation*.

8. For my present purposes I am not concerned to delineate the relationship between belief and obedience. I am assuming that true belief leads to obedience, and that true obedience is rooted in faith.

that Scripture is centrally concerned to point out the connection that exists between the state of a culture and its spiritual state. Gunton, on the other hand emphasizes the relation between the state of a culture and its *ideas* about God. If a culture had the right *ideas* about God (say, a Cappadocian understanding of the Triune God), would that culture flourish? It appears that Paul's argument is that a culture must not simply have the right *ideas* of God, that culture must also glorify God and give thanks to Him, and this latter emphasis is missing in Gunton.[9] Ideas do have consequences, but I would contend that on biblical and Christian grounds, ideas are one part of a bigger picture of human relation to the divine, and for Gunton's system to work, it would be wise for him to incorporate this bigger picture of the divine-human relationship.

Creation

The twin doctrines of creation and redemption provided a focus for chapters three and five of the monograph. I begin with those emphases and will trace out my initial criticisms with those themes in view.

The doctrine of creation is key to Gunton's scheme. Indeed, the doctrines of Trinity and creation provide the backbone to Gunton's theology. In Gunton's work, all other doctrines revolve around these two emphases. Perhaps the greatest strength of Gunton's view is that, like his mentor Irenaeus, Gunton is so ruthlessly persistent in combating a type of modern gnosticism. Gunton really does want to affirm the goodness and purposiveness of *this* created order.[10] *This* world is here for a reason, and God is working out his good purposes and designs for this world.[11] Gunton is certainly right that much of modern Christianity is subtlety gnostic.[12]

In his article, "The Doctrine of Creation," Gunton contends that the three key features of a doctrine of creation are (1) "creation as an article of the creed"; (2) "creation out of nothing"; (3) "creation as a work of the whole Trinity." Augustine certainly does affirm points one and two; creation is an article of the creed, and creation is out of nothing. However,

---

9. Gunton does speak in other places about relating to God, but this theme is never related to his overall reconstruction of the history of Western thought, and to his thesis regarding the One and the Many.

10. Among many places, see *Christ and Creation*, 91.

11. "Doctrine of Creation," 141–44.

12. For Gunton's understanding of gnosticism, see *Triune Creator*, 47–50.

as we have noted, Gunton contends that Augustine's doctrine of creation continues to be plagued by his residual neoplatonism.[13] Gunton also contends that whereas before Augustine theologians moved from "the incarnation to the goodness of the creator order," Augustine himself accepts the *conclusion* (i.e., *creatio ex nihilo*), but he does not get there by the traditional means (i.e., moving from the incarnation to the goodness of the created order). Rather, Gunton charges that Augustine's doctrine of creation out of nothing is rooted in Augustine's defense of the radically sovereign and free will of God.

Perhaps one of the first things that should be said in response to Gunton is that in Augustine's theology the created order is good, *even if it is a lesser good than ultimate spiritual realities*. That is, in Augustine there appears to be *limited* dualism, where the created order (especially the physical realm) is viewed as somewhat less than higher, spiritual realities. Creation is fundamentally *good* in Augustine's view of things.[14] Indeed, Augustine can write, commenting on Genesis 1, "when we hear, *And God saw that it was good*, we recognize that creation was approved by the benevolence of the Spirit of God; not that the work pleased the Holy Spirit as something known after it was made, rather that it pleased Him that it should remain in existence by that same Divine Goodness which previously was pleased that it should be created."[15] Even after the sin the created order remains a fundamentally good thing: "But creatures that lose their own proper beauty by sinning can in no way undo the fact that even they, considered as part of a world ruled by God's providence, are good when taken with the whole of creation."[16] Indeed, "whenever creatures individually lose their loveliness by sin, nevertheless the whole of creation with them included always remain beautiful."[17] Hence, for Augustine the creation is fundamentally good, and even after the entrance of sin into the world the creation *remains* fundamentally good.

---

13. Ibid., 74.
14. *De Moribus Ecclesia Catholicae et de Moribus Manichaeorum* II.4.
15. *De Genesis ad litteram* II.6.14.
16. Ibid., III.24.36.
17. Ibid.

Creation and God's Will

One criticism Gunton offers deserves particular attention. Gunton laments that creation for Augustine is simply the result of God's will. Gunton can write that "Augustine is a theologian of the will," and that "Augustine's stress on God's willing of the world leaves little reason except sheer will."[18] Augustine contributes to the West a tendency for the "conception of creation as the outcome of arbitrary will."[19] This charge is as serious as it is puzzling. When speaking of God, what does it mean to say that something God does is an act of "sheer" or "arbitrary" will? Several things can be said in response to this criticism. First, such a criticism, on my view, fails to consider the seriousness with which Augustine contends for the simplicity of God. One of the reasons Augustine spends so much time searching for the correct way to think and speak about God is that he affirms the *simplicity* of God, while at the same time affirming that there really are three persons who really are fully equal, consubstantial and divine. A key Augustinian insight in *De Trinitate* is that nothing is said of God "accident-wise," but rather anything that can be said of the entire Godhead is said "substance-wise."[20] God is fundamentally simple. Thus, to speak of God's "will" *is* to speak of God's being, love, etc. Thus, on Augustine's own terms, God creates because he *wills* to do so, but he *wills* to do what is loving, good, etc. That is, God creates out of his goodness. This point is most clearly illustrated from Augustine's chapter on creation in *Confessiones* (Book XIII). Augustine can write, "Your creation has its being from the fullness of your goodness."[21] Augustine writes, "Your made it [i.e., creation] not because you needed it, but from the fullness of your goodness, imposing control and converting it to receive form—but not as if the result brought you fulfillment of delight."[22] Augustine makes a similar point in *De civitate Dei*. Speaking of God and his relation to the world, Augustine suggests that the best cause for God to create is simply "that good might be created by the good God."[23] Again, in Augustine's thought

---

18. *Triune Creator*, 76.
19. *One, the Three and the Many*, 54.
20. I summarize Augustine's position on these issues in chapter 5 above. Cf. *De Trinitate*, Books V–VII.
21. *Confessiones* XIII.ii (2).
22. Ibid., XIII.iii (4).
23. *De civitate Dei* XI.21.

God's *goodness* is fundamental in God's creation of the world. Gunton is right that Augustine is a "theologian of the will," but Gunton's criticism that creation for Augustine is due to "sheer will" or "arbitrary will" appears to fail to take into consideration Augustine's clear affirmation of the simplicity of God, and that God creates out of his *goodness*.

Creation and Trinity

One of Gunton's chief charges against Augustine in relation to the doctrine of creation is that Augustine does not conceive of creation in trinitarian terms. This leads to a number of errors, one of the most significant being the charge that Augustine in effect replaces Christ with the platonic forms. Gunton writes: "the Logos was crowded out by the logoi." (The logoi being the platonic forms). These logoi, in much of (particularly Augustinian) Western thought, became "the effective mediators of creation." In short, "Christ is displaced by the forms."[24] Summarizing Augustine and those who shared in his errors, Gunton writes, "The exclusion of christological mediation is definitive for the shape the thought of this era takes, because the structuring of the created order comes to be provided not by the one who became incarnate, *Christus creator*, but by *intellectual* forms or patterns."[25]

We note that for Augustine, quite contrary to Gunton's charge, creation *is* mediated by Christ. In the famous section of *Against the Manichees*, where Augustine is responding to the question, "what was God doing before He created the world," Augustine's response is a christological response. Augustine says, "We answer them that God made heaven and earth in the beginning, not in the beginning of time, but in Christ. For he was the Word with the father, through whom and in whom all things were made."[26] In his *On the Literal Interpretation of Genesis: An Unfinished Book*, Augustine begins the book by summarizing the Catholic faith: "God the Father almighty made and established all of creation *through his only-begotten Son*, that is, through the Wisdom and Power consubstantial and

---

24. *Brief Theology of Revelation*, 42–43.

25. *Triune Creator*, 98.

26. *Against the Manichees* I.2.3. Note that in I.5.8 Augustine argues that it really *is* the Holy Spirit who is present in Gen 1:2 ("The Spirit of God was borne over the water").

coeternal to himself, in the unity of the Holy Spirit, who is also consubstantial and coeternal."[27]

Gunton might rightly respond that for Augustine the pre-existent, non-incarnate Christ is the mediator of creation, and that in Augustine's thought the reality of the incarnate Son is not brought to bear on the doctrine of creation. This more narrow criticism of Augustine would have more substance. But would it be a worthwhile criticism? It might, but as I will argue below there *is* in Augustine a sense in which redemption is the perfection of the created order, and this redemption is rooted in the cross born by the incarnate Christ.

Besides the explicit role of Christ in creation, Augustine at several points can simply state that creation is a trinitarian act. For example, Augustine can write that all things are created by God "and that there is nothing which either He Himself is not or which does not stem from Him—from Him, the Trinity, the Father, the Son begotten of the Father, and the Holy Spirit proceeding from the same Father, but being the one and the same Spirit of Father and Son."[28] Augustine can write, "by this Trinity supremely, equally, and unchangeably good, all things were created."[29] Thus, I conclude that contrary to Gunton's claims, Augustine does construe creation as christologically mediated (although the pre-existent Christ is more central her). Additionally, it would appear that Gunton's claim that creation is not construed in trinitarian terms in the theology of Augustine fails to give adequate attention to Augustine's quite explicit writings to the contrary.

Creation and Revelation

Particularly important for our purposes is the fact that for Augustine creation is *revelatory*. Gunton laments that Augustine's construal of revelation was of virtually an *unmediated* knowledge of God, which ultimately contributed to making God unknowable. In Augustine a trinitarian, christological construal of revelation was replaced by platonic forms. However, I would suggest a close reading of Augustine points us in another direction. For Augustine creation *itself* is revelatory. That is, the created order reveals God. A key text which is referred to repeatedly in

27. *De Genesis ad litteram imperfectus liber* I.2 (emphasis mine).
28. *Enchiridion* 9.
29. Ibid.

De Trinitate is Rom 1:20. Augustine can argue, "So then, as we direct our gaze at the creator *by understanding the things that are made* (Rom 1:20), we should understand him as triad, whose traces appear in creation in a way that is fitting."[30] Augustine also can write, "I quote this passage from the book of Wisdom in case any of the faithful should reckon I have been wasting time for nothing in searching creation for signs of the supreme Trinity we are looking for when we are looking for God, going step by step through various trinities of different sorts until we eventually arrive at the mind of man."[31] Augustine can also write (referring to Romans 1) that we should try and discern God's "invisible things by understanding them through the things that are made, and especially through the rational or intellectual understanding and will that God is a trinity."[32] Not only does Scripture reveal God; nature does so as well: "It is not, after all, only the authority of the divine books which asserts that God is; the universal nature of things which surrounds us, to which we too belong, proclaims that it has a most excellent founder, who has given us a mind and natural reason by which to see that living beings are to be preferred to non-living with sense to non-sentient ones."[33]

As we noted earlier in our exposition of Augustine, the created order thus reveals God, and is one step toward the goal of the Christian life: the vision of God, when the Christian will see God "face to face" (1 Cor 13:12). Thus, for Augustine the created order has a good, but limited role, as a *means* by which the Christian moves forward to the direct vision of God. In his *Confessiones* Augustine makes a similar point. In the context of a discussion about creation, Augustine writes: "God is loved in that which he has made [i.e., creation], and he is not loved except through the Spirit which he has given."[34] That is, through the Spirit, humans can see (and indeed love) God. If I have understood Augustine at this point, several things follow. First, categorizing Augustine as "platonic" in relation to his doctrine of revelation is simply inadequate. Augustine, like virtually all seminal thinkers, evidences continuity and discontinuity with the past, and Augustine also contributes new insights to the tradition of which he

30. *De Trinitate* VI.12.
31. Ibid.
32. Ibid., XV.39.
33. Ibid., XV.5.
34. *Confessiones* XIII.xxxi (46).

is a part. For Augustine the created order reveals the Triune God. This is no unmediated revelation, but just the opposite, *mediated* revelation. The created order is a *medium* through which God reveals himself. An *unmediated* revelation *is* the goal of the Christian life. But this "face to face" vision of God is future, and in the meantime the created order is *a* means by which we move toward that end. Second, as we will discuss more fully shortly, in order to achieve this "face to face" knowledge of God, we must go through an earthly, bloody cross, which was born by a truly flesh and blood man—Jesus. As Michel R. Barnes has noted, "The Son has to be(come) *really material* if he is to perform the 'mission' of bringing us to the beatific vision." In Barnes' view, whereas Augustine's (Arian) opponents could say, "'If material, then not divine,'" Augustine asserted, "'Material, in order to bring us to the divine.'"[35] Interestingly, Augustine's doctrine of the knowledge of God is as much *Aristotelian*—with Augustine's emphasis on knowing eternal realities *through* concrete objects—as it *Platonic*. The key suggestion I want to make here is that in light of Book IV and V of *De Trinitate*, where Augustine discusses the death of Christ at length, knowledge of God is *radically* and *thoroughly* mediated, because ultimately the most full knowledge of God is *only* achieved through the medium of Christ's sacrificial death.

The Order and Purpose of Creation

We have seen throughout earlier sections of the paper that Gunton criticizes Augustine for severing creation from redemption. That is, on Gunton's view, creation is an act of "arbitrary will," and creation has no organic or intrinsic relation to redemption. I would like to suggest that if Gunton wishes to see an intricate connection between creation and redemption—an emphasis Gunton admires in the theology of Irenaeus—he may find a true ally in the thought of Augustine. Although it may not be as prominent as Gunton would like, there *is* in Augustine an emphasis on redemption as the fulfilling of God's good intentions with creation. For example, Augustine can write that the very reason we are *created* the way we are is so that we can know and love God. Augustine writes of the human soul, "it is with reference to its capacity to use reason and understanding *in order to understand and gaze upon God* that it was made to the image

---

35. Barnes, "Exegesis and Polemic," 58.

of God."³⁶ That is, we are created *with the end in view* of seeing God face to face. Also, Augustine can argue that there will be a resurrection of the body, and the "bodies of the saints, then, will rise free from any blemish or deformity."³⁷ As we noted earlier, Augustine *does* see a *telos* present in the created order. A most vivid example is found in *Enchiridion*. Speaking of the aborted fetus, Augustine can ask if anyone would deny "that the act of resurrection would fill out whatever is lacking to the form?" (of the aborted fetus). Indeed, "*Nature*, then would not be defrauded of anything fitting and harmonious which the passage of days was to bring nor be disfigured by anything of an opposite kind which passage of days had added, but rather that which was not yet completed, just as that which had suffered blemish will be renewed." ³⁸ That is, there will be a renewal of all things at the resurrection, and this renewal includes the unborn and the aged and scarred. Note that in this illustration Augustine is arguing that at the eschaton the good things of *this* world are perfected. Indeed, the resurrection is the means by which God perfects and completes and perfects the imperfections found in the created order.³⁹

Augustine also makes a not so subtle connection between creation and redemption in his *Confessiones*. In the context of a discussion of creation, Augustine can write, "Your works praise you that we may love you, and we love you that your works may praise you."⁴⁰ That is, for Augustine there is an intricate connection between the created order and our own love of, or praise of God. The created order is a *means* by which man is moved to love and praise God.

In his writing on the book of Genesis Augustine is actually quite explicit that there is an order and indeed a *telos* in the created order. For example, in *De Genesis ad litteram* Augustine can write that in creation "God ordered all things."⁴¹ There is an order and *telos* in the created world. Augustine can write, "For the perfection of each thing according to the

---

36. *De Trinitate* XIV.9. (emphasis mine).
37. *Enchiridion* 91.
38. Ibid., 85.
39. For a lengthier discussion of how the Augustine's doctrine of the resurrection gives evidence of both an appreciation for the goodness of creation, as well as for the *telos* built into creation, see Marrou, *Resurrection and Saint Augustine's Theology of Human Values*.
40. *Confessiones* XIII.xxxiii (48).
41. *De Genesi ad litteram* IV.3.7.

limits of its nature is established in a state of rest, that is, it has a fixed orientation by reason of its natural tendencies, not just in the universe of which it is a part, but more especially in Him to whom it owes its being, in whom the universe itself exists."[42] Here Augustine makes clear that the whole created order has been created with an order appropriate to each thing ("according to the limits of its nature"), and that everything has a "fixed orientation" in relation to its "natural tendencies," and that as created, the created order has its ultimate coordinates in the Creator of the universe. Indeed, "the whole of creation, which as finished in six days, has a certain character in its own nature and another character in the order or orientation by which it is in God, not as God Himself is, but in such a way that there is no repose to give it its proper stability except in the repose of Him who desires nothing outside of Himself."[43] Augustine's notion of *rationes causales* or *rationes seminales* in the created order serve as a means by which Augustine can argue that there is indeed purpose in creation. Augustine can write regarding the creation of man, "For God had finished simultaneously in the perfection of the causal reasons the works He had begun, and He had begun the works *that were to be finished in the course of the ages.*"[44] Augustine also writes, "the causes of all future things were inserted in the world when that day was made on which God created all things together."[45] Augustine is explicit that it is the *Creator* who is sovereignly sustaining creation and moving it towards a goal: "Over this whole movement and course of nature [of sustaining and providing for the created order] there is the power of the Creator, who is able to do in all creatures something other than what the seminal reasons would bring about, but not something that He Himself had not originally made possible to be done by Him in them."[46]

Thus, we simply note that Gunton may truly find in Augustine a kindred spirit. An Augustinian construal of God's purposes for his creation may serve as a rich theological pool for Gunton's own theological endeavors. Put slightly differently, we might suggest that to the extent that Gunton wishes to affirm the continuity between creation redemption, this

42. Ibid., IV.18.34.
43. Ibid.
44. Ibid., VI.15.26 (emphasis mine).
45. Ibid., VI.18.29.
46. Ibid., IX.17.31.

notion is not simply to be found in Irenaeus, but is also an Augustinian insight.

Redemption

Interestingly, while Gunton's writing on redemption broadly considered includes treatments of Augustine (particularly Gunton's consistent emphasis on the continuity between creation and redemption), Gunton has little to say on Augustine's doctrine of the work of Christ. However, I want to argue that the work of Christ plays an important role in *De Trinitate*, and that Augustine's thought on the work of Christ gives us particular insights into his construal of the Trinity. I am less interested here in ferreting out a particular "theory" of the atonement, as much as I am interested in coming to terms with the *nature* of the work of Christ, and *why* the work of Christ is prominent at key points in *De Trinitate* and the rhetorical and/or polemical function which the work of Christ plays in *De Trinitate*.

Missions and Processions

First, I want to elucidate an issue raised in the previous section, namely, that the temporal missions reveal the eternal processions. This issue is central to an understanding of what Augustine is doing in *De Trinitate*. Augustine's contention is that the missions which take place *in time* reveal the processions which are *eternal*. That is, what God does in *time* reveals who God is in *eternity*. Edmund Hill can write, "The sendings of the Son and the Holy Spirit reveal their eternal processions from the Father (and the Holy Spirit's procession from the Son as well), and thus reveal the inner trinitarian mystery of God."[47] Augustine himself can write, "And just as being born means for the Son his being from the Father, so his being sent means his being known to be from him. And just as for the Holy Spirit his being the gift of God means proceeding from the Father, so his being sent means being known to proceed from him."[48] To quote Edmund Hill again, "And so this mystery of God's being is organically linked to the

---

47. Hill, *Mystery of the Trinity*, 89.
48. *De Trinitate* IV.29.

economy of salvation, above all to the mystery of the incarnation and of the saving death and resurrection of Jesus Christ."[49]

If I am interpreting Augustine faithfully at this point, certain criticisms are generated. First, to say that Augustine somehow severs the link between the immanent Trinity and the economic Trinity is misguided. Indeed, the point Augustine wishes to make in the text quoted above is that we actually *know* the immanent Trinity by means of what God has done in history. Rather than severing the immanent and economic Trinity, Augustine sees a thoroughgoing and organic connection between the two. Second, and following the discussion of the Holy Spirit above, the immanent Trinity is not "closed" in on itself. Rather, the sendings of the Son and the Spirit flow out God's trinitarian being. That is, the sending in *time* of the Son and the Spirit is not somehow discontinuous with the being of God. Quite the contrary, the sendings in *time* reflect who God truly is in *eternity*. And this leads to a third crucial point. Gunton's claim that Augustine's doctrine of God renders God virtually unknowable must be seriously questioned. In fact, quite the opposite is the case. The economy *reveals* God. That is, the economic Trinity reveals the immanent Trinity. In seeing the economy we humans are getting a radical insight into the nature of God. The economy is *revelatory* of the nature of God, and God's actions in history provide true revelation of who God is. Far from rendering God unknowable, Augustine's notion that the missions in time reveal the processions in eternity provides a rather thoroughgoing affirmation of the knowability of God. We should also note a connection to another concern of Gunton. We noted earlier Gunton's concern that revelation is always *mediated*, and Gunton argued that Augustine's doctrine of revelation was largely a doctrine of *unmediated* revelation. On Gunton's view this *unmediated* revelation ultimately leads to the loss of revelation, where God is rendered unknowable. But if I am interpreting Augustine faithfully on the issue of missions and processions, not only is God knowable, but *God is knowable through the material world* (i.e., the incarnate Christ). Rather than an unmediated platonic remembrance or illumination, we come to a true knowledge of God through what God has done in *this* world. In sum, Augustine's doctrine of missions and processions provides a rather strong reason to question some of Gunton's chief criticisms of Augustine.

---

49. Hill, *Mystery of the Trinity*, 90.

The Centrality of the Incarnation and the Cross

There is a second main point which must be made concerning the work of Christ in *De Trinitate*. In *De Trinitate* Augustine is discussing how one is to arrive at the vision of God. 1 Cor 13:12 serves as a key text for all of *De Trinitate*: "Now we see but a poor reflection as in a mirror; then we shall see face to face. Now I know in part; then I shall know fully, even as I am fully known." The pilgrimage to this "face to face" vision of God serves as an important sub-plot (if not indeed the main plot line) for *De Trinitate*, as Augustine asks how we move from our current self-centered and sinful state to the purified state where we can stand to see God "face to face." For example, Augustine questions whether one can move from man's mind to the Trinity. Augustine writes: "So then, when this image is renewed to perfection by this transformation, we will be like God because we shall see him, not through a mirror but as he is (1 John 3:2); what the apostle calls face to face (1 Cor 13:12)."[50] Likewise, Augustine can write, "But when the sight comes that is promised us face to face (1 Cor 13:12), we shall see this trinity that is not only incorporeal but also supremely inseparable and truly unchangeable much more clearly and definitely than we now see its image which we ourselves are."[51] But how is this theme significant for my critique of Gunton? I would suggest that while a central theme of *De Trinitate* is the vision of the triune God, it is also clear that the only way by which anyone will ever see God is through the cross. It is in relation to the *temporal*, *physical*, and *particular* nature of the *means* by which one sees God that I want to offer a set of criticisms of Gunton.

Augustine argues at length that the cross is absolutely central if one is going to reach the vision of God. Augustine writes, "the only thing to cleanse the wicked and the proud is the blood of the just man and the humility of God; to contemplate God, which by nature we are not, we would have to be cleansed by him who became what by nature we are and what by sin we are not."[52] As sinners this vision of God, and the purity required to attain such a vision, eludes us. We need a mediator. We could not "pass from being among the things that originated things to eternal things, unless the eternal allied himself to us in our originated condition,

---

50. *De Trinitate* XV.21.
51. Ibid., XV.44.
52. Ibid., IV.4.

and so provided us with a bridge to his eternity."[53] Augustine attempts to deflate the notion that somehow one can attain to the vision of God apart from the cross. There are "some people who think they can purify themselves for contemplating God and cleaving to him by their own power and strength of character."[54] But this is an illusion. In a powerful word picture Augustine illustrates the importance of admitting and confessing our need for the cross: "But what good does it do a man who is so proud that he is ashamed to climb aboard the wood, what good does it do him to gaze afar on the home country across the sea?" Indeed, "And what harm does it do a humble man if he cannot see it from such a distance, but is coming to it nonetheless on the wood the disdains to be carried by?"[55] Augustine's message is clear, the path to the vision of God *requires* the cross. Thus, for Augustine *this* world is God's good means by which he leads believers to himself. For Augustine, while the love of "temporal things" does keep us from grasping eternal things, he can argue that we are led to eternal things *only* through temporal things—the cross.

What should we conclude from Augustine's teaching at this point? I suggest the following. First, in light of the importance Augustine places on the cross as an *absolutely necessary* means of seeing God, it is at the least inadequate to accuse Augustine of denigrating the material world. One may be able to point to this or that quote where the physical world seems to fare poorly in Augustine's thought, but the importance of the good, material world is a necessary component of Augustine's doctrine of redemption in *De Trinitate*, and this component must be considered when making generalizations about Augustine's view of the physical, created order.

Second, Augustine's teaching at this point should make us at least rather cautious about Gunton's charge that the psychological analogies somehow denote that Augustine severs the immanent Trinity from the economic Trinity, and we should be slow to assert that somehow Augustine severs creation from redemption. That is, in Augustine's doctrine of redemption it is the *economic* Trinity—here especially the death and resurrection of Christ—which leads us to the vision of (immanent) Triune God. The sendings of the Son and the Spirit is the means by which God brings

---

53. Ibid., IV.24.
54. Ibid., IV.20.
55. Ibid.

sinners to the vision of Himself. The work of the *economy* is the *means* by which persons are brought into the presence of the *immanent* Trinity. Michael R. Barnes can write, "The Homoians claim 'If material, then not divine,' while Augustine wants to assert 'Material, in order to bring us to the divine.'"[56] Barnes also writes, "The Son has to be(come) *really material* if he is to perform the 'mission' of bringing us to the beatific vision."[57] John Cavadini sees an anti-neoplatonic polemic at work here: "the *De trinitate* uses the Neoplatonic soteriology of ascent only to impress it into the service of a thoroughgoing critique of its claim to raise the inductee to the contemplation of God, a critique which, more generally, becomes a declaration of the futility of any attempt to come to any saving knowledge of God apart from Christ."[58] Earl Muller similarly argues that "the key theological point which governs the rhetorical structure of *De Trinitate*: "*there can be no intellectus apart from the concrete sacrificial act of Christ*."[59] It is worth asking why, in Book XIII, in the middle of Augustine's exploration of the trinitarian *imago Dei* in the human mind, Augustine's turns to the cross. If Augustine's effort is to penetrate the eternal trinitarian mystery, why move back "down" to an earthy, bloody cross? Muller suggests, and I think he is right, that Augustine "*refuses to deal with anything above the human mind without first purifying his mind in the sacrifice of Christ, the only way for sinful humans to obtain the eternal.*"[60] I suggest that the notion that Augustine is offering an anti-neoplatonic polemic is fundamentally correct. Such polemic would explain why Augustine, in the middle of a discussion of Christ the mediator, determines to criticize those who believe they can attain to the vision of God apart from the mediator.[61] In *De civitate Dei* Augustine devotes Book X to a refutation of Porphyry's doctrine of redemption, and his polemic against such neoplatonism is more explicit. Augustine does not deny that purification is necessary, but he does assert that the person of Christ (particularly his death) is the only *means* of purification. Thus, Augustine can write, "It was therefore truly said that man is cleansed only by a Principle, although

56. Barnes, "Exegesis and Polemic," 58.
57. Ibid.
58. Cavadini, "Structure and Intention of Augustine's *De Trinitate*," 106.
59. Muller, "Rhetorical and Theological Issues," 359.
60. Ibid., 362.
61. *De Trinitate* IV.20–24.

the Platonists erred in speaking of the plural *principles*."⁶² What exactly was Porphyry's error? "But Porphyry, being under the dominion of those envious [i.e., demonic] powers, whose influence he was at once ashamed of and afraid to throw off, refused to recognize that *Christ is the Principle by whose incarnation we are purified.*"⁶³ Porphyry "despised Him, because of the flesh itself which He assumed, that He might offer a sacrifice for our purification."⁶⁴ It is only through the incarnate Christ that we can attain the vision of God. Again directing his polemic against Porphyry, Augustine writes, "but the incarnation of the unchangeable Son of God, whereby we are saved, and are enabled to reach the things we believe, or in part understand, this is what you refuse to recognize."⁶⁵ And in this "face to face" vision, Christians will still be *embodied* persons: "yet there is not among us the smallest doubt that [our bodies] shall be everlasting, and of a nature exemplified in the instance of Christ's risen body," and the body "shall offer not hindrance to the soul's contemplation by which it is fixed in God."⁶⁶ Thus, in *De civitate Dei* it is clear that Augustine wants to construe his own doctrine of redemption in contradistinction to a neoplatonic understanding of redemption, and I think one is justified in saying that a similar, if slightly more subtle polemic is seen in *De Trinitate*.

I suggest that Gunton has not adequately mined Augustine's doctrine of redemption, and the implications therein for Gunton's own work. Augustine's work serves to provide an impressive theological connection between the immanent and economic Trinity: the means by which the human person reaches the *immanent* Trinity is the work of the *economic* Trinity in history. Using Irenaeus' own terminology, through one of God's "two hands"—here the Son—God works in history to bring persons into the presence of God. For Augustine, the economy is *radically central* to Augustine's trinitarian theology. The work of Son *in time* not only reveals who God is *in eternity* (my point above), the *economy* is God's mean of preparing people for the more direct "face to face" vision of the *immanent* Triune God. If my criticism is legitimate, it would appear that Augustine need not be a foe of Gunton. Quite the contrary, Augustine's view of the

62. *De civitate Dei* X.24.
63. Ibid. (emphasis mine).
64. Ibid.
65. Ibid., X.29.
66. Ibid.

redemptive work of Christ affirms the goodness of *this* material world, and provides a powerful theological and conceptual link between creation and redemption, and these Augustinian emphases are actually *supportive* of Gunton's own theological concerns.

The Holy Spirit and God's Relationship to the World

Augustine's doctrine of the Holy Spirit comes under harsh criticism in Gunton's writings. First, Augustine, in his notion that the Holy Spirit is the "link" or "bond" between the Father and Son "closes" off the life of the Triune God from the created order. Ultimately, the economic Trinity is severed from the immanent Trinity. Second, Augustine tends towards a type of "intellectualism," a tendency rooted in the above noted preference for the immanent Trinity. Flowing out of these two errors is a failure in Augustine to affirm the Holy Spirit's role as the one who realizes eschatological blessings now.

Gunton is not the first contemporary theologian to note that the Holy Spirit has often been the "neglected member" of the Trinity in much of contemporary theology. In response to Gunton one of the first things that should be said is that the most tortured and difficult sections of *De Trinitate* are those sections where Augustine is trying to make sense of the Holy Spirit. Perhaps the most unconvincing argument Augustine utilizes is one that is seen when Augustine is discussing the analogy of *mens, notitia sui, amor sui* (mind, the mind's knowledge of itself, and the mind's love of itself).[67] Augustine suggests that "knowledge" can be construed as word, image or begotten. But if knowledge can be construed as word, image or begotten (clearly words which fittingly apply to the Son), why cannot the Holy Spirit *also* be called word, image or begotten? Augustine's answer is less than persuasive. "Knowledge" is a sort of "finding out what is said to be brought fourth to light," thus knowledge is appropriately called word, image or begotten. Love, however, is roughly construed as an inquisitiveness or "appetite for finding out"—i.e., that which, in a sense, elicits or births the knowledge. A sympathetic reading can try to draw out the strengths of Augustine's argument at this point, but even such a reading would generally admit that Augustine's logic is less than fully convincing.[68]

---

67. *De Trinitate* IX.18.

68. Edmund Hill is the translator of *De Trinitate* in the New City Press series and has written *The Mystery of the Trinity*, an exposition and recommendation of Augustine's

However, Gunton's criticisms are not focused on that particular argument of Augustine. Gunton's criticisms are more sweeping and thorough than simply a critique of this or that bit of strained logic. First, Gunton is dissatisfied with Augustine's whole general notion of the Holy Spirit as the "link" between Father and Son.[69] Gunton can argue that such a conception effectively "closes" an inward circle. That is, the immanent Trinity is severely demarcated from the economy. Gunton prefers thinking of the Holy Spirit as one who "seeks to involve the other in the movement of giving and receiving that is the Trinity." The Spirit's role is "*to perfect the love of the Father and Son by moving it beyond itself.*"[70] My critique of Gunton at this point is a simple one: what Gunton desires in a doctrine of the Holy Spirit *is*, on the whole, to be found in Augustine's doctrine of the Holy Spirit. I would like to suggest here that Augustine's own position is a good deal more subtle than Gunton allows, and that indeed, Augustine's construal actually *does* serve to emphasize how the Trinity is not an inward "closed" circle at all, but is directed outward toward the world. That is, in *De Trinitate*, Augustine can argue that not only does the Holy Spirit "join" the Father and Son, the Holy Spirit is also the one who brings us into relationship with God. Thus, Augustine can write of the Holy Spirit as "gift": "we find our blessedness *from him and through him and in him* [Rom 11:36], because it is by his gift that we are one with each other."[71] Here the Holy Spirit *is* the means by which believers are united with one another (and by implication with God). For Augustine the notion of the Holy Spirit as "gift" must be taken seriously. Augustine can write, "the Holy Spirit is the gift of God, in that he is given to those who love God through him."[72] The Holy Spirit is truly *given* to the world. For Augustine there is simply no need to posit a dichotomy between the "immanent" and "economic" Trinity. For example, Augustine can write that the Holy Spirit "is the gift of God insofar as he is given to those he is given to." And then he writes, "But in himself he is God even if he is not given to

---

doctrine of the Trinity. In an introductory essay in *De Trinitate* Hill can write, "Augustine is less successful, as I think he himself would be inclined to admit, in his attempts to elucidate the procession of the Holy Spirit." See his "Foreword to Books IX–XIV," in *De Trinitate*, 267.

69. "God the Holy Spirit," 124ff.
70. Ibid., 127.
71. *De Trinitate* VI.7.
72. Ibid., XV.35.

anyone, because he was God, co-eternal with the Father and the Son, even before he was given to anyone."[73] Rather than construing the Holy Spirit as *simply* the bond between the Father and Son, Augustine sees that Holy Spirit as the one who proceeds (in eternity *and* in time) from the Father and Son, and brings us into relationship with God. Augustine writes, the Holy Spirit "is from God and causes us to abide in God and him in us," and "we know this because he has given us of his Spirit, this Spirit of his is God charity."[74] The Holy Spirit is radically *outward* focused in Augustine's thought. Indeed, Augustine can write, "charity [the Holy Spirit] is poured out in our hearts through this gift, charity by which we are to love God and neighbor according to those two commandments on which the whole law depends and the prophets."[75]

I believe that Augustine's writings on the Holy Spirit found in *De Trinitate* generally diffuse Gunton's contention that Augustine's notion of the Holy Spirit as the bond between the Father and Son somehow "closes" the circle of the immanent Trinity in an inward fashion, severing the immanent Trinity from the economic Trinity. Perhaps a more fundamental question is why Gunton argues as he does. If my thesis is right, what theologic is Gunton perhaps missing in Augustine's thought? I will suggest the answer now, and wait for a full treatment below, in the section on redemption. The heart of the issue, which I believe Gunton does not appropriate, is: *in Augustine's thought the missions in time reveal the processions in eternity*. Or put differently, *what God does in time reveals who God is in eternity*. Thus, the *sending* of the Holy Spirit in time reveals the *procession* of the Holy Spirit in eternity. This theological proposal would mean that there simply is not a dichotomy between the economic and immanent Trinity. In light of Augustine's position, Gunton's suggestion that in Augustine the Holy Spirit is "a timeless function in a Platonic triad,"[76] and that the idea of the Holy Spirit as the bond between the Father and the Son "closes" the circle of the Trinity off from the world needs to be rejected.

73. Ibid., XV.36.
74. Ibid., XV.37.
75. Ibid., XV.46.
76. "Christology," 167. Gunton's work, on my view, is generally characterized by thoughtful and careful theological exegesis. I wonder, if in speaking of Augustine's view of the Spirit as "a timeless function in a Platonic triad" he was engaging in slight hyperbole.

Ontology

Chapters 3 and 5 were devoted primarily to the question of ontology in the theology of Gunton and Augustine, respectively. Without reworking Gunton's position in detail here, we will suffice to say that on Gunton's view, Augustine forfeited a profound Christian ontology which had been forged by the Cappadocian Fathers, Augustine failed to appropriate Irenaeus' affirmation of there only being two ontological realms (God and creation), and Augustine subsumed the three persons under the one essence or substance, rendering the three persons effectively superfluous.

The One and the Three

The question of unity and plurality, or of the One and the Many is central to Gunton's theological writings. The schemata of the One and the Many provides the conceptual backdrop for his own understanding of Western thought, as we have described earlier. We have also noted that Gunton is not alone in criticizing Augustine for his thorough emphasis on the *unity* of the Godhead over the *threeness*. We have noted above that scholars like G. L. Prestige,[77] Eugene Webb,[78] and T. R. Martland[79] essentially affirm Gunton's position that whereas the West—particularly Augustine—began with the one and moved to the three (and also over emphasized the one), the East began with the three persons and moved to the oneness of God.[80] However, other scholars such as Michel René Barnes,[81] Rowan Williams,[82] Lewis Ayres[83] and Edmund Hill[84] all agree

---

77. Prestige, *God in Patristic Thought*, 235, 157–78.

78. Webb, "Augustine's New Trinity," 191–212.

79. Martland, "Study of Cappadocian and Augustinian Trinitarian Methodology," 252–63.

80. In a personal conversation with Gunton (August 6, 1999, Brentwood, England), Gunton stated that he does believe Augustine began with the unity and *then* tried to make sense of the three persons. However, Gunton believes that while the Cappadocians emphasized and began with the three, they did not begin with the three and then move the one. Rather, they simply emphasized the three persons. Indeed, *in so doing* they were dealing with who God is.

81. Barnes, "Augustine in Contemporary Trinitarian Theology," 237–50.

82. Williams, "*Sapientia* and the Trinity," 317–32.

83. Ayres, "Augustine, the Trinity and Modernity," 127–33; cf. idem, "The Fundamental Grammar of Augustine's Trinitarian Theology"; idem, "Augustine on the Unity of the Triune God."

84. Hill, *Mystery of the Trinity*, 95–96, 116.

in their own way that the idea that Augustine begins with the unity and then moves to the three persons, while the East does the opposite is woefully inadequate as a faithful summary of the issues involved. Gunton's criticisms of Augustine are crucial, because so many (all?) of Gunton's complaints against Augustine flow out of Gunton's criticisms of Augustine's understanding of the Triune God. While much of Gunton's theological work is stimulating and provocative, I want to here argue that there are several fundamental weaknesses in Gunton's understanding and/or appropriation of Augustine's doctrine of God.

Three Persons, One God

One of Gunton's chief claims is that Augustine so emphasizes the oneness of God that the threeness of God is ultimately lost. Indeed, for Gunton there is a disconnect in Augustine between the one substance or essence and the three persons. In contrasting the Cappadocians and Augustine, Gunton can write, "the three persons [for the Cappadocians] are what they are in their relations, and therefore the relations qualify them ontologically, in terms of what they are." But with Augustine we see that he "continues to use relation as a logical rather than an ontological predicate," and is thus "precluded from being able to make claims about the being of the *particular persons*, who, because they lack distinguishable identity tend to disappear into the all-embracing oneness of God."[85] Augustine has failed to appropriate the Cappadocian insight that "God's being was seen to consist in personal communion."[86] In Augustine, and this is a key point I would like to address here, the being of God is "an unknown substance *supporting* the three persons rather than *being constituted* by their relatedness."[87]

I would like to offer a response to Gunton at this point. First, for Augustine there is a much closer connection between the three persons and the being of God. Here I am arguing that Gunton's claims that in Augustine the three persons are ultimately lost and that somehow the being of God is an "unknown substance" which "supports" the persons cannot be justified. How *does* Augustine speak of the relation between the being of God and the three persons? Augustine is clear that anything said

85. *Promise*, 41.
86. Ibid., 53.
87. Ibid., 43.

of the Trinity (i.e., all three persons) is said "substance-wise."[88] Indeed, the Holy Spirit "is substance together with the Father and the son," and the Holy Spirit is "great together and good together and holy together with them and whatever else is said with reference to self, because with God it is not a different thing to be, and to be great or good etc."[89] Thus, for Augustine, who wishes to affirm both the simplicity of God as well as the consubstantiality of all three persons, anything said of the Godhead "substance-wise" and applies to all three persons.

Several texts in Augustine's *De Trinitate* reveal that Augustine was indeed aware of the danger of construing the substance of God as something "underlying" or "supporting" the three persons—the charge which Gunton levies against Augustine. For example, Augustine at one point explains the weaknesses in using an analogy of three men when trying to explain the Trinity. The main weakness is that we really cannot say one *man*, three *men*; we are rather forced simply to say three men. In this context Augustine writes, "But such is the inseparability that reigns in that supreme trinity which incomparably surpasses all things, that while a triad of men cannot be called a man, *that triad is called, and is, one God.*"[90] Augustine continues, "Nor is it a triad in one God—it *is* one God. Nor is that triad like this image, man, which is one person *having* those three things; on the contrary, it *is* three persons, the Father of the Son and the Son of the Father and the Spirit of the Father and the Son."[91] In pointing out the difficulty of moving from the trinitarian *imago dei* in the human mind to the triune God, Augustine can write, "And yet, while in this image of the trinity [i.e., in man] these three [i.e., memory, understanding, love] *are* not one man but *belong to* one man, it is not likewise the case in that supreme trinity of which this is the image that those three belong to one God: they *are* one God and they *are* three persons, not one."[92] It would appear rather clear that Augustine is teaching here that the three persons *are* the one God. The substance of God does not "support" or "underlie" the three persons; the three persons *are* the one God. Augustine is equally clear when he writes, "In the nature of divinity, or of the deity if you

---

88. *De Trinitate* V–VII.
89. Ibid., VI.7.
90. *De Trinitate* XV.43. (emphasis mine).
91. Ibid.
92. Ibid.

prefer it, *that triad is what this nature is.*"[93] Augustine makes the same point when he writes, "this same three is also one."[94] Rather than speaking of the substance or essence of God apart from the three person, Augustine consistently argues that the three persons *are* the one God. He can write that "it is clear that Father and Son and Holy Spirit is what the one God is."[95] In short, Augustine seems to quite aware of guarding against severing the one from the three, and indeed seems quite concerned to affirm that there is nothing besides the three persons, and that the three persons *are* the one God.

Being and Relationship

As we have discussed in some detail above, one of Gunton's chief criticisms of Augustine is that he has failed to appropriate the ontological advance of the Cappadocians. With the Cappadocians, Gunton contends, "a new ontology is developed: for God to be is to be in communion."[96] The heart of Gunton's criticism is as follows. For the Cappadocians, "the three persons are what they are in their relations, and therefore the relations qualify them ontologically, in terms of what they are." Augustine, however, "continues to use relation as a logical rather than an ontological predicate," and Augustine is thus "precluded from being able to make claims about the being of the *particular persons*, who, because they lack distinguishable identity tend to disappear into the all-embracing oneness of God."[97] Ultimately, "the achievement of the Cappadocians, an achievement Augustine has failed adequately to understand, was to create a new conception of the being of God, in which God's being was seen to consist in personal communion."[98] In short, relationship is not something "added" to what God is; rather, *relationship constitutes what it means for God "to be."*

At least a few things should be said in response to this important criticism. One is simply the obvious response that in Augustine's own trinitarian thinking relationship *is* radically important. In Augustine's

---

93. Ibid. (emphasis mine).
94. Ibid., I.19.
95. Ibid., I.12.
96. *Promise*, 39.
97. Ibid., 41.
98. Ibid., 53.

theology it is *relationship* which distinguishes the persons from one another. We have argued just above that in Augustine there *is* nothing besides the three persons. There is no substance "supporting" the three persons. There simply is the three persons, and these three persons *are* the one God. I believe that once that point is made, Gunton's criticism we are here considering that Augustine fails to understand this relational Cappadocian ontology is a bit less persuasive. However, Gunton's criticism needs to be heard, because it helps us to ask exactly what Augustine is doing and saying in *De Trinitate*. Gunton's criticism is that in the end there is not room in Augustine's construal of being for "relationship" to play a constitutive part. Gunton is on to something here, for as we discussed earlier Augustine is trying to explore the best and truest way to speak of God, and he does so by saying everything said about God is *either* said "substance-wise" or "relationship-wise." This would seem, *pace* Gunton, to denote that relationship is something "added" to being, but is not constitutive of being itself. That is, substance words like "love," "goodness," etc., can be said of God (i.e., the Godhead as a trinitarian whole)," but that relationship words like "Father," "Son," and "Holy Spirit" cannot be said of God substance-wise, for the simple reason that the Father is not the Son, the Son is not the Spirit, and the Spirit is not the Father, etc. That is, we speak of the Father as the first member of the Trinity, and the Father really is God. However, the Father is not the Son, so, according to Augustine, we really should not use "Father" substance-wise, since "Father" only truly says something about the one member of the Trinity—the Father—and not the entire Godhead. Thus, if we follow Augustine's logic, it might appear *prima facie* that relationship indeed does *not* constitute what God is.

However, I would like to suggest another way of reading Augustine at this point. I would like to suggest that at an important level Augustine does indeed consider relationship to be constitutive of what it means for God to be. This is an aspect of Augustine's trinitarian theology which might be easily missed, given that he makes a repeated distinction between "substance" words and "relationship" words, and that this distinction might seem at first to somehow relegate relationship to second-class status in the being of God. However, note that Augustine, when wrestling with the three persons of the Trinity, is trying to discover how to speak of each person, and how to distinguish the persons from one another. Augustine argues that the chief characteristic which distinguishes the persons from each other is the different relationships the persons enter into. Thus, the *particular* relationship of Father to Son is *different* from the relationship between Father and Spirit. Father, Son and Spirit are engaged in different relationships, and these different relationship help us to distinguish the persons from one another. However, and this is the key point, relationship itself is a reality which is common to the Godhead, and as such, relationship constitutes what it means for God to be. That is, *in Augustine's trinitarian theology it is completely legitimate to call "relationship" a "substance-word."* This is a claim which is not worked out thoroughly in De Trinitate, but it is a claim which is completely consistent with the arguments Augustine proffers in the work. I believe this claim to be defensible because while the *particular* relationship of say, Father to Son is not the same as the *particular* relationship of Son to Spirit, it is nonetheless the case that relationship is constitutive of the entire Godhead, and that without relationship the Godhead would simply cease to be. Indeed, Augustine's entire teaching regarding the eternal processions and temporal missions is predicated on the assumption that the Godhead is *fundamentally relational*. The realities of "proceedings" and "missions" are at their core relational realities. Augustine's notion that the temporal missions reveal the eternal processions is predicated on the premise that the Godhead is eternally relating. The analogies from the human mind, particularly the mind remembering itself, understanding itself, and loving itself is fundamentally an *active* and *relational* analogy. If my argument here is sound, we would have a further reason to question a key component of Gunton's criticisms of Augustine.

The Trinity, the Imago Dei, and Being

Another point, following from the previous criticism, needs to be discussed. Gunton laments that Augustine seeks for the Trinity in the human mind, or psyche, rather in man's relationship with others. That is, Gunton criticizes Augustine for looking for the Trinity in the individual human person, rather than man as a relational being. Thus, Gunton can write, "*The crucial analogy for Augustine is between the inner structure of the human mind and the inner being of God, because it is in the former* [i.e., the human mind] *that the latter* [i.e., the inner being of God] *is made known, this side of eternity at any rate, more really than the 'outer' economy of grace.*"[99] Rather than thinking of the *imago Dei* in terms of

---

99. *Promise*, 45.

reason, Gunton suggests it should be thought of in terms of "the whole of human being as existing in relation to God, other human beings and the rest of the created order."[100] Gunton can write, "To be in the image of God is not, therefore, to have some timeless quality like reason, or anything else, but to exist in a directedness, between our coming from nothing and our being brought through Christ before the throne of the Father."[101] Our relationality as human persons is due to the fact that we are created beings who bear God's image. As Gunton writes, "Imaging is therefore a triune act," and since the Trinity is fundamentally relational, we also are fundamentally relational.[102] In short, "to be in the image of God is to be called to a relatedness-in-otherness that echoes the eternal relatedness-in-otherness of Father, Son and Spirit."[103] As Gunton writes, "the doctrine of the image of God represents a relation, primarily to God and secondarily to the other creatures, animate and inanimate alike."[104] Relation is central to being, both to God's being and man's being. Relation is not peripheral to our being, but actually constitutes our being: "relation constitutes who and what we are. Many of the difficulties facing the image doctrine derive from a failure to see this, and to construe the image as something characterizing us as individuals, rather than as persons in relation."[105] As we saw earlier, Augustine's error, in Gunton's view, was an individualistic construal of the image, and in not construing the image as constituted by man's relationships with God and others.[106]

At least two key responses should be made to Gunton at this point. First, one should simply say that at one level Gunton is right in his understanding of Augustine on the *imago Dei*. Augustine's understanding of the *imago Dei* gives much more emphasis to man and God than on man's relationship to the rest of the created order, human and non-human. Besides *De Trinitate*, such a reading can be seen in such works as *Two Books on Genesis Against the Manichees* (*De Genesis adversus Manicheos*),[107] *On the*

---

100. "Doctrine of Creation," 144.
101. *Christ and Creation*, 102.
102. Ibid., 101.
103. Ibid.
104. *Triune Creator*, 198.
105. Ibid., 206.
106. Ibid., 208.
107. *Two Books on Genesis Against the Manichees* I.17.27-28.

Literal Interpretation of Genesis: An Unfinished Book (*De Genesis ad litteram imperfectus liber*)[108] and *The Literal Meaning of Genesis* (*De Genesis ad litteram*).[109] For example, Augustine does indeed affirm that the image refers to the interior man: "When man is said to have been made to the image of God, these words refer to the interior man, where reason and intellect reside."[110] However, Augustine also affirms that man's authority over the rest of the created order is predicated on his being an image-bearer: "From these [i.e., the words depicting man as an image-bearer] man also has power over the fish of the sea and the birds of heaven and all cattle and wild animals and all the earth and all reptiles which creep upon the earth."[111] In short, for Augustine the fact that man was made in the image of God entails his authoritative and ruling relationship to the rest of the created order.

However, there is a more significant criticism which I would like to proffer. Gunton is correct that Augustine looks to the human mind as the *loci* of the image, for in the mind we reach the highest part of man. This certainly is Augustine's position. However, in understanding Augustine's view of the image of God, one must remember what is Augustine's *goal* in *De Trinitate*. As I have suggested throughout this monograph, Augustine is not simply offering a manual on the Trinity. He *is* trying to articulate an orthodox view of the Trinity. But he is doing more than that. He is asking how one reaches the goal of the Christian life, and that goal is to see God face to face. By going into the human mind, by travelling an interior way (*interior modo*), it is as if Augustine is seeking a small foretaste of what it will be like to see God. He already believes in the Triune God, and he believes that believers will one day see this Triune God. *De Trinitate* is thus largely an exploratory work which tries, by plumbing into the human mind, to explore who this God is whom believers will one day see face to face. If the Triune God has created man in God's image, certainly man somehow reflects that. And thus Augustine moves into the human mind on his quest.

However, as we have discussed earlier, Augustine's quest is checkered by various fits and starts. The analogies mostly are rather limited in

---

108. *De Genesis ad litteram imperfectus liber* 16.54–62.
109. *De Genesis ad litteram* 6.12.20–21.
110. *Against the Manichees* I.17.28.
111. Ibid.

what they reveal, and most of the analogies are eventually set aside, as Augustine moves to another analogy and seeks to explore its potential value. The criticism I wish to offer of Gunton at this point is a criticism which proceeds from Augustine's seemingly never-ending quest for the right analogy. The reader is given to believe that the analogy of the mind remembering itself, understanding itself and willing or loving itself is the analogy which will satisfy Augustine. Indeed, speaking of the mind remembering itself, understanding itself and loving itself, Augustine can write, "If we see this we see a trinity, not yet God of course, but already the image of God."[112] It is important to note that in this trinity Augustine is not speaking of mental *faculties*, but mental *activities*. That is, we are dealing with *activities* of the mind. Thus, if the mind is not actually engaged in the activities of remembering, understanding and loving this trinity simply, on one level at least, is not present because it is not actualized.[113]

Additionally, we must note that the image of God in man is something that is being transformed and repaired over time: "And thus the image begins to be reformed by him who formed it in the first place."[114] The image of God is present, but deformed in the sinner. With the beginning of the Christian life, the image begins to be restored, and it will be fully restored when the believer sees God face to face.

If Augustine were to stop here, and were to conclude that the best way of understanding the trinitarian nature of the *imago Dei* was that of the mind remembering itself, understanding itself and loving itself, Gunton's criticisms of Augustine at this point would be more persuasive. But Augustine indeed is *not* finished yet, and the move he makes should make us cautious of Gunton's criticism. Augustine proceeds to argue that the real image of God to be found in man is not the mind remembering, understanding and loving *itself*, but the mind remembering, understanding and loving *God*. Augustine can write, "This trinity of the mind is not really the image of God because the mind remembers and understands and loves itself, but because it is also able to remember and understand and love him by whom it was made."[115] Thus, the image of God is best seen when the mind is remembering, understanding and loving God. Thus,

---

112. *De Trinitate* XIV.11.
113. Ibid., XIV.6–10.
114. Ibid., XIV.22.
115. Ibid., XIV.15.

and here is the heart of my criticism, *in Augustine's thought man is most fully human when he is actively focused outward on God*. Stated differently, at the heart of what it means to be a human person is the Trinity and relationship. Man is in a real sense less than what he ought to be when he is focused inward. For Augustine, the image of God is not simply a static faculty such as reason. To truly image God in the fullest sense man must be focused in a loving relationship on *another*—God. Thus the "being" of man is only fully actualized when man is actively engaged in an outward focused relationship with God. As one who is created in the image of God, man does reflect the triune God. But the image is only repaired and actualized as man relates to God in a loving relationship. And this trinitarian image, which is only truly actualized when man is focused on God, will be only fully perfected when man comes to see God in a "face to face" vision. As Augustine writes, "For only when it comes to the perfect vision of God will this image bear God's perfect likeness."[116]

The implications of my argument here for Gunton's thesis should be clear. Although Augustine argues differently than Gunton, and states his position somewhat differently, for Augustine both *relationship* and *Trinity* constitute what it means for man to be. Rather than a precursor to Enlightenment individualism, Augustine offers a view of man in which man is *only* fully man when as image-bearer he is not focused on himself but on the Triune God. Relationship *does* constitute what it means when we say "man," for without this relationship to the only one who can perfect the image, man will always be less than fully human. I believe Gunton does not pay adequate enough attention to how the analogies function in *De Trinitate*. Unless the analogies are seen against the backdrop of Augustine's discussion of the face to face vision, and unless the *weaknesses* of many of the analogies are recognized, it is easy to miss what Augustine is doing. Additionally, if one does not follow Augustine's argument all the way to the end of *De Trinitate*, one might miss that in the end, *the image of God in man is only fully and truly realized when man sees God face to face*, that is, *when man's mind is off himself and directed to the Triune God in a loving relationship*.

---

116. Ibid., XIV.23.

Conclusion

In this summative, critical chapter, I have attempted to deal fairly yet critically with the thought of an important recent British theologian. In general, the criticisms have been negative. However, the criticisms do not ultimately undermine the theology of Colin Gunton, for reasons I will suggest in the concluding chapter. Having followed the general outline of the first five chapters of the monograph, I have offered a set of criticism under the general categories of the One and Many, creation, redemption and ontology. On the whole, I conclude that Gunton's interpretation and construal of the thought of Augustine is generally deficient. At times Gunton appears to misread Augustine, and to fail to take into consideration the complexity and genuine insights of Augustine's thought. Additionally, I have argued that Augustine's thought is actually quite friendly to a number of Gunton's own theological concerns. Paradoxically then, Augustine may be more of a theological friend than foe for Gunton's own theological endeavors.

CHAPTER 7

Conclusion

IN THIS MONOGRAPH I have attempted to come to terms with an important theological figure, Colin Gunton. The means I chose was the exposition and criticism of Gunton's own construal of Augustine. As I began to read the work of Gunton I was almost immediately struck by the towering presence of Augustine in Gunton's reconstruction of the history of Western thought. Throughout his work Augustine kept appearing as a foil, against which Gunton worked out his own theological proposals. As I worked through Gunton's corpus it became plain that many of the problems in the history of Western thought were to laid squarely at the feet of Augustine. Gunton's own architectonic vision of Western thought is quite impressive and is almost breathtaking in its attempt to draw theological, philosophical and ideological connections between myriad figures and movements. In all honesty, I was initially quite smitten with Gunton's theological reconstruction. I determined that in order to come to grips with Gunton's thought it would be necessary to spend some time with his chief foe, Augustine. I chose to concentrate on *De Trinitate* because it was ultimately Augustine's doctrine of God which seemed the most problematic for Gunton. However, while concentrating on *De Trinitate* it of course became necessary to take excursions into other well-known and some less well-known works by Augustine. As I began to get to know Augustine, it began to dawn on me that perhaps there were insights from Augustine that had not been appropriated or appreciated by Gunton. The more I read of Augustine this initial intuition began to be strengthened. I will not rework the previous chapters at this point, but I will suggest that my criticisms might fall under the following categories, which at times overlap.

First, some criticisms have suggested that Gunton has simply misread Augustine at certain points. For example, I have argued that, contra Gunton's interpretation of Augustine on creation, that the created order is fundamentally good. Augustine' dualism is a *limited* dualism, and the created order has a good, but limited role and purpose. Likewise, I have argued against Gunton that creation is not the act of "arbitrary" will in the thought of Augustine. Rather God's will is his being, and a *good* creation is created by a good God and is created out of God's goodness.

Second, my criticisms have attempted to show that at points Gunton is actually rather Augustinian in his theology, and that Gunton can find a *friend* not a *foe* in the bishop of Hippo. For example, I have tried to show that while Gunton laments that God is "unknowable" in Augustine's thought, in fact Augustine—particularly in his construal of the missions and processions—actually proffers a theological vision in which God is genuinely knowable indeed.

The nature of my criticisms should demonstrate that while I have ultimately been generally negative of Gunton regarding his interpretation and appropriation of Augustine, I am not trying to refute or disparage Gunton's overall theological project. On the contrary, Gunton is a unique voice in contemporary theology. A realist, an anti-modern (for the most part), a theologian not interested in embracing the latest fad, a theologian who thinks *theologically* about the dilemmas of modernity, Gunton's theology has much to commend it. Indeed, I have argued that by appropriating certain strengths in Augustine, Gunton's own theological efforts might be substantially strengthened. In particular, Gunton's own efforts might be fruitfully strengthened by the following Augustinian insights.

Augustine and Gunton

First, Augustine's doctrine of the missions and processions would seem to serve Gunton's own theological endeavors quite well. Augustine's important argument that the missions in time reveal the processions in eternity generates a number of things which would be helpful to Gunton. First, Augustine's construal of missions and processions would truly affirm Gunton's position that there should not be a dichotomy between the economic Trinity and the immanent Trinity. Indeed, that *is* Augustine's fundamental insight. God reveals himself in time as he truly is in eternity. Second, Augustine's construal of the missions and processions is in fundamental agreement with Gunton's conviction that revelation is always *mediated*, and that indeed God is knowable. Augustine's argument is that we know who God is because God has revealed himself in time. The sendings of the Son and the Spirit show us who God is.

Second, Augustine's repeated emphasis on the proper ends of the Christian life seem to concur with Gunton's own conviction that there is a fundamental connection between creation and redemption, as well as Gunton's emphasis on the centrality of relationship as fundamental to what it means for man "to be." A notion which pervades Augustine's writing, both in *De Trinitate* and elsewhere, is the notion that there is a proper *telos* or goal to the Christian life. For Augustine it is the vision of God when we will see God "face to face." Augustine's emphasis on this proper end seems to provide the purposiveness which Gunton wishes to see in creation. Similarly, Augustine's idea that the proper end of man is the vision of God seems to place relationship at the heart of what it means to be a person, and this emphasis in Augustine would seem to harmonize with Gunton's emphasis on the centrality of relationship.

Third, Augustine's emphasis on the simplicity of God may help remove some ambiguity from Gunton's own thought. I argued earlier that Gunton seems a bit unclear as to whether God "needed" to create or not. Gunton, with classical Christianity, will say that God does *not* need to create, but then he is a bit hesitant to affirm that God creates simply due to his will. A proper understanding of God's simplicity would lead one to affirm that there need not be a dichotomy between "will" and "goodness," or between "will" and any of other attributes of God, whether we are speaking of love, wisdom, etc. Because God *is* fundamentally good, one can argue *both* that creation flows out of God's goodness *and* that creation is a result of God's will. Indeed, God's will is not "arbitrary," but operates in accords with God's fundamental goodness.

Fourth, although we have not offered an explicit criticism of Gunton's view of modernity, it should be pointed out that the thought of Augustine provides a rich conceptual and theological mine of help in living in, and responding to, the modern age. I simply offer a few brief suggestions here. First, it may be that Augustine's concern for the unity of God is a *blessing* and not a *curse* at all. The fundamental unity of God would seem to be a theological affirmation which is to *treasured* rather than *disparaged*, because the fundamental unity of things may be just what is needed in a confused, disoriented age which largely seems to have no bearings at all. Second, Augustine's repeated emphasis on an ordered creation would also seem to be a welcome word to our age. The idea that there are *limits* which are simply part of the created order, and that these limits should be respected is an idea which might seem foreign to our age. That the world has actually has an order and a moral structure *inherent* to it and not imposed haphazardly by the human creature is an idea which would certainly have consequences if it ever found receptive soil. Finally, the notion that there is a *telos* to the created order, and that this *telos* has been shaped by a good and sovereign Lord, and that there is a proper end for man is a potentially powerful message. This message that could also bear fruit, if ever truly recognized and affirmed.

In short, Augustine need not be a foe of Gunton. Indeed, key Augustinian insights seem quite friendly to Gunton's theological project, and Gunton seems himself to be an Augustinian at key points in his own thinking, even if this indebtedness is not completely recognized.

Possibilities for Further Research

There are several possibilities for further research which could follow from this study, and which could treat in further detail issues which have been broached here. First, a more in-depth exploration of the trinitarian theology of the Cappadocians and Augustine could be very fruitful. Having spent some time with Augustine for this monograph it has become evident that a rethinking of the common way of construing the differences between the Cappadocians and Augustine is necessary. The received view that Augustine began with the one and moved to the three while the Cappadocians began with the three and moved to the one needs to be rethought, if not outright rejected. Augustine's thought is too complex for such a simple summary, and the Cappadocians are also done less than justice in such a schema. Such contrasts of "West" and "East" appear to ignore the commonalities which existed during the first four to five centuries of the Christian Church, and appear to impose a construct which is less than faithful to the intricacies of these theological traditions.

Second, further research could examine Augustine with a sharper eye to his particular style of discourse. *De Trinitate* reads very differently from later works such as Thomas' *Summa Theologiae*, and certainly differently from theological manuals, whether they be Melancthon's *Loci Communes* or later systematic theologies. I suspect Augustine is prone to misinterpretation because interpreters have sought to pull out certain theological truths in isolation from the overall plan of *De Trinitate*. In particular, if one seeks simply to summarize Augustine's view of the Trinity by listing key analogies, one is very likely going to miss Augustine's teaching. Augustine is seeking the vision of God, and it is crucial to remain with him to the end of the volume, for then one learns that the *imago Dei* which reflects the Trinity is only fully realized when one is directed off oneself and towards God. That is, Augustine's doctrine of the image of God is fundamentally other-centered and relational. Further research on Augustine needs to pay close attention to the overall purpose and goal of his text, and that Augustine can at times raise possible solutions to problems only to drop them several pages later, when the potentially helpful idea has proved unsuccessful.

Third, further research could be done in terms of a project of retrieval. That is, how can Augustine speak today? I have outlined very briefly above how key Augustinian insights might speak to the contemporary milieu. Augustine moved in a world quite different from our own. The benefit of spending time with a pre-modern theologian is that one is granted the freedom to bracket, at least for a time, and to a certain degree, certain contemporary issues that can predominate theological discussion. By spending time with an Augustine one is in a sense freed up to think theologically without getting bogged down in the often sterile and troubled world of modern theology. If Christian theology is to speak today with a meaningful message, it will be because it has spent time with figures like Augustine, and has learned from the experience.

Bibliography

Adam, Peter. "The Trinity and Human Community." In *Grace and Truth in the Secular Age*, edited by Timothy Bradshaw, 52-65. Grand Rapids: Eerdmans, 1998.
Allen, Diogenes. "Christianity and the Creed of Postmodernism." *Christian Scholar's Review* 23 (1993) 117-26.
Allers, Rudolf. "The Notions of Triad and of Meditation in the Thought of St. Augustine." *The New Scholsticism* 31.4 (October 1957) 499-525.
Anderson, James F. *St. Augustine and Being: A Metaphysical Essay*. The Hague: Martinus Nijhoff, 1965.
Andrews, Robert. "Boethius on Relation in De Trinitate." In *Editing of Theological and Philosophical Texts from the Middle Ages*, edited by Monika Asztalos, 281-89. Stockholm: Amquist & Wiksell, 1986.
Anselm. *Monologion*. In *Anselm of Canterbury: The Major Works*, edited by Brian Davies and G. R. Evans, 5-81. Oxford: Oxford University Press, 1998.
Aquinas, Thomas. *Summa Theologiae: A Concise Translation*. Translated by Timothy McDermott. Westminster, MD: Christian Classics, 1989.
Arendt, Hannah. *The Life of the Mind*. Vol. 2, *Willing*. New York: Harcourt Brace Jovanovich, 1978.
Aristotle. *Metaphysics*. Vol. 1. Translated by H. Tredennick. Vol. 2. Translated by H. Tredennick and G. Cyril Armstrong. Loeb Classical Library. Cambridge: Harvard University Press, 1933.
Armstrong, A. H. "St. Augustine and Christian Platonism." In *Augustine: A Collection of Critical Essays*, edited by R. A. Markus, 3-37. Garden City, NY: Anchor, 1972.
Arnold, Duane W. H., and Pamela Bright, editors. *"De Doctrina Christiana": A Classic of Western Culture*. Christianity and Judaism in Antiquity. Notre Dame: University of Notre Dame Press, 1995.
Augustine. *Against Julian (Contra Julianum)*. Translated by Matthew A. Schumacher. The Fathers of the Church 35. Washington, DC: Catholic University of America Press, 1957.

———. *The City of God* (*De civitate Dei*). Translated by Marcus Dods. New York: Modern Library, 1950.

———. *Confessions* (*Confessiones*). Translated by Maria Boulding. Edited by John E. Rotelle. The Works of Saint Augustine: A Translation for the 21st Century. Brooklyn: New City, 1991.

———. *De Trinitate*. Corpus Christianorum Series Latina 51–52. Turnholti: Brepols Editores Pontificii, 1968.

———. *Eighty-Three Different Questions* (*De diversis quaestionibus octoginta tribus*). Translated by David L. Mosher. The Fathers of the Church 70. Washington, DC: Catholic University of America Press, 1982.

———. *Faith, Hope, and Charity* (*Enchiridion de fide, spe et caritate*). Translated by Bernard M. Peebles. The Fathers of the Church 21. Washington, DC: Catholic University of America Press, 1947.

———. *Letters 1-82* (*Epistulae*). Translated by Sister Wilfrid Parsons. The Fathers of the Church 1. Washington, DC: Catholic University of America Press, 1951.

———. *The Literal Meaning of Genesis* (*De Genesi ad litteram*). Translated by John Hammond Taylor. Ancient Christian Writers 41–42. New York: Newman, 1982.

———. *On Faith and the Creed* (*De fide et symbolo*). Translated by S. D. F. Salmond. *Nicene and Post-Nicene Fathers* 3. Peabody, MA: Hendrickson, 1994.

———. *On Teaching Christianity* (*De Doctrina Christiana*). The Works of Saint Augustine: A Translation for the 21st Century I/11. Edited by John E. Rotelle and translated by Edmund Hill. Hyde Park, NY: New City, 1992.

———. *On the Literal Interpretation of Genesis: An Unfinished Book* (*De Genesi ad litteram imperfectus liber*). Translated by Roland J. Teske. The Fathers of the Church 11. Washington, DC: Catholic University of America Press, 1991.

———. *On the Nature of the Good* (*De natura boni*). Translated by Richard Stothert and Albert H. Newman. Nicene and Post-Nicene Fathers 4. Peabody, MA: Hendrickson, 1994.

———. *The Retractions* (*Retractationes*). Translated by Sister Mary Inez Bogan. The Fathers of the Church 60. Washington, DC: Catholic University of America Press, 1968.

———. *The Teacher* (*De Magistro*). Translated by Joseph M. Colleran. Ancient Christian Writers 9. New York: Newman, 1949.

———. *The Trinity* (*De Trinitate*). Translated by Edmund Hill. The Works of Saint Augustine: A Translation for the 21st Century I/5. Brooklyn: New City, 1991.

———. *Two Books on Genesis Against the Manichees* (*De Genesi adversus Manicheos*). Translated by Roland J. Teske. The Fathers of the Church 19. Washington, DC: Catholic University of America Press, 1991.

Ayer, A. J. "The Concept of Person." In *The Concept of a Person and Other Essays*. London: Macmillan, 1963.

Ayres, Lewis. "Augustine, the Trinity and Modernity: Review of *The One, the Three, and the Many* by Colin E. Gunton." *Augustinian Studies* 26:2 (1995) 127–33.

———. "The Discipline of Self-Knowledge in Augustine's De trinitate Book X." In *The Passionate Intellect: Essays on the Transformation of Classical Traditions*, edited by Lewis Ayres, Rutgers University Studies in Classical Humanities 7, 261–96. New Brunswick: Transaction, 1995.

———. "The Fundamental Grammar of Augustine's Theology." In *Augustine and His Critics*, edited by R. Dodaro and G. Lawless, 51–76. New York: Routledge, 2000.

———. "'Remember that you are Catholic' (serm. 52.2): Augustine on the Unity of the Triune God." *Journal of Early Christian Studies* 8 (2000) 39–82.
Barnes, Michel R. "The Arians of Book V and the Genre of *De Trinitate*." *Journal of Theological Studies* NS 44 (1993) 185–95.
———. "Augustine in Contemporary Trinitarian Theology." *Theological Studies* 56 (1995) 237–50.
———. "Exegesis and Polemic in Augustine's *De Trinitate* I." *Augustinian Studies* 30 (1999) 43–59.
Barth, Karl. *Church Dogmatics*. Edited by G. W. Bromiley and T. F. Torrance. Translated by G. T. Thomson and Harold Knight. Edinburgh: T. & T. Clark, 1956.
———. *The Holy Spirit and the Christian Life: The Theological Basis of Ethics*. Translated by R. Birch Hoyle. Louisville: Westminster John Knox, 1993.
———. *Protestant Thought: From Rousseau to Ritschl*. Translated by Brian Cozens. New York: Harper, 1959.
Bartholomew, Craig. "The Healing of Modernity: A Trinitarian Remedy? A Critical Dialogue with Colin Gunton's *The One, the Three and the Many: God, Creation and the Culture of Modernity*." *European Journal of Theology* 6:2 (1997) 111–30.
Basil of Caesarea. *Letters*. Translated by Sister Agnes Clare Way. The Fathers of the Church 13 and 28. Washington, DC: Catholic University of America Press, 1951 and 1955.
Blocher, Henri. "Immanence and Transcendence in Trinitarian Theology." In *The Trinity in a Pluralistic Age: Theological Essays on Culture and Religion*, edited by Kevin J. Vanhoozer, 104–23. Grand Rapids: Eerdmans, 1997.
Booth, Edward. "From Augustine to Aristotle." *Augustiniana* 27 (1977) 70–104.
———. *Saint Augustine and the Western Tradition of Self-Knowing*. The St. Augustine Lecture 1986. Villanova, PA: Villanova University Press, 1989.
———. "St. Augustine's De Trinitate and Aristotelian and Neo-Platonist Noetic." In *Studia Patristica*, vol. 16.2, edited by Elizabeth Livingstone. Berlin: Akademie-Verlag, 1985.
———. "St. Augustine's *notitia sui* Related to Aristotle and the Early Platonists." *Augustiniana* 27 (1977) 70–132, 363–401; 28 (1978) 183–221; 29 (1979) 97–124.
Bourassa, Francois. "Le don de Dieu." *Gregorianum* 50 (1969) 201–37.
Bourke, Vernon J. *Augustine's Question of Wisdom: Life and Philosophy of the Bishop of Hippo*. Milwaukee: Bruce, 1947.
———. *Augustine's View of Reality*. The Saint Augustine Lecture 1963. Villanova, PA: University Press, 1964.
———. "The Body-Soul Relation in Early Augustine." In *Collectanea Augustiniana: "Second Founder of the Faith,"* edited by Joseph C. Schnaubelt and Frederick Van Fleteren, 435–50. New York: Peter Lang, 1990.
Bradshaw, Timothy. *Grace and Truth in the Secular Age*. Grand Rapids: Eerdmans, 1997.
———. *Trinity and Ontology: A Comparative Study of the Theologies of Karl Barth and Wolfhart Pannenberg*. Rutherford Studies Series Two: Contemporary Theology. Edinburgh: Rutherford, 1988.
Bray, Gerald. *The Doctrine of God*. Contours of Christian Theology. Downers Grove, IL: InterVarsity, 1993.
———. "The Patristic Dogma." In *One God in Trinity*, edited by Peter Toon and James D. Spiceland, 42–61. Westchester, IL: Cornerstone, 1980.
Brown, David. *The Divine Trinity*. London: Duckworth, 1985.
Brown, Peter. *Augustine of Hippo: A Biography*. Berkeley: University of California Press, 1967.

Buckley, Michael. *At the Origins of Modern Atheism*. New Haven: Yale University Press, 1987.
Calvin, John. *The Institutes of the Christian Religion*. 2 vols. Translated by Ford Lewis Battles. Edited by John T. McNeill. Library of Christian Classics. Philadelphia: Westminster, 1960.
Campenhausen, Hans von. *The Fathers of the Church*. 2 vols. Translated by Manfred Hoffman. Peabody, MA: Hendrickson, 1998.
———. "Neuere Augustin-Literatur." *Theologische Rundschau* N.S. 17 (1948–1949) 51–72.
Carson, Donald A. *The Gagging of God: Christianity Confronts Pluralism*. Grand Rapids: Zondervan, 1996.
Cavadini, John. "The Structure and Intent in Augustine's *De Trinitate*." *Augustinian Studies* 23 (1992) 103–23.
Chia, Ronald. "Trinity and Ontology: Colin Gunton's Ecclesiology." *International Journal of Systematic Theology* 9 (2007) 452–68.
Clark, Mary T. *Augustinian Personalism*. Villanova, PA: Villanova University Press, 1970.
———. "Augustine's Theology of the Trinity: Its Relevance." *Dionysius* 13 (1989) 71–84.
———. "The Trinity in Latin Christianity." In *Christian Spirituality: Origins to the Twelfth Century*, edited by Bernard McGinn, John Meyendorff, and Jean Leclercq, 276–90. New York: Crossroads, 1985.
Clarke, Paul A. B. "On Modernity." In *Theology, the University and the Modern World*, edited by Paul A. B. Clark and Andrew Linzey, 91–136. London: Lester & Crook, 1988.
Cochrane, Charles N. *Christianity and Classical Culture*. New York: Oxford University Press, 1944.
Colyer, Elmer M. *The Promise of Trinitarian Theology: Theologians in Dialogue with T. F. Torrance*. Lanham, MD: Rowman & Littlefield, 2002.
Conyers, A. J. *God, Hope, and History: Jürgen Moltmann and the Christian Concept of History*. Macon, GA: Mercer University Press, 1988.
Corpus Augustinianum Gissense. CD-ROM. Basel: Schwabe AG, 1995.
Crouse, R. D. "St. Augustine's *De Trinitate*: Philosophical Method." In *Studia Patristica* 16.2, edited by Elizabeth Livingstone, 501–10. Berlin: Akademie, 1985.
Cruickshank, Colin John. "Saint Augustine in Early New England." PhD diss., University of Maine, 1996.
Cunningham, David S. *These Three are One: The Practice of Trinitarian Theology*. Challenges in Contemporary Theology. Malden, MA: Blackwell, 1998.
Daniélou, Jean. *The Origins of Latin Christianity*. Translated by David Smith and John Austin Baker. A History of Early Christian Doctrine before the Council of Nicaea 3. Philadelphia: Westminster, 1977.
Davies, Brian. *The Thought of Thomas Aquinas*. Oxford: Oxford University Press, 1993.
De Régnon, Theodore. *Études de théologie positive sur la Sainte Trinité*. Paris: Victor Retaux, 1892 / 1898.
Du Roy, Olivier. *L'Intellegence de la Foi en la Trinité Selon Saint Augustin*. Paris: Études Augustiniennes, 1966.
Durrant, Michael. *Theology and Intelligibility*. Boston: Routledge & Keagan Paul, 1973.
Erickson, Millard J. *God in Three Persons: A Contemporary Interpretation of the Trinity*. Grand Rapids: Baker, 1995.
Evans, G. R. *Anselm*. Outstanding Christian Thinkers. Wilton, CT: Morehouse-Barlow, 1989.

Fleteren, Frederick Van, Joseph C. Schnaubelt, and Joseph Reino, editors. *Augustine: Mystic and Mystagogue*. Collectanea Augustiniana. New York: Peter Lang, 1994.
Fortman, Edmund J. *The Triune God: A Historical Study of the Doctrine of the Trinity*. Philadelphia: Westminster, 1972.
Frame, John M. *The Doctrine of the Knowledge of God: A Theology of Lordship*. Phillipsburg, NJ: Presbyterian & Reformed, 1987.
Fredriksen, Paula. "Vile Bodies: Paul and Augustine on the Resurrection of the Flesh." In *Biblical Hermeneutics in Historical Perspective: Studies in Honor of Karlfried Froehlich on His Sixtieth Birthday*, edited by Mark S. Burrows and Paul Rorem, 75–87. Grand Rapids: Eerdmans, 1991.
Fuller, Peter. *Theoria: Art and the Absence of Grace*. London: Chatto & Windus, 1988.
Gay, Peter. *The Enlightenment: An Interpretation*. Vol. 1: *The Rise of Modern Paganism*. New York: Knopf, 1966.
———. *The Enlightenment: An Interpretation*. Vol. 2: *The Science of Freedom*. New York: Knopf, 1969.
Gilson, Etienne. *The Christian Philosophy of Saint Augustine*. Translated by L. E. M. Lynch. New York: Random House, 1960.
———. *The Spirit of Medieval Philosophy*. Gifford Lectures, 1931–1932. New York: Scribner's, 1949.
Gondek, Adela Jessica. "On the Origin of Modern Liberalism in Medieval Christian Thought: A Comparative Study of Augustine, Thomas, and Aristotle." PhD diss., Harvard University, 1981.
Grabowski, Stanislaus J. *The All-Present God: A Study in St. Augustine*. St. Louis: Herder, 1954.
Green, Bradley G. "The Protomodern Augustine? Colin Gunton and the Failure of Augustine." *International Journal of Systematic Theology* 9 (2007) 328–41.
Guitton, Jean. *The Modernity of Saint Augustine*. Translated by A. V. Littledale. Baltimore: Helicon, 1959.
Gunton, Colin E. *The Actuality of Atonement: A Study of Metaphor, Rationality, and the Christian Tradition*. Grand Rapids: Eerdmans, 1989.
———. "Augustine, the Trinity and the Theological Crisis of the West." *Scottish Journal of Theology* 43 (1990) 33–58.
———. *The Barth Lectures*. Edited by P. H. Brazier. London: T. & T. Clark, 2007.
———. "Barth on the Western Intellectual Tradition: Towards a Theology After Christendom." In *Theology Beyond Christendom: Essays on the Centenary of Karl Barth, May 10, 1886*, edited by J. Thompson, 285–301. Allison Park, PA: Pickwick, 1986.
———. *Becoming and Being: The Doctrine of God in Charles Hartshorne and Karl Barth*. Oxford: Oxford University Press, 1978.
———. *A Brief Theology of Revelation*. The 1993 Warfield Lectures. Edinburgh: T. & T. Clark, 1995.
———, editor. *The Cambridge Companion to Christian Doctrine*. Cambridge: Cambridge University Press, 1997.
———. *Christ and Creation*. The Didsbury Lectures, 1990. Grand Rapids: Eerdmans, 1992.
———. "The Christian Doctrine of God: Opposition and Convergence." In *Heaven and Earth: Essex Essays in Theology and Ethics*, edited by Andrew Linzey and Peter Wexler, 11–22. Worthing, England: Churchman, 1986.

———. *The Christian Faith: An Introduction.* Cambridge: Blackwell, 2001.

———. "Christology: Two Dogmas Revisited—Edward Irving's Christology." In *Theology Through the Theologians: Selected Essays 1972–1995*, 151–68. Edinburgh: T. & T. Clark, 1996.

———. "Christus Victor Revisited: A Study in Metaphor and the Transformation of Meaning." *Journal of Theological Studies* NS 36 (1985) 129–45.

———. "The Church on Earth: The Roots of Community." In *On Being the Church: Essays on the Christian Community*, edited by Colin E. Gunton and Daniel W. Hardy, 48–80. Edinburgh: T. & T. Clark, 1989.

———. "Creation and Recreation: An Exploration of Some Themes in Aesthetics and Theology." *Modern Theology* 2 (1985) 1–19.

———. "The Doctrine of Creation." In *The Cambridge Companion to Christian Doctrine*, edited by Colin E. Gunton, 141–88. Cambridge: Cambridge University Press, 1997.

———. *Enlightenment and Alienation: An Essay Towards a Trinitarian Theology.* Grand Rapids: Eerdmans, 1985.

———. "A Far-Off Gleam of the Gospel: Salvation in Tolkien's Lord of the Rings." *King's Theological Review* 12 (1989) 6–10.

———, editor. *God and Freedom: Essays in Historical and Systematic Theology.* Edinburgh: T. & T. Clark, 1995.

———. "God the Holy Spirit: Augustine and His Successors." In *Theology through the Theologians: Selected Essays 1972–1995*, 105–28. Edinburgh: T. & T. Clark, 1996.

———. "God, Grace, and Freedom." In *God and Freedom: Essays in Historical and Systematic Theology*, edited by Colin E. Gunton, 119–33. Edinburgh: T. & T. Clark, 1995.

———. "Historical and Systematic Theology." In *The Cambridge Companion to Christian Doctrine*, edited by Colin E. Gunton, 3–20. Cambridge: Cambridge University Press, 1997.

———. *Intellect and Action: Elucidations on Christian Theology and the Life of Faith.* Edinburgh: T. & T. Clark, 2001.

———. "Knowledge and Culture: Towards an Epistemology of the Concrete." In *The Gospel and Contemporary Culture*, edited by H. Montefiore, 84–102. London: Mowbray, 1992.

———. "Mozart the Theologian." *Theology* 94 (1991) 346–49.

———. "No Other Foundation: One Englishman's Reading of Church Dogmatics, chapter V." In *Reckoning With Barth: Essays in Commemoration of Karl Barth's Birthday*, edited by Nigel Biggar, 61–79. London: Mowbray, 1988.

———. *The One, the Three and the Many: God, Creation and the Culture of Modernity.* The 1992 Bampton Lectures. Cambridge: Cambridge University Press, 1994.

———. "The Political Christ: Some Reflections on Mr. Cupitt's Thesis." *Scottish Journal of Theology* 32 (1979) 521–40.

———. *The Promise of Trinitarian Theology.* Edinburgh: T. & T. Clark, 1991.

———. *The Promise of Trinitarian Theology.* 2nd ed. Edinburgh: T. & T. Clark, 1997.

———. "Proteus and Procrustes: A Study in the Dialectic of Language in Disagreement with Sallie McFague." In *Speaking the Christian God: The Holy Trinity and the Challenge of Feminism*, edited by A. Kimel Jr., 65–80. Grand Rapids: Eerdmans; Leominister, 1992.

———. *Revelation and Reason.* Edited by P. H. Brazier. London: T. & T. Clark, 2008.

———. Review of *Justitia Dei: A History of the Christian Doctrine of Justification, I: Beginnings to 1500*, by Alister E. McGrath. *Expository Times* 99 (1987) xiii, 252.

———. "The Sacrifice and the Sacrifices: From Metaphor to Transcendental?" In *Trinity, Incarnation, and Atonement: Philosophical and Theological Essays*, edited by Ronald J. Feenstra and Cornelius Plantinga Jr., 210–29. Notre Dame: University of Notre Dame Press, 1990.

———. "Time, Eternity and the Doctrine of the Incarnation." *Dialog* 21 (1982) 263–68.

———. *Theology through Preaching*. Edinburgh: T. & T. Clark, 2001.

———. *Theology through the Theolgians: Selected Essays 1972–1995*. Edinburgh: T. & T. Clark, 1996.

———. "The Trinity in Modern Theology." In *Companion Encyclopedia of Theology*, 937–57. London: Routledge, 1995.

———. *The Triune Creator: A Historical and Systematic Study*. Grand Rapids: Eerdmans, 1998.

———. "Two Dogmas Revisited: Edward Irving's Christology." *Scottish Journal of Theology* 41 (1988) 359–76.

———. "Universal and Particular in Atonement Theology." *Religious Studies* 28 (1992) 453–66.

———. "Using and Being Used: Scripture and Systematic Theology." *Theology Today* 47 (1990) 248–59.

———. *Yesterday and Today: A Study of Continuities in Christology*. Grand Rapids: Eerdmans, 1983.

Gunton, Colin E., and Daniel W. Hardy. *On Being the Church: Essays on the Christian Community*. Edinburgh: T. & T. Clark, 1989.

Hanby, Michael. *Augustine and Modernity*. Radical Orthodoxy Series. London: Routledge, 2003.

Harnack, Adolf. *History of Dogma*. 7 vols. Translated by Neil Buchanan. 1894–1900. Reprint, Eugene, OR: Wipf & Stock, 1997.

Henry, Paul. *Augustine on Creation*. The 1967 Saint Augustine Lectures, unpublished.

———. *Saint Augustine on Personality*. The Saint Augustine Lecture 1959. New York: Macmillan, 1960.

Hill, Edmund. *The Mystery of the Trinity*. Introducing Catholic Theology 4. London: Geoffrey Chapman, 1985.

———. "Our Knowledge of the Trinity." *Scottish Journal of Theology* 27 (1974) 1–11.

Hill, William J. *The Three Personed God*. Washington, DC: Catholic University Press, 1982.

Houston, James. "Spirituality and the Doctrine of the Trinity." In *Christ in Our Place: The Humanity of God in Christ for the Reconciliation of the World: Essays Presented to Professor James Torrance*, edited by Trevor A. Hart and Daniel P. Thimell, 48–69. Allison Park, PA: Pickwick, 1989.

Jenson, Robert W. "The Triune God." In *Christian Dogmatics*, vol. 1., edited by Carl E. Braaten and Robert W. Jenson, 83–191. Philadelphia: Fortress, 1984.

———. *The Triune Identity: God According to the Gospel*. Philadelphia: Fortress, 1982.

Jones, E. Michael. *Degenerate Moderns*. San Francisco: Ignatius, 1995.

Jüngel, Eberhard. *The Doctrine of the Trinity*. Translated by Horton Harris. Edinburgh: Scottish Academic, 1976.

———. *God as the Mystery of the World: On the Foundation of the Theology of the Crucified One in the Dispute between Theism and Atheism*. Translated by D. L. Guder. Edinburgh: T. & T. Clark, 1983.

Kany, Roland. "Fidei contemnentes initium: On Certain Positions Opposed by Augustine in De Trinitate." In *Studia Patristica* 18, edited by Elizabeth A. Livingstone. Leuven: Peeters, 1993.

Knight, G. A. F. *A Biblical Approach to the Doctrine of the Trinity*. Scottish Journal of Theology Occasional Papers No. 1. Edinburgh: Oliver & Boyd, 1953.

La Croix, Richard. "Augustine on the Simplicity of God." *The New Scholasticism* 51 (1977) 468–69.

———. "Wainwright, Augustine and God's Simplicity." *The New Scholasticism* 53 (1979) 124–27.

LaCugna, Catherine Mowry. Review of *The Promise of Trinitarian Theology*, by Colin E. Gunton. *Modern Theology* 9 (1993) 307–9.

Landesman, Charles, editor. *The Problem of Universals*. New York: Basic, 1971.

Lasch, Christopher. *The True and Only Heaven: Progress and Its Critics*. New York: Norton, 1991.

Lawless, George. "Augustine and Human Embodiment." In *Collectanea Augustiniana: Melanges T. Van Bavel*, edited by B. Bruning, M. Lamberigts, and J. Van Houtem, 167–86. Leuven: University Press, 1990.

———. "Augustine of Hippo and His Critics." In *Augustine: Presbyter Factus Sum*, 3–28. New York: Peter Lang, 1993.

Leff, Gordon. "Wyclif and the Augustinian Tradition: With Special Reference to His De Trinitate." In *Studies in Medieval and Renaissance Culture: Essays In Honor of Samuel Harrison Thomson*, edited by Paul M. Clogan, 29–39. Cleveland: Press of Case Western Reserve University, 1970.

LeMoine, Fannie, and Christopher Kleinhenz, editors. *Saint Augustine the Bishop*. Garland Reference Library of the Humanities. New York: Garland, 1994.

Lienhard, Joseph T., Earl C. Muller, and Roland Teske, editors. *Augustine: Presbyter Factus Sum*. Collectanea Augustiniana. New York: Peter Lang, 1993.

Livingstone, Elizabeth A., editor. *Studia Patristica*. Vol. 22, *Cappadocian Fathers, Chrysostom and Greek Contemporaries, Augustine, Donatism, Pelagianism*. Louvain: Peeters, 1989.

Lloyd, G. E. R. *Aristotle: The Growth and Structure of His Thought*. Cambridge: Cambridge University Press, 1968.

Lorenz, Rudolf. "Augustinliteratur seit dem Jubiläum von 1954." *Theologische Rundschau* N.S. 25 (1959) 1–75.

———. "Zwölf Jahre Augustinusforschung (1959–1970)." *Theologische Rundschau* 40 (1975) 227–61.

Loux, Michael J. *Universals and Particulars: Readings in Ontology*. Notre Dame: University of Notre Dame Press, 1976.

MacIntyre, Alasdair. *Three Rival Versions of Moral Enquiry: Encyclopaedia, Genealogy, and Tradition*. Notre Dame: University of Notre Dame Press, 1990.

Macmurray, John. *Persons in Relation*. London: Faber & Faber, 1961.

Manchester, Peter. "The Noetic Triad in Plotinus, Marius Victorinus, and Augustine." In *Neoplatonism and Gnosticism*, edited by Richard T. Wallis and Jay Breman, 209–24. Studies in Neoplatonism: Ancient and Modern 6. New York: SUNY Press, 1991.

Marrou, Henri. I. *The Resurrection and Saint Augustine's Theology of Human Values*. Translated by Maria Consolata. The Saint Augustine Lectures 1965. Villanova, PA: Villanova University Press, 1966.

Martin, Elaine Mary. "Seek God's Face Evermore: A Study of the Structure and Common Themes in Augustine's 'De Trinitate' and Langland's 'Piers Plowman.'" PhD diss., Yale University, 1986.

Martland, Thomas Rodolphe. "Study of Cappadocian and Augustinian Trinitarian Methodology." *Anglican Theological Review* 47 (1965) 252–63.

Mayer, Cornelio, and Karl Heinz Chelius, editors. *Augustinus-Lexicon*. Vol. 1. Basel: Schwabe AG, 1986–1994.

McCormak, Bruce L. "The One, the Three and the Many: In Memory of Colin Gunton." *Cultural Encounters* 1.2 (2005) 7–17.

McGrath, Alister A., editor. *The Blackwell Encyclopedia of Modern Christian Thought*. Oxford: Blackwell, 1995.

McWilliam, Joanne, editor. *Augustine: From Rhetor to Theologian*. Waterloo, Ontario: Wilfrid Laurier University Press, 1992.

Meagher, Robert. *Augustine: An Introduction*. New York: Harper Colophon, 1978.

Metzger, Paul Louis. *Trinitarian Soundings in Systematic Theology*. London: T. & T. Clark, 2005.

Milbank, John. "An Essay Against Secular Order." *Journal of Religious Ethics* 15 (1987) 199–223.

———. "'Postmodern Critical Augustinianism': A Short *Summa* in Forty Two Responses to Unasked Questions." *Modern Theology* 7 (1991) 225–37.

———. *Theology and Social Theory: Beyond Secular Reason*. Oxford: Blackwell, 1990.

———. "Theology Without Substance: Christianity, Signs, Origins." [Part One] *Journal of Literature and Theology* 2 (1988) 1–17.

———. "Theology Without Substance: Christianity, Signs, Origins." [Part Two] *Journal of Literature and Theology* 2 (1988) 131–52.

———. *The Word Made Strange: Theology, Language and Culture*. Oxford: Blackwell, 1996.

Miles, Margaret Ruth. *Augustine on the Body*. American Academy of Religion Dissertation Series. Missoula, MT: Scholars, 1979.

Moltmann, Jürgen. *God in Creation: A New Theology of Creation and The Spirit of God*. The Gifford Lectures 1984–1985. San Francisco: HarperSanFransisco, 1991.

Moltmann, Jürgen. *The Crucified God*. London: SCM, 1974.

———. *The Trinity and the Kingdom*. London: SCM, 1981.

Mourant, J. A. "The *Cogitos*: Augustinian and Cartesian." *Augustinian Studies* 10 (1979) 27–42.

Muller, Earl C. "Rhetorical and Theological Issues in the Structuring of Augustine's *De Trinitate*." In *Studia Patristica* 27, edited by Elizabeth A. Livingstone. Leuven: Peeters, 1993.

———. "Trinity and Marriage in Paul: Theological Shape as Ground for a Scriptural Warrant for a Communitarian Analogy of the Trinity." PhD diss., Marquette University, 1987.

Murphy, Nancey, and James Wm. McClendon Jr. "Distinguishing Modern and Postmodern Theologies." *Modern Theology* 5 (1989) 191–214.

O'Daly, Gerald. *Augustine's Philosophy of Mind*. Berkeley: University of California Press, 1987.

O'Donovan, Oliver. *Resurrection and Moral Order: An Outline for Evangelical Ethics*. 2nd ed. Grand Rapids: Eerdmans, 1994.

O'Leary, Joseph Stephen. "Overcoming Augustine." In *Questioning Back: The Overcoming of Metaphysics in Christian Tradition*, 165–202. Minneapolis: Winston, 1985.

O'Meara, John J. "Studies Prepatory to an Understanding of the Mysticism of St. Augustine and His Doctrine on the Trinity." *Augustinian Studies* 1 (1970) 263–76.

O'Toole, Christopher J. *The Philosophy of Creation in the Writings of St. Augustine*. The Catholic University of America Philosophy Series. Washington, DC: Catholic University of America Press, 1944.

Oberman, Heiko A., and Frank James III, editors. *Via Augustini: Augustine in the Later Middle Ages Renaissance and Reformation: Essays in Honor of Damasus Trapp*. Studies in Medieval and Reformation Thought. Leiden: Brill, 1991.

Olson, Roger. "Trinity and Eschatology: The Historical Being of God in Jürgen Moltmann and Wolfhart Pannenberg." *Scottish Journal of Theology* 36 (1983) 213–27.

———. "Wolfhart Pannenberg's Doctrine of the Trinity." *Scottish Journal of Theology* 43 (1990) 175–206.

Osborne, Catherine. "The Nexus Amoris in Augustine's Trinity." In *Studia Patristica* 22: *Cappadocian Fathers, Chrysostom and Greek Contemporaries, Augustine, Donatism, Pelagianism*, edited by Elizabeth A. Livingstone. Leuven: Peeters, 1989.

Pannenberg, Wolfhart. *Systematic Theology*. Vol. 1. Translated by G. W. Bromiley. Grand Rapids: Eerdmans, 1988.

Pelikan, Jaroslav J. "Canonica Regula: The Trinitarian Hermeneutics of Augustine." In *Collectanea Augustiniana*, edited by J. Schnaubelt and F. Van Fleteren, 327–43. New York: Peter Lang, 1990.

Plantinga, Cornelius, Jr. "The Fourth Gospel as Trinitarian Source Then and Now." In *Biblical Hermeneutics in Historical Perspective: Studies in Honor of Karlfried Froehlich on His Sixtieth Birthday*, edited by Mark S. Burrows and Paul Rorem, 303–21. Grand Rapids: Eerdmans, 1991.

———. "The Hodgson-Welch Debate and the Social Analogy of the Trinity." PhD diss., Princeton Theological Seminary, 1982.

Portalie, Eugene. *A Guide to the Thought of Saint Augustine*. Translated by Ralph J. Bastian. Chicago: Henry Regnery, 1960.

Prestige, G. L. *God in Patristic Thought*. London: SPCK, 1959.

Rahner, Karl. "Remarks on the Dogmatic Treatise De Trinitate." In *Theological Investigations*, vol. 4: *More Recent Writings*, translated by Kevin Smyth, 77–102. Baltimore: Helicon Press, 1966.

———. *The Trinity*. Translated by Joseph Donceel. London: Burns & Oates, 1970.

Richard of St. Victor. *The Trinity*. Translated by Benjamin Minor. London: SPCK, 1979.

Rist, John M. *Augustine: Ancient Thought Baptized*. Cambridge: Cambridge University Press, 1996.

Rondet, Henri. "Bulletin augustinien." *Recherches de Science Religieuses* 53 (1965) 643–59.

———. "Bulletin augustinien." *Recherches de Science Religieuses* 55 (1967) 252–56.

Rosen, Stanley. *The Ancients and the Moderns: Rethinking Modernity*. New Haven: Yale University Press, 1989.

Rushdoony, Rousas J. "The One and the Many Problem—The Contribution of Van Til." In *Jerusalem and Athens: Critical Discussions on the Theology and Apologetics of Cornelius Van Til*, edited by R. Geehan, 339–48. Phillipsburg, NJ: Presbyterian and Reformed, 1971.

Rutler, George William. *Beyond Modernity: Reflections of a Post-Modern Catholic.* San Francisco: St. Ignatius, 1987.
Ryba, Thomas. "Augustine's Trinitology and the Theory of Groups." In *Augustine*, edited by J. Lienhard, 151–68. New York: Peter Lang, 1993.
Schaeffer, Hans. *Createdness and Ethics: The Doctrine of Creation and Theological Ethics in the Theology of Colin E. Gunton and Oswald Bayer.* Berlin: de Gruyter, 2006.
Scharlemann, Robert P. "Hegel and Theology Today." *Dialog* 23 (1984) 257– 62.
Schleiermacher, Friedrich. *The Christian Faith.* Edited and translated by H. R. Mackintosh and J. S. Stewart. Edinburgh: T. & T. Clark, 1989.
Schmaus, Michael. *Die Psychologische Trinitätslehre des Heiligen Augustinus.* Münster: Aschendorffsche, 1927.
Schmid, H. H. "Creation, Righteousness, and Salvation: 'Creation Theology' as the Broad Horizon of Biblical Theology." In *Creation in the Old Testament*, edited by Bernhard W. Anderson, 102–17. Issues in Religion and Theology 6. Philadelphia: Fortress, 1984.
Schwindler, Alfred. *Wort und Analogie in Augustine Trinitätslehre.* Tübingen: Mohr, 1965.
Sell, Alan P. F. Review of *The Actuality of Atonement: A Study of Metaphor, Rationality and the Christian Tradition*, by Colin E. Gunton. *Irish Theological Quarterly* 57 (1991) 82–84.
Stead, Christopher. "The Concept of Divine Substance." In *Substance and Illusion in the Christian Fathers*, 1–14. London: Variorum, 1985.
———. *Divine Substance.* Oxford: Clarendon, 1977.
———. *Philosophy in Christian Antiquity.* Cambridge: Cambridge University Press, 1994.
———. *Substance and Illusion in the Christian Fathers.* London: Variorum, 1985.
Studer, Basil. *Trinity and Incarnation: The Faith of the Early Church.* Translated by Matthias Westerhoff. Edited by Andrew Louth. Edinburgh: T. & T. Clark, 1993.
Sullivan, John E. *The Image of God.* Dubuque, IA: Priory, 1963.
Sweeney, Leo. "Augustine and Gregory of Nyssa: Is the Triune God Infinite in Being?" In *Augustine: Presbyter Factus Sum*, edited by Joseph T. Lienhard, Earl C. Muller, and Roland J. Teske, 497–516. New York: Peter Lang, 1993.
Taylor, Charles. *Sources of the Self: The Making of the Modern Identity.* Cambridge: Cambridge University Press, 1989.
TeSelle, Eugene. *Augustine the Theologian.* London: Publisher, 1970.
———. "Works in Augustinian Studies." *Quarterly Review* 7 (1987) 80–90.
Teske, Roland J. "Augustine's Use of 'Substantia' in Speaking about God." *Modern Schoolman* 62 (1985) 149.
———. "Properties of God and the Predicaments of *De Trinitate* V." *Modern Schoolman* 59 (1981) 1–19.
Thielicke, Helmut. *Modern Faith and Thought.* Translated by Geoffrey W. Bromiley. Grand Rapids: Eerdmans, 1990.
Timiadis, Emilianos. "The Holy Trinity in Human Life." *One in Christ* 21 (1985) 1–18.
Toon, Peter, and James D. Spiceland, editors. *One God in Trinity.* Westchester, IL: Cornerstone, 1980.
Torrance, Alan J. *Persons in Communion: Trinitarian Description and Human Participation.* Edinburgh: T. & T. Clark, 1996.
Torrance, James B. *Worship, Community, and the Triune God of Grace.* Downers Grove, IL: InterVarsity, 1996.

Torrance, Thomas F. "Calvin's Doctrine of the Trinity." In *Trinitarian Perspectives: Toward Doctrinal Agreement*. Edinburgh: T. & T. Clark, 1994.

———. *Divine and Contingent Order*. Oxford: Oxford University Press, 1981.

———. "The Doctrine of the Holy Trinity in Gregory Nazianzen and John Calvin." In *Trinitarian Perspectives: Toward Doctrinal Agreement*, 21–40. Edinburgh: T. & T. Clark, 1994.

———. *Theology in Reconciliation*. London: Geoffrey Chapman, 1975.

———. *Transformation and Convergence in the Frame of Knowledge: Explorations in the Interrelations of Scientific and Theological Enterprise*. Belfast: Christian Journals, 1984.

———. *The Trinitarian Faith*. Edinburgh: T. & T. Clark, 1988.

Toulmin, Stephen. *Cosmopolis: The Hidden Agenda of Modernity*. Chicago: University of Chicago Press, 1990.

Van Dusen, Henry P. "The Trinity in Experience and Theology." *Theology Today* 15 (1958) 377–86.

Vanhoozer, Kevin J. *The Trinity in a Pluralistic Age: Theological Essays on Culture and Religion*. Grand Rapids: Eerdmans, 1997.

Voegelin, Eric. *The New Science of Politics: An Introduction*. 1952. Reprint, Chicago: University of Chicago Press, 1987.

Volf, Miroslav. *After Our Likenes: The Church as the Image of the Trinity*. Grand Rapids: Eerdmans, 1997.

———, editor. *Theology and Western Values*. Grand Rapids: Eerdmans, 1997.

Wainwright, Arthur. *The Trinity in the New Testament*. London: SPCK, 1969.

Wainwright, William J. "Augustine on God's Simplicity: A Reply." *New Scholasticism* 53 (1979) 118–23.

Walker, Graham. "Antique Modernity: Augustine's 'Liberalism' and the Impasse of Modern politics." In *Saint Augustine the Bishop*, edited by F. LeMoine and Christopher Kleinhenz, 201–2. New York: Garland, 1994.

Warfield. Benjamin B. "Calvin's Doctrine of the Trinity." In *Calvin and Augustine*, edited by Samuel G. Craig, 189–284. Philadelphia: Presbyterian and Reformed, 1956.

Wassmer, Thomas A. "Trinitarian Theology of Augustine and His Debt to Plotinus." *Scottish Journal of Theology* 14 (1961) 248–55.

Weaver, Richard M. *Ideas Have Consequences*. Chicago: University of Chicago Press, 1948.

Webb, Eugene. "Augustine's New Trinity: The Anxious Circle of Metaphor." In *Innovation in Religious Traditions: Essays in the Interpretation of Religious Change*, edited by Michael A. Williams, Collett Cox, and Martin S. Jaffee, 191–213. Berlin: de Gruyter, 1992.

Webster, John. "Systematic Theology After Barth: Jungel, Jenson and Gunton." In *The Modern Theologians: An Introduction to Christian Theology Since 1918*, 3rd ed., edited by David Ford and Rachel Muers, 249–64. London: Wiley-Blackwell, 2005.

Wendebourg, Dorothea. "From the Cappadocian Fathers to Gregory Palamas: The Defeat of Trinitarian Theology." *Studia Patristica* 17 (1982) 194–98.

Wesche, Kenneth Paul. "The Triadological Shaping of Latin and Greek Christology." [Part 1] *Pro Ecclesia* 1 (1992) 63–75.

———. "The Triadological Shaping of Latin and Greek Christology." [Part 2] *Pro Ecclesia* 2 (1993) 84–105.

Wethersfield Institute. *Christianity and Western Civilization*. San Francisco: Ignatius, 1995.
Wiles, Maurice. "Some Reflections on the Origins of the Doctrine of the Trinity." *Journal of Theological Studies* N.S. 8 (1957) 92–106.
Williams, Rowan. "'Good for Nothing'? Augustine on Creation." *Augustinian Studies* 25 (1994) 9–24.
———. "Sapientia and the Trinity: Reflections on De Trinitate." In *Augustine: Second Founder of the Faith*, edited by B. Bruning, 317–32. New York: Peter Lang, 1990.
Williams, Stephen. *Revelation and Reconciliation: A Window on Modernity*. Cambridge: Cambridge University Press, 1995.
Wills, Garry. *Saint Augustine*. New York: Viking, 1999.
Wolfson, Harry Austryn. *The Philosophy of the Church Fathers*. Vol. 1, *Faith, Trinity, Incarnation*. 3rd ed. Cambridge: Harvard University Press, 1970.
Yu, Carver T. *Being and Relation: A Theological Critique of Western Dualism and Individualism*. Edinburgh: Scottish Academic, 1987.
Zizioulas, John D. *Being as Communion: Studies in Personhood and the Church*. Crestwood, NY: St. Vladimir's Seminary Press, 1985.
Zizioulas, John D. "On Being a Person. Towards an Ontology of Personhood." In *Persons, Divine and Human: King's College Essays in Theological Anthropology*, edited by Christoph Schwöebel and Colin E. Gunton, 33–46. Edinburgh: T. & T. Clark, 1992.

Index

Abraham, 160
accident, 145, 146, 148, 164, 175
accident-wise, 175
act, 7, 14, 28, 33, 34, 39, 41, 43, 64, 65, 90, 115, 120, 126, 127, 130, 132, 137, 140, 175, 177, 179, 180, 186, 197, 203
Adam, 32, 63, 78, 115, 119–22
Ambrose, 124, 125, 137
analogy, analogies (Trinitarian), 4, 13, 21, 25, 31, 37, 49, 56, 61, 83, 85, 86, 87, 101, 103–6, 108, 116, 147, 185, 188, 193, 196, 198–200
angels, 40, 81
Anselm, 10–12, 59, 113, 114
anthropology, 20, 23, 41, 47, 63, 76–78, 87, 153
anti-Arian, 127
anti-Augustinian, 169
anti-foundationalism, 45
anti-incarnational, 81, 154
anti-material, anti-materialism, 81, 85, 169
anti-modern, 203
anti-neoplatonic, 126, 127, 186
apophatic theology, 39
Aquinas, Thomas, 8, 11–16, 20, 21, 23, 205
Arendt, Hannah, 88

Aristotle, Aristotelian, 35, 49, 140–46, 163, 164, 179
Arius, Arianism, 3, 98, 124, 125, 127, 132, 148, 149, 156, 166, 179
Athanasius, 16, 27, 28, 72, 73, 137
Atheism, 48
atonement, 30, 43, 58, 59–62, 97, 109, 113, 114, 118, 119, 128, 132, 182
attributes of God, 90, 139, 142, 159
Augustinian, Augustinianism, 10–12, 14, 15, 46, 47, 68, 76, 77, 135, 140, 153, 157, 161, 175, 176, 181, 182, 188, 191, 203, 205, 206
autotheos, 16, 17
Ayres, Lewis, 84, 137

baptism, 15, 63, 81, 97, 129, 164
Barnes, Michel René, 68, 94, 124, 125, 136, 166, 179, 186, 191
Barth, Karl, 15, 17, 19, 20–22, 25, 46
Basil, 8, 16, 36, 39, 40, 62, 73, 75, 84, 85, 101, 129, 137
begetting, begotten, 13, 14, 97, 104–6, 148, 149, 151, 153, 156, 176, 177, 188

Index

being, 2–8, 12–14, 16, 17, 22–24, 27–31, 34, 35, 37–45, 47, 49, 50, 52–54, 56–58, 60, 62, 64, 67, 69–83, 85–87, 91, 92, 95, 100, 102, 110–15, 117–22, 124, 128, 129, 131, 134, 135, 137, 139–67, 175–77, 181–84, 187, 191, 192, 194–200, 203
Boethius, 11
Booth, Edward, 127, 141, 164
Bourke, Vernon J., 139, 140
Bray, Gerald, 15
Buckley, Michael, 48
Bultmann, Rudolf, 46

Calvin, John, 15–17
Cappadocians, Cappadocian Fathers, 4, 7–10, 15–17, 24, 27, 28, 30, 40, 45, 50, 67–76, 79, 80, 82–86, 134, 135, 137–39, 146, 154, 158, 160, 161, 167, 169, 173, 191, 192, 194, 195, 205
Cavadini, John, 125, 126, 186
Chadwick, Henry, 141n36
Chalcedon, Chalcedonian Christology, 15, 54, 96, 100
Christocentric, Christological, Christology, 30, 33, 34, 40, 47, 48, 50–55, 63, 67, 84, 89, 92, 96, 97, 100, 125, 129, 176, 177, 190
Chrysostom, John, 137
church, 1, 5, 17–21, 23, 28, 30, 32, 43, 46, 50, 51, 57, 58, 60–63, 69, 71, 78–80, 84, 85, 87, 88, 92, 124, 128, 129, 131, 135, 136, 152, 153, 161, 205
Clark, Mary T., 153
coeternal, 13, 46, 101, 104, 177
communion, being-in-communion, 5, 8, 27, 28, 29, 60, 69, 70, 74, 75, 77–80, 103, 104, 109, 192, 194
community, 2, 4, 23, 24, 34, 42, 45, 57, 60–63, 75, 128, 129, 152, 154
Confessiones (*Confessions*), 89, 90, 139, 141, 175, 180
consubstantial, constubstantiality, 16, 98, 101, 102, 104, 108, 112, 132, 157, 175, 176, 193
Conyers, A. J., 24n96
creatio ex nihilo, 132
creation, 2, 4–9, 21, 23, 28, 30–51, 53–67, 69–73, 76–79, 82, 84–86, 88–93, 95, 97–99, 101, 103, 105, 107, 109–13, 115, 117, 119, 121, 123, 125, 127–33, 138, 151, 154, 169, 170, 173–82, 185, 188, 191, 197, 201, 203–5
creator, 33, 34, 37–45, 47, 49, 50, 55, 59, 64, 65, 71, 72, 78, 81, 93, 129, 147, 158, 173–76, 178, 181, 197
Crouse, R. D., 123
Cunningham, David S., 2, 21, 171, 172

Davies, Brian, 12
De civitate Dei (*City of God*), 89, 90, 92, 119, 175, 186, 187
De diversis quaestionibus ad Simplicianum (*Diverse Questions to Simplicius*), 90
De doctrina Christiana (*On Christian Doctrine*), 147
De Fide et Symbolo (*On Faith and the Creed*), 90
De Magistro (*The Teacher*), 48, 50
De Moribus Ecclesia Catholicae et de Moribus Manichaeorum (*On the Morals of the Catholic Church and the Morals of the Manichees*), 91, 174

De quantitate animae (*On the Greatness of the Soul*), 95
de Regnon, Theodore, 136
De vera religione (*On True Religion*), 90, 91
Derrida, Jacques, 140
Descartes, Rene, 84, 97
devil, 80, 114, 115, 119–22, 129
divine simplicity, 82, 139, 152, 156, 157, 161, 164, 165, 175, 176, 193, 204
double-procession, 26
Durrant, Michael, 144, 145

ecclesiology, 69, 84
Economic Trinity, 22, 27, 55, 84, 110, 138, 183, 185, 187, 188, 189, 190, 203
Enchiridion ad Laurentium de fide spe et caritate (*Enchiridion*), 91, 96, 130, 177, 180
epistemology, 46, 47, 50, 56
Epistulae (*Letters* 1–82 of Augustine), 95, 96
eschatology, eschatological, 24, 28, 35, 43, 55–57, 61–65, 76, 85, 89, 101, 129, 130, 132, 147
esse, 148
essence, essences, 2, 4, 15, 17–19, 37, 74, 80, 82, 85, 92, 133, 134, 136, 137, 139, 142, 145, 146, 148, 157–59, 161, 163–67, 191, 192, 194

Feuerbach, Ludwig, 87
Filiation, 14
filioque, 11
forms (platonic), 46, 47, 51, 89, 92, 96, 136, 142, 143, 172, 176, 177
Fortman, Edmund J., 68
Frei, Hans, 46

gnostics gnosticism, 38, 79, 132, 173

Grabowski, Stanislaus J., 1, 2
Gregory Nazianzen, 15, 16, 50
Gregory Nyssen, 16
Gregory of Nazianzus, 15
Guillou, M. J. Le, 125

Harnack, Adolf Von, 69, 141
Heraclitus, 2, 3, 31, 76, 170
Hexaemeron (Basil), 73
Hilary, 124, 125
Hill, Edmund, 14, 83, 110, 111, 127, 137–39, 157, 166, 182, 183, 188, 189, 191
Holy Spirit, 4, 5, 7, 11–14, 16–20, 22–24, 26, 27, 34–36, 38–42, 44–47, 49, 50, 53–62, 64, 70–72, 76, 78, 79, 81, 84, 85, 89, 91, 92, 96–98, 101–6, 108–12, 122, 124, 128–30, 132–34, 150–53, 156, 157, 161, 164, 165, 174, 176–78, 181–83, 185, 188–90, 193–97, 204
homoians, homoianism, 94, 124, 125, 186
homoousion, homoousios, 4, 54, 72
hypostasis, hypostases, 16, 28, 53, 74, 79, 83, 158

image, 5, 21, 23, 24, 34, 35, 40–44, 47, 58, 63, 77–79, 94, 95, 105–8, 122, 123, 129, 154, 163, 179, 184, 188, 193, 197–200
imago Dei, 24, 40, 42, 43, 58, 76–78, 95, 154, 186, 193, 196, 197, 199, 206
immutability, 5, 142, 148, 156, 164, 165
incarnation, 4, 11, 19, 34, 47, 50, 51, 53, 63, 72, 81, 97, 99, 100, 111–13, 118, 121, 125, 127, 131, 132, 133, 174, 176, 177, 183, 184, 187

Institutes of the Christian Religion (John Calvin), 15–17
interpenetration, perichoresis, 23
Irenaeus, 7, 8, 10, 30, 34, 37, 38, 44, 47, 49, 50, 61, 62, 65, 71, 72, 73, 86, 129, 133, 138, 169, 173, 179, 182, 187, 191
Irving, Edward, 53

Jenson, Robert W., 8, 82, 138
justification, 15, 33, 114, 115, 187, 192
Justin Martyr, 35, 71, 72, 138

Kany, Roland, 124
knowledge, 21, 35, 41, 44, 46, 48, 50, 51, 63, 80–82, 84, 92, 105, 106, 122, 126, 128, 132, 134, 147, 148, 164, 177, 179, 183, 186, 188

Lawless, George, 95, 124
Lloyd, G. E. R., 142–44

Macmurray, John, 77
Malet, A., 125
Marius Victorinus, 124, 125, 141
Martland, Thomas Rodolphe, 68, 135, 136, 191
Miles, Margaret, 95, 96
missions (of the Son and Spirit), 35, 56, 94, 99, 100, 104, 110–12, 116, 125, 133, 179, 182, 183, 186, 190, 196, 203, 204
manicheism, 900
modalism, 3, 4, 19, 67, 74, 82, 159, 163, 167
model (God as), 7, 8, 32, 44, 53, 63, 65, 71, 76–79, 113, 114, 121, 128, 152–54
modern, modernism, 1–7, 10, 11, 15, 17, 20, 24, 25, 31, 32, 37, 48, 50–53, 66, 68, 70, 74, 76, 79, 84, 123, 137, 169, 173, 191, 203, 204, 206
modification-wise, 148, 149
Moltmann, Jürgen, 22–24
Monologion, 11
Morris, William, 2
Muller, Earl C., 125–27, 186
Nebridius, 95
neoplatonic, neoplatonism, 4, 37, 80, 82, 85, 86, 89, 90, 95, 125–27, 132, 133, 141, 164, 174, 186
Nicaea, Nicene Creed, 4, 124
Novatian, 138

O'Leary, Joseph Stephen, 140
O'Toole, Christopher, 89–91
one and the many, 2–8, 10, 12, 14, 15, 20–23, 30–32, 36, 37, 43, 44, 47, 61, 66–69, 76, 80, 108, 116, 132, 144, 160, 164, 169–73, 175, 176, 185, 191, 192, 194, 201
ontology, ontological, 4, 7–9, 24, 26, 28, 31, 37–39, 42, 43, 45, 47, 51, 54, 66–87, 134, 135, 137–39, 141, 143, 145–47, 149, 151–55, 157–59, 161, 163, 165, 167, 169, 170, 191, 192, 194, 195, 201
Origen, 6, 36, 72, 73
ousia, 53, 74, 83, 127, 143, 148, 158, 164
Owen, John, 57

Paissac, H., 125
Pannenberg, Wolfhart, 24–28
Parmenides, Parmenidean, 2, 3, 31, 32, 76, 170
particulars, particularity, 6, 7, 11, 15, 17, 24, 32, 34, 36, 37, 41, 44, 47, 51, 53, 57–59, 63, 66, 67, 75, 83, 85, 89, 95, 97, 101, 102, 110, 116, 132, 133, 135,

particulars, particularity (*cont.*)
138, 142, 143, 158, 166, 167, 171, 175, 182, 184, 189, 192, 194, 196, 203, 205
Pelagius, Pelagianism, 20
perichoresis, 24, 27, 161
person, personhood, 1, 3, 4, 8–10, 12–20, 22, 24, 27–29, 31, 34, 40–44, 53, 55, 58, 60, 67–70, 74, 75, 77–80, 82, 83, 85, 86, 92, 96–102, 108, 111, 116, 118, 119, 125, 128, 130, 133, 135–39, 144, 145, 152–55, 157–63, 165–68, 175, 186, 187, 191–97, 200, 204
Philo, 38, 72
Philoponos, John, 35
Plato, Platonism, 4, 6, 32, 35, 36, 46–49, 51, 55, 56, 71–73, 79–81, 86, 89, 92, 95, 96, 116, 127, 142, 144, 146, 154, 164, 169, 176–79, 183, 186, 187, 190
Plotinus, 90, 95, 127
pneumatology, pneumatological, 34, 47, 48, 61, 63, 84, 85
Polanyi, Michael, 44
Porphyry, 127, 186, 187
Portalie, Eugene, 113, 114
postmodernism, postmodernity, 15, 24
Prestige, G. L., 134, 191
privatio boni, 19, 91
proceed, processions, 9, 11, 13, 14, 16, 22, 23, 26, 46, 48, 56, 58, 68–70, 74, 76, 103–5, 108, 110–12, 124, 132, 133, 150, 169, 182, 183, 189, 190, 196, 199, 203, 204

Rahner, Karl, 21, 22, 27, 36, 55, 110
Ratzinger, Cardinal Joseph, 28
relations, relationality, 2, 4, 6–10, 13, 14, 24, 26, 27, 29, 31, 33, 34, 36, 38–45, 47–50, 52, 54, 56, 59, 61–64, 69–71, 74–80, 82–89, 95, 101, 102, 110, 111, 124, 127, 136, 138, 139, 141, 142, 144, 146, 149–57, 160–63, 165, 171–73, 175, 176, 178, 179, 181, 184, 188–190, 192, 194–98, 200, 204, 206
relationship-wise (words used of God), 102, 149, 150, 195
resurrection, 58, 63, 64, 94–96, 111–14, 127, 129, 130, 132, 180, 183
Retractationes (*Retractations*), 95, 96
Richard of St. Victor, 11, 12
Rushdoony, Rousas John, 2n6

Sabellius, Sabellianism, 19, 159
sacraments, 114
sacrifice, 59, 63, 64, 113, 115, 116, 118, 121, 127, 132, 186, 187
Schleiermacher, Friedrich, 17, 18, 19
Schmid, H. H., 33
self-knowledge, 44, 84, 164
sin, 18, 34, 40, 43, 44, 59, 95, 107, 112–15, 119–22, 174, 184
Socrates, 143
Soliloquia (*Soliloquies*), 139
Son, Sonship, 4, 5, 7, 11–14, 16, 17, 23, 24, 26, 27, 34, 35, 41, 42, 44, 47, 49, 53, 55–57, 60, 70–72, 75, 76, 78, 91, 94, 97, 98–106, 108–12, 118, 121, 124, 125, 132–34, 148–52, 155–57, 161–63, 165, 166, 176, 177, 179, 182, 183, 185–190, 193–97, 204
soteriology, soteriological, 54, 126, 186
spiration, procession of Holy Spirit, 14
Stead, Christopher, 142–44, 146, 157, 158

Stephen, Joseph, 140
subordinationism, 127
subsistence, subsistence relation, 14, 23, 42, 77, 78
substance, 3, 20, 75, 80, 83, 85, 91, 96, 97, 99, 102, 108, 111, 112, 136, 138, 139, 141–46, 148–52, 154, 156–60, 162–67, 175, 177, 191–96
substance-wise, substance-word, substantialiter, 102, 148–50, 157, 175, 193, 195, 196
Sullivan, John E., 95n39
Summa Theologiae (Thomas Aquinas), 13

teleology, teleological, 34, 35, 40, 55, 62, 63, 89, 101, 109, 117, 129, 130, 180, 204, 205
Tertullian, 113, 138, 160
Teske, Roland J., 148, 164, 165
Theophanies (Augustine's understanding of), 81

Thomas Aquinas, 8, 11–16, 20, 21, 23, 205
Torrance, James, 8
Torrance, Thomas F., 8
transcendental, transcendentals, 138

unbegotten, unbegottenness, 148, 149, 156

vestiges, vestigial (of the Trinity), 20, 21, 76, 77, 81, 132
Volf, Miroslav, 28, 32, 63

Warfield, Benjamin Breckendridge, 16
Webb, Eugene, 134, 191
William of Ockham, 47
Williams, Rowan, 84, 130, 136

Zizioulas, John, 8, 10, 28, 29, 45, 57, 69, 70, 77, 79, 80, 138

www.ingramcontent.com/pod-product-compliance
Lightning Source LLC
Chambersburg PA
CBHW062018220426
43662CB00010B/1383